"Your book is fantastic—direct, passionate, and a real page-turner!"

Eugene Izotov, Principal Oboe, San Francisco Symphony

"Joe Robinson has penned an extraordinary memoir that will be fascinating to musicians and the rest of the public as well. It reads like a novel—gripping and colorful. Not a word is wasted; his style is clever, spare, eloquent, and often humorous . . . Robinson has made his story of an audacious, upstart oboist an adventure for all—inspiring and uplifting. A Hero's Life!

Your book would make a good movie!"

Elaine Douvas, Principal Oboe, Metropolitan Opera,
Head of Woodwinds at Juilliard

"The writing is excellent . . . this memoir is terrific!"

Ervin Duggan, former FCC Commissioner and
President of PBS

"Joe Robinson's memoir is a celebration of tenacity in pursuit of artistic excellence by a musician entranced with the love of language. He has the captivating ability to describe the exhilaration of 'a few good notes' to untutored laymen. His is a fable for all who dream large, then succeed by rigorous training, determined resilience, and a refusal to compromise with excellence."

Hon. Wyche Fowler, former U.S. Senator from Georgia and
Ambassador to Saudi Arabia

Long Winded
An Oboist's Incredible Journey to the New York Philharmonic

by

Joseph L. Robinson

Joshua Tree Publishing

• Chicago •

Long Winded

An Oboist's Incredible Journey to the
New York Philharmonic

by

Joseph L. Robinson

Joshua Tree Publishing
• Chicago •
JoshuaTreePublishing.com

13-Digit ISBN: 978-1-941049-54-9

Front Cover Image: Oboe © alenavlad
Picture Zubin Mehta: Used with Permission

Disclaimer:
This book is designed to provide information about the subject matter covered. The opinions and information expressed in this book are those of the author, not the publisher. Every effort has been made to make this book as complete and as accurate as possible. However, there may be mistakes both typographical and in content. Therefore, this text should be used only as a general guide and not as the ultimate source of information. The author and publisher of this book shall have neither liability nor responsibility to any person or entity with respect to any loss or damage caused or alleged to be caused directly or indirectly by the information contained in this book.

Printed in the United States of America

Dedication

I dedicate this book gratefully to

Four men who gave me my life in music:
Capt. James C. Harper
Dr. James C. Pfohl
John Mack
Marcel Tabuteau
and
Four Women who shared it most:
Mary Kay, my wonderful wife, and
Katie, Jody and Becky, our amazing daughters

Contents

Prelude

"Yes . . . Hello?" The lilt in his voice was as distinctive as curry.

"Mr. Mehta? This is Joe Robinson, the oboist who wrote you a letter at the New York Philharmonic . . ."

I envisioned the handsome maestro standing on the patio of Steve McQueen's former home in the Brentwood section of Los Angeles, looking west across his swimming pool toward the Pacific. NEWSWEEK had recently put a photograph of Zubin Mehta, a matador in white tie and tails, on its cover under the headline, "Macho Maestro!" He was one of a trio of brilliant rising star conductors dubbed "the Exotics—Mata, Muti, Mehta!" NEWSWEEK quoted the Philharmonic's Executive Director, Carlos Moseley, as saying, "God did not create many people who possess the requisite qualities of a successful major orchestra leader." The New York Philharmonic's Music Director designate, he asserted, was one of them.

"Oh, I know who you are. Your letter piqued my interest in speaking to you about your audition. When I heard you play last week, I thought your tone sounded forced."

"In retrospect, I'm sure it did, Mr. Mehta. We both know that Harold Gomberg was the most dramatic oboist in the world and I was second-guessing the audition committee, playing with the biggest tone possible. I may have overdone it."

Harold Gomberg was indeed an icon in America's oldest orchestra. Subscribers who never guessed that the New York Philharmonic was founded the same year as the Vienna Philharmonic, recognized Gomberg as one of New York's stars—its principal oboist for thirty-five years until his retirement in 1976. They had watched him dozens of times performing on television with Leonard Bernstein and knew that no oboist in the world played with bigger range or more heroic aspiration.

"That's a good point. By the way, you were on the Avery Fisher Hall stage a long time. I hope I didn't push you too hard."

"No, but I appreciate your giving me extra time before that Tchaikovsky Fourth solo. I could hardly keep my lips on the reed by then!"

Orchestra auditions normally happen in elimination rounds of no more than ten minutes per candidate, with excerpts precisely indicated ahead of time—only a few of which are actually performed. In my audition a week earlier, I had played for thirty minutes through all of the music in the audition folder, then taken a break and returned for more.

"I can tell you, Mr. Robinson . . . I rather liked your phrasing."

"Thank you, Sir. There's something else I would like to explain. I never would play so much repertory on the same reed. It was just the audition. In concerts with you I would use a lighter reed for Mozart and a heavier one for Brahms. I can vary my tone quite a lot."

"Hmm . . . of course, you are right." (as if he hadn't thought of that!) *"Thanks for your call. I look forward to hearing you play again at Lincoln Center next month."*

* * *

How did a North Carolina farm boy who never attended conservatory arrive at this point—persuading one of the world's greatest conductors to give him a second chance at one of the world's most coveted orchestra positions? Answering that question is the purpose of this book. It describes an improbable odyssey that affirms the value of liberal learning as much as of God-given musical talent; the significance of good luck as much as hard work; the power of private philanthropy as much as enlightened public policy; and the importance of faithful apprenticeship as much as courageous self-realization.

Musical secrets are revealed along the way and authentic witness given to the influence of the epic transformations of American culture in the third quarter of the twentieth century.

andante con moto

Love in the afternoon

Davenport Junior High School in 1952 looked like a brick monolith beneath tall oak trees on a hill near the center of Lenoir, North Carolina. In fact, there were two structures up there: a smaller one with Doric columns facing north that hinted at past glory for a place that once housed a junior college but which now provided only rehearsal space and storage rooms for the junior high school band, and a larger, prosaic academic building.

At my desk in one of the upstairs classrooms, I sweltered in un-air-conditioned September heat as bleeps and squawks from the rehearsal next door interrupted my reverie. Linda Broyhill, Lenoir's twelve-year-old version of Elizabeth Taylor, upset careful plans when she joined the band instead of sitting next to me in this last-period study hall. Disappointed, I doodled in the margins of a notebook and dreamed of Linda over there learning to play the oboe.

My hometown of around eight thousand inhabitants called itself "Gateway to the Blue Ridge Parkway"—a sobriquet unnecessarily modest, since Lenoir was a major center of wood furniture manufacture in the United States. And the most important of the dozen or so factories turning hardwoods into dressers and tables and chairs was Broyhill Furniture Company.

The Broyhills were the plutocrats of Lenoir. Patriarch T. H. had acquired for pennies an acre during the Depression vast holdings of timberland, from which he extracted a seemingly endless supply of maple, oak, cherry and walnut for an already-established industry manned by Scots-Irish mountaineers contemptuous of labor unions. "Haystacks" of wooden boards cured in the open air all over Caldwell County, waiting to enter the factory assembly lines that shaped, bolted, lacquered and glued them, and filled the inverted air in the geologic bowl east of Grandfather Mountain known as "The Globe" with noxious fumes and smoke.

Above most of this pollution and noise, on a hill on the other side of town, T. H.'s younger brother, J. E Broyhill, accessed his home up a driveway that curved through protective pines. It was Lenoir's "Xanadu," gleaming white in the center of green grassy skirts that fell away from it on all sides. Behind was a wondrous marble pool, in which a few of the town's Caucasian children were sometimes invited to swim.

Linda Broyhill is the first girl I remember kissing—when I was ten years old during a movie at the Center Theater. Tickets cost a quarter and the box of popcorn a dime. My quest for a furtive peck on Linda's cheek required such concentration I have no idea what we were watching. When I reached over and took her hand and she stayed put, I landed my little kiss.

Linda and I were publicly paired in a presumption of prepubescent affection because of our partnership in something called "The Pantomime Club"—an amusing showcase of lip-syncing children dressed up like adults pretending to be popular singers of the day. It was a production conceived and directed by Grady Kincaid, principal of East Harper Elementary School. Usually dressed in a plaid sport coat and bow tie, he was an irrepressible grade school impresario. He taught us the Schottische and the Virginia reel and how to "put your little foot right out!"

One-day Grady barged into our fourth-grade classroom with poster paper under his arm and yardsticks for everyone. He demonstrated in an hour how to draw with perspective, so that smaller objects receded into the distance in a realistic way. He even entrusted the 16-mm projector to favored students during assemblies and the freezer with Popsicles for sale to others at lunchtime. Late one spring afternoon Grady announced over the school intercom: "Teachers and students! Stop what you are doing right now and come to the auditorium for an experience you will never forget!" After everyone assembled, he led a pudgy little kid onto the stage and stepped back to see what would happen. Michael Rabin tucked his violin under his chin with wondrous nonchalance, and instead of playing "Twinkle, Twinkle Little Star," churned out smoking hot Paganini "Caprices" for us right on the spot! This astonishing prodigy was only eleven years old. And Grady was right—I never forgot

But the Pantomime Club was Grady's biggest success. We mimes stood at a microphone mouthing words to music that played behind us on 45 rpm discs, gesticulating as grandly as we dared. I was Bing Crosby, crooning with son Gary (Dennis Rash) "On Moonlight Bay," and at other times Nelson Eddy pledging my love to Jeanette McDonald (Linda Broyhill). It was the love duet that prompted Tom Greer, an honored older gentleman of Lenoir, to invite Linda and me to pose on his front lawn dressed as we had been for a performance at the Rotary Club the night before. I had to find an uphill place to stand to avoid looking half a foot shorter than Linda in that photograph; but people said we were "a right cute couple" after that.

In 1951, we were invited to appear on television. It was at WBTV, the CBS affiliate station in Charlotte, for an afternoon variety show hosted by Fred Kirby with the theme song, "Roll out the Barrel and We'll Have a Barrel of Fun." I was so impressed with the whole urban adventure that I drew detailed pictures for my parents of the tall buildings in Charlotte, our television studio, and the cameramen who did the filming. The Pantomime Club was my introduction to show business.

Bored back in study hall, I resolved to follow Linda Broyhill and join the junior high school band. When I spoke to director George Kirsten (whose sister Dorothy was a leading soprano at the Metropolitan Opera) about it, he told me to come back "tomorrow" and choose an instrument. That evening, watching Jimmy Dorsey on television with my dad, we both admired Jimmy's playing so much I chose the alto sax.

My first notes on the saxophone were immortalized in the memory of my best friend's father, who was forced to listen to them during a sleepover at his house that night. Years later Lloyd Rash was still telling everyone I had NO musical talent!

Linda dropped out of band at the end of that school year.

Childhood Compensations

"I don't think he can hear me, Roy," my mother said to her young husband after work one day. "Of course, he does, Nina," replied my dad; and he would have smacked his hands together or banged the kitchen table with his fist to prove the point. I imagine Eddie turned his infant head around in response to noises like that.

My brother was born 362 days ahead of me, thanks to the c-section that spared my mother another thirty-hour labor and put all five pounds four ounces of me into an incubator ahead of schedule. That is why for three days each year Ed and I are the same age. In June when we both got Mickey Mouse watches for our birthday and checked into a Myrtle Beach motel, we confounded the clerk who couldn't understand how we were both "six years old" and not twins.

November, 1944

Ed was indeed severely "hard of hearing." Nerve damage was the reason most often given my frantic parents, who drove everywhere to meet with specialists in search of relief or remedy.

"Don't send a boy like that to the 'Deaf and Dumb School' in Morganton," was the persuasive verdict of most of them. "He hears just well enough to survive public school with everyone else."

I still remember when Ed appeared in class red-faced one morning, wearing a large hearing aid in a holster around his neck.

Taller, stronger, and just as smart as my friends and me, Ed was beset by terrible asthma attacks until he outgrew the worst of them in young adulthood. Family reunions in the mountains and overnight trips anywhere would trigger attacks, and of course, hayrides were the worst; but my parents and I never knew when wheezing and gasping and crying would awaken us and prompt a call to Dr. Troutman for a shot of life-saving adrenalin. Bright lights and fear and commotion disturbed many nights in the room we shared growing up.

Despite obvious disadvantages, Ed was learning to play the cornet when I brought my saxophone home. He reacted with anger and wept out on the front porch one afternoon when he told Mother he failed to make the band.

Something worse than sleepless nights and school disappointments haunted our childhood. No one knows why Caldwell County was a state leader in per capita contractions of polio, but epidemics of terrifying intensity cycled through our community every three or four years, always in the summertime. Public gathering places such as the movie theater were off limits and community swimming pools had to be closed. Hardly a week passed without a report of another affliction, and grown-ups whispered earnestly among themselves when they speculated about how the infection had spread or "how far the paralysis would go."

My dad's younger brother Luther lived nearby in Whitnel, a few miles southeast of Lenoir. He was principal of West Lenoir Elementary School and a deacon in the First Baptist Church. His wife Mildred operated a flower shop out of the basement of the stone house Luther himself had built. They had two daughters who were a few years older than Ed and me. Anita was senior of the two, genial but prim and bookish, while Alta was prettier and more outgoing.

One Saturday afternoon in the summer of 1953 while Uncle Luther was supervising injections of immunity-boosting gamma globulin for children at his school, nineteen-year-old Alta slipped in her bathroom getting ready for a date and was unable to stand up. An ambulance transported her as quickly as possible a hundred miles west to the Orthopedic Hospital in Asheville, where special equipment alleviated some of the worsening effects of polio as it ravaged her neurons. There was nothing to do but watch the disease run its course. Anita, meanwhile, complaining of an unbearable headache, admitted herself to Caldwell County Memorial Hospital for observation. Eight days later, after Uncle Luther and Aunt Mildred raced back to Lenoir from their younger daughter's bedside, Anita died overnight.

The third of Benjamin Britten's "Six Metamorphoses after Ovid" for Solo Oboe is entitled "Niobe—Who, Lamenting the Death of her Fourteen Children, was turned into a Mountain." In the months that followed Anita's death and Alta's return to her home in an iron lung, where she lay in the living room for seventeen years able only to wiggle three fingers on her right hand and move her head and speak between artificial puffs of breath, Alta's mother, overcome by grief, instead of turning into a mountain, froze within her own catatonic cave. Throughout my career, whenever I performed "Niobe," I have mentioned my Aunt Mildred. Uncle Luther devoted the rest of his life to serving his younger daughter and writing a book entitled *We Made Peace With Polio* about his family's suffering and their Christian faith.

I visited Alta as a matter of course throughout high school and college years, always feeling guilty when she begged reports from me about the world beyond her collection of little glass figurines—my vast and thrilling world which she could only imagine from her peek at it through a single living room window. I still believe Alta Robinson to be my personal guardian angel.

Two years after Alta and Anita contracted polio, Dr. Jonas Salk produced a vaccine that effectively ended its scourge in America.

Penton Avenue

Flame retardant asbestos was used everywhere by the military during World War II, a time when carpet fire-bombing was being perfected on the cities of Europe. Asbestos had civilian applications too. It was touted by home builders as a perfect siding material—tough, safe, cheap, easy to install; and our first house on Penton Avenue in Lenoir, which cost a little more than $5,000 brand new, was made of it.

The house sat near the back of a narrow lot that sloped down in front and had a one-car garage and a brick chimney facing the street. When we lived in it, it was painted white. Its front porch looked east across Lower Creek directly at Hibriten Mountain. A sidewalk in front served as my brother's and my tricycle race track. Pretending to be intrepid explorers, Ed and I ventured into no-man's land around the corner onto Norwood Street one day, disobeying our parents' orders not to go that far away from home. Giddy with excitement, we pedaled faster and faster towards a spooky cement archway that marked the outer limits of our territorial imagination. Just then we heard Mother yelling from the corner behind us, "Come back here, you boys! Right this instant!" She was brandishing a hairbrush and running in her high heel pumps towards us up Norwood Street. Ed and I u-turned and raced back—our little legs churning furiously. In the moment she was upon us, we swerved in opposite directions and left her standing. We were squealing like a couple of piggies when we careened back onto Penton Avenue and raced for home. Just then we heard gravel rolling and a loud thump behind us. Mother had twisted her ankle and fallen in a heap at the corner. She was scraped, dirty and mad as a hornet when she caught up with us at the house. POW! It was the first time she ever slapped me!

(The other time was in Dennis Cook's dentist's office closet, into which I fled during a fearful, screaming tantrum.)

Canines were part of Creation as soon as I could perceive anything. A Boston bulldog terrier named Bob was my first baby-sitter and blanket companion. Mike and Kitty, two Brittany spaniels Dad kept for quail hunting, lived chained up to a dog house in the back yard most of the time. Through the years we had mongrels and purebreds—collies and Cocker spaniels. But there was always a dog.

Mimosa trees thrived in the 1940s before a virus suppressed them for the next fifty years or so. In our yard, there was one that spilled sticky pink flowers onto the lawn and produced green fronds we stripped and played with. A climbable maple tree stood out front; I knocked myself breathless when I fell flat on my back out of it one day. Best of all was the ubiquitous honeysuckle, a Southern vine that filled our spring and summer air with the most delicious fragrance in all of Nature. We learned to pick off the little yellow blossoms and suck nectar out of them from behind.

Inside the house my crib was placed against a wall in a tiny second bedroom. When I tried to climb out of it, I broke my collar bone. Naps were compulsory whether I was sleepy or not. As a consequence, I spent many hours during early childhood contemplating the wallpaper next to my bed. It had an intricate blue and white floral pattern that taught me a lot about spatial organization, texture, form and symmetry; and blue is still my favorite color.

In addition to wooden furniture manufactured in Lenoir and the nearby towns of Hickory, Morganton, and High Point, textiles and cigarettes dominated the economy of North Carolina. Cotton was still king in the eastern part of the state, and every stream that could be dammed for power spawned a textile mill. Often those company towns had nothing in them but rows of identical white-washed shacks for the workers and a large brick factory that clicked and hummed with the noise of its looms and sewing machines alongside a railroad track. Hanes, Blue Bell, Burlington and Cannon Mills were just a few of the North Carolina brands that dominated the textile industry in America.

Bright-leaf tobacco grew wherever cotton did not in Eastern North Carolina, but burley from smaller mountain plots was said to be more highly prized by cigarette manufacturers. American Tobacco Company was a colossal monopoly when it was broken up by Teddy Roosevelt and the Clayton Antitrust Act. After that, its progeny—R. J. Reynolds, Liggett and Myers, Brown and Williamson, and

Phillip Morris continued to be among the biggest tobacco companies in the world.

"Cigarettes will stunt your growth" was a familiar parental mantra when I was growing up; but every adult I knew smoked, and all of them seemed tall enough. Maybe they were the ones lucky or smart enough to wait until after puberty to start smoking. Print media, radio and television ads everywhere relentlessly glamorized the pleasures of puffing. My parents both smoked two packs a day, which was not unusual; and Dad and his friends sometimes lit a pipe. During the winter, our car with its windows rolled up tight often transported my parents and two other grown-ups all smoking at the same time; and Ed and I rode half-hidden in the haze among them. Bridge parties always littered our living room with overflowing trays of ashes and cigarette butts, leaving the house a smelly mess.

I was three or four when I crawled onto my Dad's lap one afternoon and asked if I could try what he was doing.

"Sure!" he answered, placing his lit cigarette carefully between my lips. "Now suck real hard on this thing."

Burning and choking and coughing hit me instantly, with violent nausea close behind. For the next hour, I threw up and gasped, convinced to the marrow of my bones that I would never do that again. And I never did.

A good thing, too, because Dad died of emphysema and my mother lost half her left lung to cancer.

Instrumental Transition

My mother's father was called "Captain Jones," despite never earning military rank or finishing high school. A teenager when he signed on as an apprentice for Virginia Bridge and Iron Company, he worked his way up over the years to job boss at construction sites for power plants, dams and bridges in Piedmont North Carolina. His was "learn-on-the-job" engineering. I have a pocket notebook in which my grandfather penciled estimates of the cost of cement and steel and labor for some of the big projects he supervised. Despite the absence of formal schooling, he must have engineered pretty well. Mother always boasted as she drove across a particular trestle south of Lenoir, "Boys, your grandfather built this bridge!" Captain Jones also owned the Ford Agency in Granite Falls, where a nickel in the resident soft drink machine delivered a Cheerwine every time I visited.

By standards of the day Captain Jones married well too, choosing his wife from among the prosperous Hayes's of Granite Falls—farmers with good bottom-land along the Catawba River. My grandmother Bessie produced eight children who lived (twins and another daughter died in childbirth); and of all the survivors my mother was the Captain's favorite. Nina Jones grew up as spoiled as a small-town princess. She studied English and Voice at white-gloved Greensboro College and finished with highest honors just three weeks past her twentieth birthday. A Baldwin Acrosonic was the wedding gift that arrived from my grandfather soon after his bright-eyed girl married my dad, and Nina accompanied herself on it when she sang in our living room on Penton Avenue. Because Mother could barely play two notes at a time, it is the clickety-clack of her long fingernails on the keys that I remember more than the tone of the piano.

Perhaps that's why I could never learn to play. Shirley Michael tried earnestly to teach me on two occasions—once when I was six and again when I was eleven. The first attempt ended in a springtime recital rendition of "She'll Be Comin' 'Round the Mountain"—a duet she and I performed from the last pages of John Thompson's *Teaching Little Fingers to Play* red book; and the second with a portentous solo performance of "Dangerous Journey" from John Schaum's purple book. Miss Michael told my mother both times it was hopeless: I would never be a pianist. Her judgment was prescient. A dozen years later, when I was the only graduate fellow seeking a Master of Music degree at the University of Maryland, my piano teacher, whenever he saw me approaching, leaned his head against the door-frame as if to say, "Lord, deliver me from this hour!" And I felt exactly the same way.

My mother's early habit of tapping out the rhythm of the Toreadors' Song from "Carmen" on my back when she put me in my crib at night failed also. In the second-grade rhythm band, I flunked bells and sand blocks before being demoted to chopsticks along with other unmusical classmates.

Saxophone at age twelve was more promising, although everyone who has learned to play a musical instrument other than piano and percussion knows how terrible it sounds in the beginning. Even a foreign language has some efficacy when first spoken, but one wonders how any music can be perceived in the early squeals of a violin or brays of a French horn. Miraculously it is. Following months of fumbling with keys to learn the notes and holding long tones to develop breath control, I joined the saxophone section of the junior high school band for my first rehearsal and honked my way through "Somewhere over the Rainbow." I thought it was just about the most wonderful thing I ever heard!

A year later at a springtime joint concert following our band's turn on stage, standing with other junior high-schoolers on the sidelines of Cook Stadium listening to a transcription of part of "Cavalleria Rusticana" played at twilight by the big kids in the high school band, suddenly I heard, tossed like a surfboard above a wave of soaring operatic melody, four little notes that pierced my soul!

They were the poignant plaint of an oboe solo.

The Lenoir High School Band was an audacious experiment in music education, wrought by a single individual whose hobby became his lifelong vocation. East and West Harper Avenues are Lenoir's main streets, named appropriately for a founding family of the town; and East Harper Elementary is the school I attended grades one through six. So, when James C. Harper returned to Lenoir following World War I with an officer's commission, he confounded hometown expectations that he would devote his life as his father had done to banking, business and community leadership, by fatuously purchasing instruments he thought American Legionnaires would be able to play as they marched around Lenoir's Civil War monument on

Armistice Day, and then by donating all of them to create one of the first high school bands in North Carolina. That was in 1924—the same year the Curtis Institute of Music opened its mansion doors in Philadelphia. Captain Harper promised to stay with the instruments for one year to get things started, and he stayed for fifty.

Captain James C. Harper

This remarkable educator invested his family fortune and bet his life on a premise I have often said no foundation board of directors would ever have accepted—namely, that youngsters in a little mountain town deserved to have a conservatory attached to their high school, complete with the finest instruments money could buy, ample practice and rehearsal spaces in a three-story brick building, three sets of uniforms and a fleet of buses to transport them throughout the region. When I was in it, the band's woodwind teacher was a former student of the great principal clarinetist of the Philadelphia Orchestra, Ralph McLean, and the brass teacher once performed as cornet soloist with the Sousa Band. Captain Harper, a Davidson College graduate who had no training in music except to teach himself to play the flute (which he did for many decades every Sunday morning in the First Presbyterian Church his grandfather founded in 1852), was the first high school band director elected President of the American Bandmasters Association. His achievements speak for themselves: professional performers and teachers out of proportion to any demographic probability issued from the Lenoir High School Band for sixty-one years, proving that extraordinary musical potential exists within all of us, only awaiting discovery and development in an educational program fully equipped and committed to excellence.

Not every talented participant successful in the band stayed with it, fortunately for me. One of those was William Happer, the group's principal oboe player. William's parents were physicians from Scotland who ran the Caldwell County public health clinic, and they considered 33% of their brilliant son's school day—two periods out of six devoted to music— too much time spent on "frivolous" activity. Consequently, they pulled William out of the band and set him to learning Russian, or something equally challenging. (William Happer became Professor of Electrical Engineering at Princeton University and a national leader in his field.) His departure set the stage for my transition from alto saxophone to oboe—a conversion my teacher assured me would access a universe of symphonic treasures by Mozart, Haydn, Beethoven and Brahms, *et.al.*, which I might otherwise never discover.

I resisted his entreaties for months. The oboe looked like an anorexic clarinet to me, and I wanted nothing to do with it. Nevertheless, in December 1954 I walked into John Kaufman's office and said "Okay," and there waiting for me on the front edge of his desk were a Lorée oboe from Paris and a box of magic reeds made by a secret supplier. There was also a piece of music he assigned me to learn over Christmas break—"The Last Rose of Summer." At almost exactly the same time one year earlier, the legendary oboist Marcel Tabuteau, my future teacher—whose students occupied every important symphonic position in the United States, retired after thirty-nine years as Principal Oboe of the Philadelphia Orchestra and sailed home to France.

Life in the Country

In 1946 hoping relocation away from Lower Creek would improve my brother's health, Dad bought a hilltop house and twelve acres of pasture land on the Wilkesboro Road five miles northeast of Lenoir. Ed and I rode standing up in the back of a truck with some of the furniture when we moved. As we bounced along, I noticed on our side of the road the sky filled with horizontal black streaks—telephone wires that connected as many as thirteen families to a single party line. Our ring was "two shorts and a long." When I answered calls, I had to stand on tiptoe to speak into the shiny black mouth of the oak box that hung on our wall.

All his life my dad had a love-hate relationship with the mountains he grew up in. When his forbears were flooded out of farms they owned on the Yadkin River, they loaded surviving essentials into a wagon and moved west to the headwaters of the highest stream in North Carolina. They planted themselves atop an ancient Cherokee Indian battleground next to the Tennessee line. Uncle Clay told me the family's collection of arrowheads increased every time he plowed. Clearing steep slopes and farming rocky soil at 4,000 feet required back-breaking work Dad never forgot nor entirely forgave. He used to say he hoped heaven would provide him a flat patch of black-loam farmland to hoe. As a child, he lived with his grandmother in front of the family home in a little wooden cabin, where she cooked over an open fire. Sometimes they awoke on winter mornings to find the floor dusted with snow; and he really did trudge miles to school. His mother died in the flu pandemic of 1918. Dad was the first member of his family to go to college.

After he left Watauga County and looked back at it through a remote lens, Dad's view of his birthplace softened. On hot summer weekends in Lenoir, he often rounded us up and headed for the mountains, where the air was cool and delicious. We patrolled the Blue Ridge Parkway, stopping at every overlook to "ooh and ah" at the majestic cascading vistas. On those trips when my mother packed and spread a picnic, she would exult in the beauty of the ferns and wildflowers growing in profusion all around us. In 1957, the year doctors at Duke University Hospital diagnosed Dad's emphysema, he bought thirty acres on the Aho Road between Blowing Rock and Boone. Ed and I helped him construct a summer cabin and watched expectantly as a pond was dug for fishing and swimming.

I sometimes resented dropping everything and tagging along when Dad commanded, "Let's go!" But my aesthetic sensibilities were undoubtedly formed and refined by contemplation of the infinitely curving, sapphire counterpoint of the beautiful Blue Ridge Mountains.

In 1946, our "new" house on the Wilkesboro Road came with a chicken coop and a sty that was occupied by three monstrously pregnant sows. It was my job after supper to tote buckets of slop through a gate up a path to the pigs' feeding troughs, hoping not to be flogged by a nasty rooster that guarded the place. When piglets were born in the fall, we kept one for slaughter. Mother actually brushed its little teeth in the sink before boiling its head for liver mush. (She was more at home with "Hamlet" than ham hocks.) Other farm experiments came and went—garden vegetables mostly eaten by rabbits; Rhode Island reds and game chickens all lost to a marauding fox one morning; a stingy, obdurate Jersey cow that kicked me when I milked it; and Hereford cattle for meat.

My pets in the country included a steer and a little black lamb. When Dad fenced the front pasture, I held the pine planks he measured, sawed and hammered; and afterwards I helped him paint them white. During summer twilights, the two of us often sat on the front porch listening to foxhounds run or watching in awe as thunderstorms blustered up the valley towards us from Lenoir.

Joe, Christmas 1949

The one house that could be seen from our front porch was a severely-weathered unpainted shack built into the side of a mountain directly across from us on the other side of the Wilkesboro Road. A boy our age lived in it with his parents; and if I stood on the fence and yelled as loud as I could and the wind was just right, he would hear me calling and come over to play. His father was a rough-hewn man in overalls who worked at one of the mills in town, and his mother had no teeth. She compensated with a lump of snuff that was always a bit too large for her lower lip. Brown juices oozed from the corners of her mouth, and her half-swallowed chin gave her the appearance of wearing a perpetual grin. Words issued indistinctly from behind the bolus when she spoke, almost as if she had no tongue.

Their front yard was swept dirt. In the middle of it a covered well—wood casing, windlass, bucket and all. An outhouse that served its necessary functions was mercifully situated downwind a few feet below the house. Some of Dad's mountain relatives lived difficult lives close to the "frontier," but Ed and I had never seen Appalachian poverty like this. From our neighbors' perspective, we must have looked like lords of a manor across the road, with our grazing cattle and gleaming white fence, telephone service and indoor plumbing. Despite the difference in social station that worried my mother, Ed and I sometimes crossed the road to visit our neighbor. We discovered when we did that he was wealthy in one respect—beneath his bed and inside a closet, he had the biggest stash of comic books we had ever seen!

A treasure I coveted more than comic books in those days was the same as Ralphie's in *A Christmas Story*—a Red Ryder BB rifle. It's the first thing I actually saved my own allowance money to be able to buy. Of course, I had heard the familiar admonition for years: "You can't have one; you'll shoot your eye out!" But eventually I got my own gun, and as soon as I set out for some serious bird hunting and an unlucky brown thrasher alit on a fence post in front of me, I hit it squarely in the breast. The wounded creature flapped around from place to place in the pasture with me in sadistic pursuit. I shot it again and again until it died at my feet. When I picked it up, staring at the bloody, feathery carcass and gagging from pity and remorse, I decided never to go hunting again.

In 1950 Ed returned from a disastrous semester at Hargrave Military Academy in Virginia, where the predicted improvement in his asthma not only did not occur, abuse by older classmates and teachers terrified him. He and I frequently played in the unfinished basement of our house in the country. One morning with me steering our little red wagon and Ed pushing from behind, we raced around the steel poles supporting the first floor of the house as fast as we could. Suddenly the wagon tilted to the side, and my head bounced off the cinder-block wall like a cantaloupe. Wailing, as I climbed the stairs to tell Mother what happened, darkness fell like a curtain across my vision. Because the family car was with dad in town, only the good luck of a neighbor's willingness to drive us to Dula Hospital saved me. A dangerous spinal tap a few days later relieved pressure on my occipital lobe and restored my sight.

Soon afterwards, Mother resumed teaching Senior English at Lenoir High School and Dad bought her a 1939 Buick sedan for the commute.

In 1955, we moved back to town.

Salesmanship

Dad attended Appalachian Teacher's College (now Appalachian State University) in Boone, North Carolina for two years before entering Wake Forest College, a liberal arts school founded by Southern Baptists east of Raleigh.

At Wake Forest, he encountered a professor named Dr. Benjamin Sledd who instilled in him such a love of literature— English Romantic poetry and Shakespeare in particular— that he determined to devote his life to teaching. He earned the tuition for his senior year sanding wooden chassis bodies for ten months in a Cleveland automobile factory—activity that undoubtedly contributed to the emphysema that killed him fifty years later.

He was twenty-six years old when he graduated in 1928, one year before the year the stock market crashed. Dad was lucky to land a job coaching basketball and teaching senior English in Hudson, a cotton-mill town halfway between Lenoir and Granite Falls. Six years after that my mother joined him on the English faculty and a year later became his wife.

In his last year at Hudson High School, Dad earned $540. Even in the midst of the Great Depression, that was nowhere near enough to repay college loans and start a family.

So, he decided to try selling life insurance. He learned the business at Pilot Life in Greensboro and later joined Security Life and Trust Company—a firm just getting started in Winston-Salem. Officials there appointed him General Agent and assigned him to Lenoir. Throughout his career, he considered Security founders Tully and Bob Blair, and later CEO J. Ed Collette, to be the finest men he ever knew.

Roy Robinson

Possessing fair-mindedness, quick wit and natural friendliness, Dad was really good at his new job. He became a top producer in the company, earning convention trips for himself and Mother to the Grove Park Inn in Asheville (the first grand hotel I ever visited) and to New Orleans and New York City. Determined to develop professionalism in his field, he became an ardent student of salesmanship. *How to Win Friends and Influence People* by Dale Carnegie was practically holy writ in our house! I was six-years-old when Dad sent me toddling up Norwood Street with *Reader's Digest* subscriptions and Christmas card order forms knocking on strangers' doors. It is part of the family lore that I started my sales pitch by asking "Don't you think I have pretty eyes?"

Mother also encouraged and demonstrated friendliness. "You can always brighten a person's life," she would say; and throughout most of her life, her "default setting" was a smile!

During my last two years in high school, I worked as

a salesman Friday afternoons and on Saturdays at a men's clothing store on North Main Street. The store was presided over by Ralph Triplett, Lenoir's handsome Beau Brummell, who often stood arms akimbo at the store's entrance, flirting with the young women of the town as they sauntered by. Inside he taught me how to fold and hang inventory; measure and mark trousers and sleeves on men's suits; and most of all, how to push "related sales." When Ralph's father introduced Triplett Dairy Milk pasteurized and homogenized in cartons my senior year, he pulled me from the clothing store and put me at the dairy counter of a local grocery store to hawk the family's new products. Carton in hand, I stepped in front of shoppers and said, "Excuse me, Ma'am. Please put that Sealtest back in the cooler and try my new Triplett Dairy milk—one-hundred-percent Jersey with more butter fat content than the 3.2% minimum U.S. government standard!" Kraft cheese representatives watched me work one Saturday and hired me on the spot.

Throughout my career I have believed that performance on stage is another kind of salesmanship.

Exotica

Television came to Lenoir in the late 1940s, and our family was among the first to buy a set. Dad rationalized the expensive decision on grounds that my brother might improve his speech and social skills if he used earphones while watching it. In order to receive a signal, he crawled onto the roof of our house in the country and attached to the chimney a gangly aluminum antenna that never pointed in the right direction for long. Down in the living room, the Admiral console's bright eye fluttered behind dancing horizontal lines and falling snow. Most of the time it revealed only an Indian's hazy profile (the station's test pattern), before and after the few programs that were broadcast from Charlotte. When transmission improved, television brought not only Buster Brown, The Lone Ranger and Amos and Andy into our lives, but also great art, drama and classical music. Parishioners would speak excitedly on Sunday after church about the prospect of seeing Leonard Bernstein and the New York Philharmonic on Omnibus or watching soprano Patrice Munsel on The Firestone Hour. With so little choice, everybody with a set watched pretty much the same programs, and in those days, producers still believed in television's power to educate, enlighten, and ennoble.

My mother's youngest sister was Aunt Helen—in the Women's Army Corps dressed in khaki's and a garrison cap when she first marched into Ed's and my life. Like Othello wooing Desdemona, she charmed us with fantastic stories of the war and exotic places she had visited. One time she brought a scrapbook full of war bond posters, jingoistic cartoons (one of Tojo that was especially rodent-like and nasty), pictures of tanks and airplanes, and postcards from Europe and Asia. Another time she gave us the first 78 rpm recordings of classical music we ever received—Beethoven's 5th conducted by Toscanini with the NBC Symphony for Ed and Tchaikovsky's *Nutcracker Suite* by Stokowski and the Philadelphia Orchestra for me. Always she arrived with two dachshunds, a six-pack of beer, and Nanita Gaither, her flamboyant older companion from Mexico who drove Dad up the wall! Because Helen never married, we understood after a while that she and Nanita were a couple; but no one spoke openly about those things in 1948. Aunt Helen was tiny, feisty and brash, and she clanged around in our conservative domicile like a rock in a tin can. Mother always felt bruised and diminished by her by the time she left. A graduate of Duke University and brilliant, Aunt Helen spent most of her life working at a top-secret biology lab in Oak Ridge, Tennessee. She definitely expanded our horizons.

Red-brick First Methodist in Lenoir was one of those steeple-less churches that could have been a synagogue except that there was only one Jewish family in Lenoir. Set between sprawling yellow-brick First Baptist on the right and demure white-brick First Presbyterian on the left, it occupied high ground overlooking the town as sternly as a judge. Dula Hospital was across the street. The two most memorable things about First Methodist Church were its tradition of "altar calls" at the end of services, when parishioners came forward and knelt at the chancel rail to recommit their lives to Jesus—something I felt guilty about when friends did it and I did not, and a soprano soloist who dominated the choir. Gertrude Blackwell forsook a New York operatic career to "marry for love" when she moved to Lenoir. She was the town's true diva—larger than life in every way, with a voice too big for our sanctuary and hats too big for the pews. Gertrude demonstrated and taught serious vocal art in Lenoir for decades. Even though I never took lessons from her, when I was in high school, I joined her and my mother in the Methodist Church Choir.

No one was in the store when Ralph Triplett emerged from the stock room with a little plastic disc in his hand which he flipped neatly across the pants rack. It was so new it was practically still smoking off the Wham-O catalogue! And for me it was love at first toss. Flipping and counting catches, Dennis Rash—a star of the high school track team and an acrobatic maniac who risked his life not to drop the Frisbee—and I set "world records" repeatedly in front of our house in town, once even surpassing the "1,000-toss barrier." By 1958 I probably was one of the best Frisbee players in America.

Bob Blair was Dad's district sales manager. He had movie star good looks and an irresistible personality. Whenever he came for dinner out in the country, he brought unusual gifts, such as a heavy toy brass cannon that could make a terrific bang he knew my brother would enjoy. One day Bob flew from Winston-Salem to Lenoir in his own single-engine airplane and invited Ed and me to go with him for a joy ride. We took off one boy at a time from a runway on the decommissioned U.S. Army airfield just off the Morganton Road and circled around nearby fields and woods—never far out of sight of our parents holding their breath down below. After that introduction Ed and I never were afraid to fly.

Classmate Angela Talton's mother was a painter. In the summer of 1952, just before I followed Linda Broyhill to the junior high school band, Mother enrolled me in Marjorie Talton's Saturday morning art classes. Both of my parents had encouraged me to draw from the time they thought I demonstrated some ability at about age three. That summer I learned a lot about chiaroscuro and three-dimensional perspectives as well as form and composition.

My still-life charcoals and pastels impressed my teacher (and especially my dad) enough to persuade them that I should have been a painter instead of a musician. Dad would have been thrilled, years after his death when I was a member of the New York Philharmonic, to know that my only oil painting was chosen by judges for exhibit in the Lincoln Center Art Show.

Even Lenoir had a concert series in the 1950s that was affiliated, like so many others in small towns across America, with Columbia Artist Management. The Longine Symphonette came to town one winter evening, and Mother and I attended the performance in the high school auditorium. Because it was my first encounter with a professional orchestra, I could hardly wait to run backstage and meet the first oboe player. He was a rotund New York freelancer whose tone, thanks to those anonymous "magic" reeds Hans Moennig sent the Lenoir High School Band, sounded thinner than mine.

John Kaufman was an inscrutable man of indeterminate age—unmarried, swarthy, and taciturn. He was my high school idol. If Capt. Harper on the podium was an impassive human metronome, Kaufman, when he conducted woodwind rehearsals, was catlike, commanding and intense. He never shouted or insulted anyone. Instead, he teased motivation out of us with understated compliments or insinuated reproofs. His office in the Band Building Library was a wonderland of musical possibilities, where I spent hours on weekdays after school and on Saturday mornings when I wasn't working at Triplett's. John Kaufman drove the instrument truck on band trips to the North Carolina-Virginia football games or our own high school games away, and he always invited me to ride with him. In the cab, he regaled me with stories of Leopold Stokowski, Marcel Tabuteau, and other stars of the Philadelphia Orchestra.

Life in the Band

Walking into the Lenoir High School Band building from street level in September 1954, one entered a kind of sanctuary. Huge photographs of the "Great Gate of Kiev" and of the Maryland State flag (a reminder of inauguration-day parade years earlier) greeted the visitor, along with a display of nearly two dozen bronze plaques representing consecutive "Superior" ratings in the highest grade level of the annual North Carolina State Band Contest. Executive offices on the right were occupied by the cheerful band secretary Phoebe Stallings and by Capt. Harper. On the left were uniform and instrument storage rooms, with boys' and girls' locker rooms farther down the hall. A wide stairway led up to the second-floor entrance at the high school ground level, through which we usually entered across a paved area separating it from the classroom building. More than a dozen practice rooms with intercoms were on this level. The spacious band rehearsal room was upstairs on the third floor. Its amphitheater risers faced Captain Harper's podium and a state-of-the-art high fidelity system, out of which resounded Lenoir's own recorded legacy of symphonic transcriptions for band. We all venerated the bandsmen who had gone before us. (Years later, no matter who was conducting the New York Philharmonic, I would think of Carolyn Thornburg's interpretation of an oboe solo in the last movement of Tchaikovsky's Fifth Symphony and try to emulate it.) String basses stood like Swiss guards along the back wall near the timpani and snare drums, and additional percussion instruments were stored in corner rooms in the back.

Also on the third floor was the library, occupied by woodwind instructor John Kaufman. Its file cabinets were packed with band and chamber music and dozens of miniature scores, and its shelves laden with LP recordings. Brass teacher Ralph Ostrom and his students had their special space also, and George Kirsten led the high school's marching program in addition to conducting the junior high school band. Altogether there were five full-time band faculty members serving a public high school with fewer than four hundred students. All of the instruments, uniforms, and music we used were free of charge.

The Lenoir High School Band Building

My dad paid only for the magic oboe reeds ($2.25 apiece) that came to the band as a result of John Kaufman's ongoing relationship with master woodwind repairman Hans Moennig, purveyor of the many Buffet clarinets, Heckel bassoons, Powell and Haynes flutes, and Lorée oboes sold to Captain Harper and reconditioned in Philadelphia every summer by Moennig himself.

During football season, the marching band snapped to attention in Cook Stadium at precisely 7:28 a.m. each school-day morning. I arose at 6:15 and tiptoed downstairs to fix myself a breakfast of pancakes and bacon before trudging across town by myself to school. As leader of the color guard, I had to learn the manual of arms and march in front of the band carrying a World War I rifle with lead in its bore.

Out of six school-day periods, one that substituted for

band members' study hall was used for individual practice of scales, long tones, etudes or concert music. The full band rehearsed during sixth period, after which some of us even stayed to play chamber music. A military chain of command enforced discipline and proper conduct. On the boys' side, traditional freshman hazing involved shining upper-class men's shoes before school each morning and enduring a dreaded "belt-line" at the end of marching season—a torture that was suspended when Dickie Keever's hand smashed through the frosted glass window in the center of the boys' locker room door one day.

In September 1957, a large piece of white poster paper appeared taped on a wall in the second-floor entry. The names of woodwind players were listed down the left-hand side with time blocks marked in seconds across the top. Black ribbons from left to right indicated the length of time each player sustained a single note. We had a month to extend our range, with as many tries as we wanted so long as John Kaufman held his stopwatch and certified the results. I expected to win, but a younger, smaller guy named Edward Tuttle beat me with his tenor saxophone (Where did all that air come from?). Kaufman's long-tone contest was a brilliant idea that improved everyone's breath control.

A more important contest happened each spring. It was the North Carolina State Band Contest (our "Super Bowl") heralded in April by trumpet daffodils. They signaled the time for Captain Harper to schedule evening rehearsals and exhort us even more earnestly to defend Lenoir's long-standing reputation. Expectations were so high in 1955 that no member of the band could imagine lowering the standard.

Unfortunately, I almost did!

Between "The Last Rose of Summer" and the middle of April, there was little time for me to learn how to play a new instrument, much less make a double reed contribution at the state band contest. But Capt. Harper surprised everyone by assigning me a short English horn solo in the band transcription of Verdi's *Sicilian Vespers Overture*. I was beside myself with excitement and had barely fallen asleep when

Mother shook me awake at 4:30 a.m. on contest day. She dressed me in the black wool suit with its discreet red and white piping that was our concert uniform and prepared a quick breakfast. Then she walked with me in pre-dawn darkness down our long gravel driveway to the Wilkesboro Road (since we had not yet moved back to Lenoir) to await a caravan of band vehicles. When they arrived, I climbed aboard the boys' bus and rode two hours to Aycock Auditorium on the campus of the University of North Carolina in Greensboro. The campus was already swarming with brightly-uniformed bandsmen when we arrived.

Outstanding directors from across America judged the competition, and participating bands were organized throughout the day by size, instrumentation and skill level. Grade 6 bands always competed late in the day, with Lenoir given the honor of performing last. Almost everyone stayed and filled the auditorium to hear what we would do. The program order was the same for each group: a march and major composition of the band's own choosing, followed by a piece the judges selected from two others on the menu. When Lenoir's turn came, a judge sang out, *"Sicilian Vespers Overture,* please!" Trembling, I tightened my English horn neck strap and put the reed in my mouth to soak it. My fingers were so wet, they slipped around searching for the right keys, but my mouth was dry as toast! Captain Harper waved his arms and the band began to play. Wait a minute! My solo was coming up . . . I counted, "Six, two, three, four; seven, two, three, four; eight, two . . . Now!"

"PFFT, WHEEZE, WONK!" went the English horn!

Good grief! My reed had glued itself to my parched lips instead of to the top of the English horn and was wobbling around on the bocal. No matter how far I stretched my neck forward and blew harder to keep the tone going, it sputtered like the FM signal on Dad's old Philco radio. Usually unflappable Capt. Harper almost stopped conducting! Thank heaven the moment passed quickly and merciful judges declared that—despite a minor break in the line, Lenoir's assault with Verdi had once again carried the day. Lenoir had indeed won another "Superior" rating in the State Band Contest. I was just about the happiest boy in North Carolina coming home on the bus that night.

High School

My brother and I received Raleigh 3-speed English bikes for Christmas, and mine quickly became my favorite possession. I learned to take it apart and put it back together again, repair the brakes and gear shift mechanism, and keep the wheels and handlebars aligned. I rode it everywhere—but mostly to and from new tennis courts that were constructed during the summer of 1955 in a city park at the north end of Norwood Street. Those courts aroused curiosity and inspired wonder, because almost nobody in Lenoir had ever seen tennis before they were built. It was a grant from one of the furniture factories that paid for them. As soon as the courts were constructed, we went to Bernhardt-Siegel's on Main Street to buy $15.00 Wilson rackets, and, holding them like fly-swatters smacked tennis balls sometimes over the net and sometimes over the fence into Capt. Harper's yard!

An impromptu league developed. Doubles teams that assembled early could play until they lost two sets—after which they usually waited courtside, drinking RC Colas or Upper-10s until their turn came around again. The trick, of course, was to find the strongest partner in the first place. Lights surrounded the courts, and for twenty-five cents an hour we could play after dark until 11:00 each evening. I often rode my bike home for supper and pedaled back again.

Tennis in that fashion was my summer obsession for two years. If I wasn't at the courts in the park, I was banging a ball noisily against the garage door at home. When Lenoir's first Junior Tennis Tournament was staged the summer of 1957, I won, beating long-winded Edward Tuttle in the finals. Only eight of us competed, to be sure, but the prizes were impressive—a jacket from Triplett's and a book on tennis by the legendary Australian Donald Budge. It's the book that did me in! A photograph in the first chapter revealing the so-called "handshake grip," ninety degrees different from the one I had been using, made me incredulous. Had I really been holding my racket incorrectly all this time? Thinking it too late to start over, I decided to stick with my old fly-swatter grip and make the best of it. Frisbie was my game after all.

I thought my big lungs might have made me a pretty good cross-country track man, but band preempted any participation in formal high school extra-curricular sports. As a result, I shot hoops in Welborn Alexander's back yard (perfecting a wicked left-hand hook shot to stay in games of "HORSE") and played Saturday morning football in Johnny Hollifield's yard (hiking the ball to the quarterback in order to be chosen for a team). During summers, caddying for Dad and his buddies, I sometimes got to hit a few golf shots so long as I did not cut the grass.

Shiny new reeds with wire on them arrived one day. They quacked and shrieked when I blew on them.

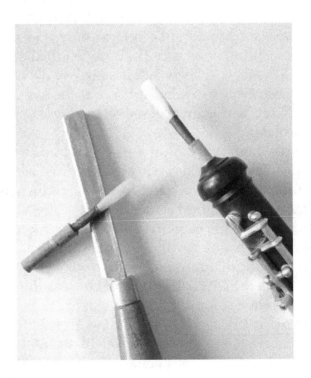

"I can't play on these horrible things!" I exclaimed, running into John Kaufman's office in a panic.

"I know," Kaufman replied. "Hans Moennig says he can't get the good ones right now."

That is when I realized how important reeds are to an oboe player: how much everything—tone, response, intonation—depends upon those two little pieces of grass tied onto a metal extension of the instrument's bore and scraped with a knife until cigarette-paper thin. For centuries, oboe reeds have been hand-crafted to maximize their vibration, requiring oboe players to subdue them by biting. Richard Bates's venerable *History of the Oboe* even describes the reed as the "vibrator" and the instrument as the "resonator." Marcel Tabuteau was the first oboist to conceive of the reed and construct it successfully, as an instrument complete in itself—with inherent attributes of sonority, responsiveness and stable pitch. By doing so he made it possible for oboists to play with a full, rich tone almost as easily as if they were whistling. Late in his career Marcel Tabuteau imparted his revolutionary reed-making secrets to only one student at the Curtis Institute of Music. That unidentified student, in exchange for access to new Lorée oboes and other favors from Hans Moennig in Philadelphia, was the one who made the "magic" reeds Moennig passed on as a favor to the Lenoir High School Band.

Only one hour of classical music could be heard on the radio in Lenoir in those days. It was broadcast at 11:00 p.m. each evening by WMIT on 6,600-foot Mount Mitchell from a tower that was the highest structure east of the Mississippi. Long after my parents went to bed, I sat at our kitchen table with my head in my hands and the sound turned down low, and listened hungrily until midnight to whatever music was transmitted. Then Santa delivered another favorite Christmas present—a portable Motorola hi-fi the size of a typewriter that came with two LPs featuring the New York Philharmonic (Brahms' Fourth Symphony conducted by Bruno Walter and *Scheherazade* conducted by Leonard Bernstein). Most other recordings that joined my collection as soon as I could find them in a bin at Bocock-Stroud's in Winston-Salem were those of my favorite composer, Johannes Brahms.

Girls obsessed me as much as most other teenage boys during high school, but in those years before the "pill," sexual discovery was constrained by unwritten rules limiting "how far one could go." Even the imprint of a walleted condom signaled a boy's lascivious intentions, and no respectable girl would date a guy who carried one. Yet, without it, the unthinkable consequence of "going too far" could be unintended pregnancy and a "shotgun" marriage like the one my brother Ed had to annul a few years later. I came of age in an unnatural "no-man's land" between thwarted consummation and continual horniness—between vestigial Victorianism and the Sexual Revolution!

The other great danger of my teenage years was the automobile. Following Friday night football games, bouncing wildly around on unbelted innerspring bench seats, we careened over mountain roads playing a game of chase we called "car tag." Ed was more obsessed with cars and car engines (which he could hear more clearly than anything else) than the rest of us, and he drove like a madman through corn fields, up road embankments, across back yards—anywhere to avoid being "tagged." Once the Morganton bypass was constructed in Lenoir, providing a perfect quarter-mile-long drag strip, our family car became mysteriously more powerful every time Ed drove it. Word soon spread around Lenoir High School that a souped-up blue and white 1957 V-8 Ford station wagon could beat just about anything in town!

In my junior year, we dressed the best we could for my first and Ed's only Junior-Senior Prom. Ed took his girlfriend, Janiel Melton, and I went with the senior first clarinetist of the band, Franklyn Noll. When Frankie and I arrived home after the dance and found her locked out of her house, I hoisted her up, crinolins and all, and pushed her indelicately through an open bedroom window before whispering "Good night."

By now my enthusiasm for the oboe was worrying my mountaineer parents. They considered artistic life "Bohemian"—therefore "dangerous" on moral as well as economic grounds. Dad called me over to him one afternoon and, tugging at my sleeve, whispered earnestly, "Son, this music business is like religion. Just don't go off the deep end!" His well-intentioned caveat, like so many others before and after, only increased my determination to demonstrate that musical success did not have to be incompatible with the good citizenship and middle-class values he and my mother cherished.

A compelling sense of vocation was beginning to form within me.

Cincinnati Conservatory

"Come meet someone who wants to hear you play," John Kaufman said to me during my practice period. "You might win a scholarship."

There was no time to prepare a real audition, so I gathered whatever music was at hand and played a few notes for the recruiter, after which he invited me to attend a six-week summer band and orchestra camp at the College-Conservatory of Music in Cincinnati. It was the first scholarship I ever received and an exciting opportunity to study at a conservatory and live in a large city. My parents were apprehensive but said they would drive me to Ohio.

In mid-June we headed northwest across the Appalachians, arriving in Corbin, Kentucky at supper time. A filling station attendant told Dad, "If ye-un's want somethin' to eat, thar's a purty good place for fried chicken up the road yonder." We found the restaurant and were about to enter it when a goateed man in a white suit swung the door open and invited us in. Nobody had yet heard of Col. Harland Sanders, but my mother liked the fried chicken so much, she begged him to give her his recipe.

"I'm sorry, ma'am," he told her. "I can't do that. I've just sold it to someone for a franchise." (We didn't understand the concept.) "Would you like my recipe for pecan pie instead?"

"Oh yes! Thank you," Mother answered. And she never prepared pecan pie for us any other way.

Continuing to Cincinnati the next morning, we discovered at the corner of Highland and Oak Streets massive dark stone buildings and stately old trees that could have been the setting for a movie about Count Dracula. While I checked in, Dad paid some remaining fees. Then we collected information about my roommate—a violinist named Darnell Jones from Tennessee; my oboe teacher—an English hornist for the Cincinnati Symphony named Ferd Prior who had once been Assistant Principal Oboe of the New York Philharmonic; and my class schedule for band, orchestra, choir, oboe, conducting and theory.

I had experienced week long boy-scout and church camps, but this summer program was a different kind of challenge away from home. Barely seventeen when I arrived in Cincinnati, I was amazed and intimidated by a city so much bigger and busier than Charlotte. It was fun drinking malted milk shakes and eating White Castle hamburgers for the first time; attending Cincinnati Reds baseball games in Crosley Field when Frank Robinson was a rising star; and seeing fully-staged operas in the zoo. But grumbling and complaining opera orchestra musicians who really seemed to hate their jobs were disenchanting.

Back at the conservatory, where I was performing in an orchestra for the first time and loving it, an eccentric, crook-pipe-smoking genius named Carl Ellis sat first chair. He had the ability to float enchanting phrases that reminded me of little white clouds in a summer sky, making me wonder, "How in the world does he do that?"

The other member of our double reed section was a graduate assistant named Patricia McGaff—"Mother McGaff" to me after she took me under her wing later on in a time of crisis. She usually played English horn. (In her professional career later on, Pat McGaff Nott would perform in the Pennsylvania Ballet and participate at the Marlboro Music Festival; administer the Marcel Moyse Flute Seminars and John Mack Oboe Camp; and become dean of the New World Symphony in Miami, Florida.)

High school students came from everywhere to Cincinnati for the College-Conservatory's summer program, many of whom were living away from home for the first time; and they wasted no time exploiting their freedom in the city. Drunkenness—something I had never witnessed or experienced before—was at the top of the list. My mother may have tasted champagne once or twice in her life, but for reasons she never felt the need to explain to anyone, she didn't drink; and while my dad wished he could, even bourbon and ginger ale upset his stomach. So, when paramedics filled our dormitory hallway late one night, their red ambulance lights strobing eerily from the street below, our student concertmaster lay almost naked, unconscious and covered with his own vomit inside a dresser drawer as if he had been poured there. It was a ghastly, traumatic scene I would never forget.

Growing up in a small town in North Carolina and completely naive about other things as well, I was used to being a "teacher's pet" but not the teacher's "Pat!" My theory teacher had become increasingly "handsy" over the weeks, making me nervous; and stories were circulating in the dorm about an assistant dean's weekend parties "for boys only." Pat McGaff clued me in one night in the laundry room where we were rehearsing oboe-English horn duets when she stopped mid-phrase, took the reed from her lips, and asked suddenly, "I don't know you very well, but you DO like girls, don't you?"

"Of course, I do!" I replied in astonishment.

"Well," she lowered her voice, "you should know that the

"queers" around here are pretty excited about you!" ("Gay" was not used in those days.) Stunned, I searched my imagination for some concept of what it meant to be sexual prey instead of predator, and came up empty. I had no idea how to react.

"Come home right now!" was my dad's advice. "Can't you talk to anybody official about this?"

Mentally checking the list, from the dean right down to the resident advisor on my hall, everybody at the school with any authority was said to be queer. Only my oboe teacher might understand, I thought; but Ferd Prior smiled dismissively when I told him about it. With only a week remaining in the summer program, I put a deadbolt lock on the dormitory door and decided to stick it out.

On the morning of the last day of classes, Pat McGaff telephoned me to tell me about a rumor that was circulating: "You are to be the guest of honor at the last all-boys' party tonight!" She said not to tell my roommate or anyone else, just collect my things and come spend the night with her and her boyfriend. I slept fitfully on her living room couch that night wondering what had become of Darnell Jones.

The Southern Railroad still had passenger service from Cincinnati through Asheville to Morganton, North Carolina in 1957. Taking the train home by myself the next day, I was shaken by a new sense of vulnerability. Conservatory life and the brief view it gave me of the professional world of music had confirmed Dad's dismal opinion of life in the arts. One thing felt certain: I would not go to a conservatory after high school. And I doubted if I would ever again even consider a career in music.

Senior Year

Fall of my senior year in the only election I ever won, I became president of the Lenoir High School band. Aside from presiding at routine officers' meetings on Monday afternoons, the position gave me little authority not conveyed by tenure, except that on one bus trip returning from a football game in Shelby, I stood off some junior boys determined to bully the high school Principal's freshman son.

Despite the Cincinnati disappointment, my music-making continued unabated. I performed in the state Solo and Ensemble Contest; sang every week with the Methodist church choir; worked feverishly on *Scheherazade* in a transcription for the State Band Contest; and when spring came, I took a road trip with Capt. Harper and seven other bandsmen to Deland, Florida—the home of a very good high school band as well as Stetson University. The trip reciprocated an exchange program begun when five Deland instrumentalists joined us in Lenoir the previous year. On the way to Florida, Wilfred Roberts (future Principal Bassoon and Personnel Manager of the Dallas Symphony) and I sat facing backwards in the rear seat of Capt. Harper's station wagon, tossing cherry bombs out the window when he wasn't looking. At intermission of my final high school band concert in May of 1958—representing all of us on stage, I presented Capt. Harper a sterling silver bowl to acknowledge his formal retirement as director. He stayed on for many years after that as Director Emeritus.

From the time Dad took my brother and me to our first Wake Forest football game, we were enrolled as future Demon Deacons. Like just about everybody in North Carolina, we were practitioners of the region's folk "religion," Atlantic Coast Conference basketball(!); and we always rooted for Wake Forest against Duke and North Carolina State and University of North Carolina. Some of my earliest memories are of listening to basketball games with Dad as he chased an FM signal around our house in the country with the radio at his ear. Trustees had voted in the early 1950s to make Wake Forest College a university and move it to Winston-Salem onto land that R. J. Reynolds donated, but it took a long time to design and build the new campus. I must have seen every new building's cornerstone set, and Ed was in the second class of freshmen to enroll on the new campus.

Lenoir High School hosted a "College Fair" every March, too late for most application schedules, but a few representatives always showed up anyway. Behind stacks of brochures and banners hung from tables in the cafeteria, they sat waiting for upperclassmen like me to wander in. After joining a long queue at the Wake Forest table, I noticed a recruiter sitting all alone nearby and decided to go over and say "Hello."

The man was Edmund White, Assistant Dean of Admissions at Davidson College, a Presbyterian men's school north of Charlotte that had an outstanding academic reputation. Capt. Harper was a graduate of Davidson College and a trustee, but I had always been too committed to Wake Forest even to consider applying somewhere else. Within fifteen minutes of meeting Dean White, however, I accepted his invitation to apply to Davidson and tour the campus. It was a love-at-first-sight visit that changed my mind about where to go to college. Concerned about disappointing Dad, I did not tell him right away; but when I did, his reaction surprised me more than my announcement surprised him.

"Good idea, Son!" he said. "Davidson is more like the old liberal arts school I attended than the 'new' Wake Forest anyway."

Since our agreement had always been that he would pay for college if I covered any additional educational expenses that followed, we shook hands and closed the deal: Davidson College it would be!

An unforgettable experience my senior year was a trip my best friend Dennis Rash and I took to Charlotte to eat Italian food at "The Open Kitchen" and attend a concert by the Philadelphia Orchestra in Ovens Auditorium. I still have the concert program signed by John DeLancie, William Kincaid, Mason Jones, and other legendary players of the orchestra.

Later that spring an item appeared in the Lenoir NEWS-TOPIC announcing a competition for two full scholarships to Transylvania Music Camp. John Kaufman and my mother both encouraged me to apply. Brevard, N.C., site of the camp, was the county seat of Transylvania County (hence the camp's name) and a modest community situated in the mountains southwest of Asheville. Nearby, flowing pristinely out of Pisgah National Forest was the Davidson River—a stream with water so pure it prompted Acusta, the largest producer of cigarette paper in the world, ironically to locate its factory there. At about the same time, the beautiful mountain setting and cooler summer weather enticed founder/director James Christian Pfohl to re-locate his summer band camp from the Queens College campus in Charlotte to Transylvania County.

Since WBTV provided the scholarships, the station hosted the competition. On the appointed day, I drove from Lenoir to Charlotte with my piano accompanist, played the first movement of the Mozart Oboe Concerto from memory and won! Dr. Pfohl himself congratulated me. The other judge—an oboist named Frank West who was coincidentally the band director at Davidson College—awarded me a $50 scholarship from the Music Department on the spot. The winner of the other Transylvania scholarship was a singer and trombone player named William Workman whose father headed the Psychology Department at Davidson. Many other Davidson College connections were soon to enrich my life . . .

For our high school yearbook, the 1958 "Bearcat," I was asked to draw a whole series of mascot figures introducing different sections of the book. They contributed to my designation as "Most Talented" among the "Senior Superlatives."

"I know his name!" John Kaufman exclaimed excitedly just before graduation. "John Mack makes those 'magic' reeds we get from Hans Moennig! He is the young first oboist of the New Orleans Philharmonic." I never learned how Kaufman did it, but unmasking John Mack was the best graduation gift I could have received in 1958. It gave me hope of a continuing connection to the only oboe reeds I could play on.

Graduation a few days later felt indeed like "commencement"—the beginning of life as a young adult rather than the end of something (except for the band) that I regretted leaving. While classmates cried and embraced each other all around me, I walked confidently out of Lenoir High School into a radiant spring night.

James Christian Pfohl

Jim Pfohl (pronounced "foal") was a phenomenon, and music is only half the story! The son of a Moravian bishop, he had grown up in a massive stone manse next to God's Acre graveyard in Old Salem, North Carolina—site of the first symphony orchestra in Colonial America. His classmate and rival, Thor Johnson, the son (only) of a Moravian minister, was born in Wisconsin but later moved as a child to North Carolina. Both men earned undergraduate degrees at the University of North Carolina and master's degrees from the University of Michigan. Thor was in Serge Koussevitzky's inaugural Conducting Seminar at Tanglewood with Leonard Bernstein in 1940. Seven years later he became the youngest American-born conductor of a major orchestra when he was appointed Music Director of the Cincinnati Symphony. Jim Pfohl, meanwhile, was only nineteen years old when he created the first applied music major at an all-men's liberal arts school in America (at Davidson College in 1933). Within one-year Pfohl organized, trained and directed a concert band, an orchestra, and an acclaimed chorus on campus. The Charlotte *OBSERVER*, acknowledging his youthful achievements in a 1934 editorial, opined that it was not unusual for genius to reveal itself at an early age in the field of music. "Just look at Mozart!" it said.

Moravians trace their roots back to Jan Hus, a Bohemian priest influenced in the late fourteenth century by the writings of the English cleric John Wycliffe, who opposed Roman Catholic Church doctrines discounting personal piety as a means of salvation, forbidding priests to marry, and granting absolution by means of purchased "indulgences." Hus was one of the first reformers to urge translation of the Bible into the vernacular. In July 1415, when he refused to recant beliefs adjudged by the Council of Constance to be heretical, he was burned at the stake.

His martyrdom set off rebellions all over Czechoslovakia that sowed the seeds of the Protestant Reformation one hundred years before Martin Luther. Two centuries after his death, Hus adherents worshiped with translated Bibles, their own hymnody and a unique surviving liturgical element known as the "love feast." They were among the 30,000 Protestants routed at the battle of White Mountain in 1620, the third year of the Thirty Years' War. Those who survived fled west to the estate of Count Nikolaus Ludwig von Zinzendorf of Saxony, where they founded a community called Herrnhut. From that time to the present-day, Moravians have expressed core beliefs in one simple epigram: "In essentials, unity; in non-essentials, liberty; and in all things, love."

Moravians were among the first Protestant denominations to dispatch missionaries, but they directed their evangelism to people they considered remote and un-churched—in places like Greenland, St. Thomas and Tanzania. When they sailed to North America, it was with the prisoners who colonized Georgia. From there they migrated north into Pennsylvania and New York, ministering to the Algonquin and Mohican Indians. In 1766, they settled in North Carolina on 100,000 acres of farmland purchased from a representative of King George III. There, in the red clay of the Piedmont, Moravians established their patterns of simple communal living, liturgical worship, daily prayer, and musical performance, just as they had in Bethlehem, Pennsylvania, and would again in Ephraim, Wisconsin.

By the time Thor Johnson and Jim Pfohl were growing up in Old Salem, Moravian churches pervaded the region, and their Easter celebrations distinguished Winston-Salem in the Southeast almost as much as Mardi Gras did New Orleans. On the night before Easter, congregational brass bands clustering on street corners all over town played chorales until just before dawn. They then led processions of parishioners and visitors to the Salem village square in front of Home Moravian Church, where at the center of a throng of believers, old Bishop Pfohl (Jim's father) strained unsteadily atop a ladder to see the first rays of dawn. As soon as the sun appeared, he lifted his right arm high and wheezed triumphantly, "Christ has risen!" to which ecstatic congregants responded as one, "Christ is risen indeed!"

It was out of this fecund tradition of piety that Thor Johnson and James Christian Pfohl both emerged as two of the most important American musicians of their generation.

At Michigan, Jim Pfohl played piano, organ, trumpet and string bass. He also studied conducting. Soon after graduation, in addition to his work at Davidson College, he became organist and choirmaster of Myers Park Presbyterian Church, one of the largest congregations in the city, and simultaneously founded and headed the Music Department of Queens College, Davidson's sister school for women in Charlotte. He conducted the Charlotte Symphony Orchestra, created and conducted the Charlotte Opera, founded the Reston Music Center in Virginia, and later became Music Director and Conductor of the Jacksonville (Florida) and York (Pennsylvania) Symphony Orchestras. Throughout his life, in many different directions, Jim Pfohl demonstrated that he was an imaginative, resourceful and irrepressible "Johnny Appleseed" of musical institutions!

And to give effective expression to his entrepreneurial ideas, Dr. Pfohl employed a unique operational principle: "Anything that can be imagined can be printed; and anything that is printed is real!" Here was a bishop's son with faith in the word—the printed, secular word! For years I watched him translate ideas into reality with a persuasive brochure. The Brevard Music Center would be his most enduring institutional legacy.

In 1934 Jim Pfohl created a band camp like the one he had attended at Interlochen, Michigan, five years earlier. It was a way to keep his "Davidson boys" practicing during their long summer vacations, and it thrived until the U.S. Army took over Davidson's campus in 1942, forcing Pfohl to move to Queens College in Charlotte. Meanwhile, Dr. Pfohl scoured Western North Carolina for a permanent summer home in the mountains. In 1944, he and two business partners discovered the perfect site—a failing boys' recreational camp around a pristine lake on 180 acres in Transylvania County. Co-educational Transylvania Music Camp, the germ of The Brevard Music Center, was born!

Transylvania Music Camp

"Service to Youth through Music" was the motto of James Christian Pfohl's band and orchestra camp, which put priorities straight as far as I was concerned. Even though I had never visited Brevard, the town and its lovely mountains made me feel right at home. Years later I would write from a park bench in Cologne, Germany, about my first night at Transylvania Music Camp—when "a thousand-noted symphony of night things" murmured all around me and a creosote-scented chill in the evening air made me shiver.

Was it just excitement?

From the stone-pillared entrance to the camp, a picturesque lake and lodge with an expansive veranda came into view—then a campus as random as a pioneer settlement. Boys' cabins climbed the hill on the left side of the large, wood-frame dining hall; girls' cabins hid in the trees on the right. Driving across a dam and around the dining-hall, one crunched into a wide gravel parking lot adjoining an open-sided gym crudely converted into a concert hall. Buildings that functioned as library, infirmary, teaching studios and rehearsal rooms, and huts and lean-tos for campers' individual practice were scattered everywhere. Wooden dorms and a rehearsal shed for the junior high-school kids known as "hill-toppers" perched up above the parking lot. Faculty members lived in cabins all around the perimeter of the camp, where without air-conditioning their only luxury was a screened-in porch.

"Reveille" woke everyone a bit too early each morning. More than 250 campers washed in cold water, dressed, swept their cabins and made their bunk beds ready for inspection—then raced to get to breakfast on time. Theory classes began at 8:15 and orchestra rehearsals at 9:00. (Bands and the chorus rehearsed in the afternoon.) After lunch during a compulsory rest period, letters home to parents were assigned. Recreation—swimming in the lake, softball or tennis—happened at different times during the day, as did private lessons for all instruments (including piano and voice) scheduled individually with the faculty. Attendance was required for everyone at evening concerts, insuring that even the worst performers had an audience. "Call to quarters" sounded soon enough not to allow TOO much time for "making out" behind the hydrangeas; and "Taps" bade a haunting, nostalgic farewell to the day.

Transylvania Music Camp was inspired by Joseph Maddy's National Music Camp at Interlochen, Michigan, which James Pfohl himself attended in 1929. A different pedagogy developed at Brevard when Dr. Pfohl discovered that student ensembles improved more quickly and sold tickets more successfully if faculty members participated in them. Since teachers could not totally supplant tuition-paying students, an ingenious compromise placed faculty members in principal chairs during early rehearsals before moving them to assistant positions for concerts. Emulating their teacher's artistry in the orchestra proved to be an even more effective way for students to learn than face-to-face in private lessons. Timothy Galway would confirm this in his best-seller, *The Inner Game of Tennis*; but it was Dr. Pfohl's model of orchestral imitative learning that directly inspired the enormously successful pedagogy of the Grand Teton Orchestral Seminar in Jackson Hole, Wyoming, thirty years later.

The Lenoir High School Band's Lorée oboe and some John Mack reeds easily won me first chair in the Transylvania Symphony in 1958. Theodora Overture by Handel and Tchaikovsky's 4th Symphony were on the opening concert. My teacher was Philip Koonce, a good-natured University of Illinois graduate student, who obliged graciously whenever Dr. Pfohl asked him to move down in the oboe section.

Transylvania Music Camp was in all ways a reflection of Southern culture in the 1950s. There were no black students, only "Mr. Hugh" and "Miss Beulah" who worked as custodians and lived in quarters somewhere behind the auditorium's Green Room. "Yes Sir" and "Yes Ma'am" were the expected response to instructors, and "Y'all's" were heard all over camp. Crawford Best, a bassoonist and Angier B. Duke Scholar at Duke University (later Principal Bassoon and Personnel Manager of the New Orleans Philharmonic and Santa Fe Opera), was the camp's "Mayor" in 1958; and Sheila Simpson, a raven-haired beauty from Mississippi who played the horn, was often chosen "Miss Transylvania" and reigned at the "Transylvania Ball." Mandatory Christian vesper services that took place every Sunday evening were staged in an amphitheater on the other side of the lake. They were led by Dean of Students John Guiton, a sometime preacher who was wrestling coach at The Citadel in Charleston, South Carolina. He and Dr. Pfohl enforced camp rules strictly enough to insure that any infraction would bring a student's dismissal and quick trip home.

Served family-style in the dining hall, Sally Dick's meals made school lunches taste gourmet. Thank goodness teenage appetites, hard work, and mountain air helped the food go down! As an antidote, on especially hot afternoons, Sally sometimes hauled watermelons from a stream that fed the lake and spread luscious slices all around.

Monday afternoons were free. Campers could walk along Prospect Street down to Brevard to do their laundry or to get a toasted pimento cheese sandwich and a milk shake at the drug store. From there it was a short drive past Biltmore Dairy Bar's famous black walnut ice cream to the entrance of Pisgah Forest, where NC 276 wound alongside the Davidson River past Looking Glass Falls up to the Blue Ridge Parkway. Parents who got permission would sometimes take their sons and daughters on Sunday mornings out of camp to Berry's Restaurant for blueberry pancakes before church, or to Sliding Rock for a swim and a campground cook-out in the forest.

Mid-summer an olive-skinned photojournalist named Constantine "Gus" Manos arrived and asked me to pose for a feature story he was producing for AMERIKA—the State Department magazine published for the Soviet Union during the Cold War. Dr. Pfohl was happy to grant permission and give me time off for the venture. During several days Gus posed me in picturesque places around camp, oboe in hand, while he clicked away. One night, visiting our cabin after call to quarters, he whispered conspiratorially to my bunk-mates and me until taps about his disdain for the "crass" world of business and his idealistic devotion to the art of photography. We thought he was a really cool guy!

Dr. Pfohl invited me to join him at a Rotary Club luncheon in nearby Hendersonville the last week of camp. He warned me to be ready to give a little testimonial about my experiences at Transylvania. After Dr. Pfohl made his practiced, compelling appeal for support of "Service to Youth through Music," he introduced me. Arising beside my plate, I surprised myself by sounding also like a country preacher. I proclaimed with gusto how inspired I was and how happy it had made me to perform the world's greatest music in one of the world's most beautiful places!

Alexander Pope once penned an insightful couplet: "Just as the twig is bent, the tree's inclined" that surely anticipated my little Rotary Club speech in Hendersonville—one that bent me in the direction of unembarrassed advocacy on behalf of the arts, education, and religion for the rest of my life.

In his final report, faculty oboist Phillip Koonce summed up our work together, calling me "an exceptional talent" who might become "a first-rate professional oboist," despite my being perhaps "too involved in the emotional mood of the music." My cabin counselor, in another assessment sent to my parents at the end of camp, wrote the following: "In my opinion, Joe is our outstanding student this summer."

It was tennis playing, however, ("fly-swatter grip" notwithstanding) that earned me my only award in 1958—"Best Boy Athlete"—which I shared with a horn player named Ronald Coleman. I probably won because my opponent all summer was flutist Charles Delaney, the most popular member of the faculty, whom Dr. Pfohl could watch playing with me through his office window. A native of Winston-Salem and also a Davidson College graduate, Charlie (pictured below with oboist Alfred Genovese) was Professor of Flute at the University of Illinois and a brilliant performer who had studied in Switzerland. He was my new hero—an all-American, all-around "good guy" who demonstrated that musical virtuosity and solid middle-class values were compatible after all.

Davidson College: Freshman Year
"Initiation"

"My name is Grier Martin. What's yours?" asked the tall, handsome man who encountered me in front of Chambers building at the center of Davidson's campus one splendid afternoon in early September. "I'm your new president," he said, smiling broadly. "That makes BOTH of us freshmen." (My red beanie gave me away.) "Come around and see me whenever you want—my office door will always be open to you." I had a feeling he meant it.

Fewer than a thousand Caucasian males were enrolled at Davidson College in the school year 1958-59. Tuition, room and board cost my dad $1,500 for each of the two semesters, and I have a postcard I wrote home to him apologizing for spending $50 on textbooks. Black stewards in white jackets cleaned our dorm rooms and straightened our beds, and laundry service was free. Situated under towering oak trees, the campus with its Georgian red brick buildings stretched along the east side of NC 21 twenty miles north of Charlotte. The town of Davidson itself occupied little more than three nondescript blocks on the other side of the roadway. Gas at a nearby Kirby filling station was 25 cents a gallon.

Founded in 1837 by Presbyterians for Presbyterians, Davidson College took its religious heritage seriously. Chapel services were required of all students an hour on Monday, Wednesday, and Friday mornings, with attendance confirmed on the basis of students' occupancy of assigned seats in the auditorium as well as in church pews for compulsory Vespers every Sunday evening. My freshman advisor, Max Polley, was a biblical scholar just beginning his career as a college professor. Because everyone had to take two years of Religion, I signed up for his course in Old Testament. Other subjects were English literature, Principles of Mathematics, European history, and German.

Physical Education and ROTC were additional requirements for freshmen and sophomores. I nearly drowned passing the swimming test and needed twelve minutes to run the only mile of my life; but ROTC was the biggest challenge. Years of precision marching and practicing the manual of arms in the Lenoir High School Band made me sure I could jump over beginner drills and land in the elite ROTC Honor Guard instead. It was a bad idea. Our upper-class commander was so offended by my participation in his company he punished me continually for joining. My accumulated drill demerits may be a record still standing at Davidson; they account for the only "C" on my college transcript.

Home visitations which rotated among faculty members

on Sunday evenings were a tradition of gracious hospitality at Davidson, and my German teacher and his wife were my first hosts. I walked the short distance to their home after Vespers, eager to see how they lived and hoping to score some "brownie points" with one of my new teachers.

When Professor Walter Robinson discovered my passion for oboe playing, he suggested, "Decide right now to win a Fulbright to Germany. That way you can go to Europe for free and discover for yourself the wellsprings of Western classical music." It was the seed of an idea that blossomed successfully four years later; even if in that first week of college, there seemed little chance it would sprout at all.

Before arriving on campus, I worried whether Lenoir High School had prepared me well enough for the rigors of Davidson College. Gertrude Whitehead's algebra classes were challenging to be sure, but most of the courses I took in high school were a joke, and mischief grew in them like mold on weeks old bread. Three of my classmates and I survived Jay Allen's Physics class by forming a breath-holding relay team, using a stopwatch to time heroic efforts that eventually broke the ten-minute barrier (training that certainly improved my oboe playing). We also put an alarm clock in Jay Allen's lab coat one morning and set it to go off five minutes before the end of class. When the clock started ringing, Jay jumped from his desk shouting "Far dree-ul!" "Far dree-ul!" and dashed to the door to hold it open for us. We flew past him down three floors to a parking lot behind the school. There, waiting for other students who never came, some of us stood laughing in self-incriminating convulsions. We could still hear the alarm clock clanging in the classroom above us.

A new interdisciplinary seminar entitled "Humanities" was being offered at Davidson in 1958, and Max Polley advised me to apply. To get in I would have to write a timed essay in response to the question, "In a democracy, are we our brother's keeper?" I remember sitting pen-in-hand at my desk during the exam pondering vacantly what to write. My high school senior thesis came to mind—the one entitled

"The Profession of Psychiatry" which I produced in one weekend, using only unattributed Reader's Digest articles as research materials. My stomach was churning.

"Study two hours outside of class for every hour in," Dad had said when he abandoned me and my trunk on the fourth floor of Watts Hall a week earlier. "Just do your best."

At the time, I didn't think he had set the bar too high; but now I wasn't so sure. My pathetic answer to that Humanities question placed me in Basic English where colorful Instructor George Lloyd quickly slapped a grade of C-minus on the first essay I wrote for him. That is when I realized I had some serious catching up to do.

Fraternities were literally "Greek to me." I knew nothing about them and was astonished to learn that 90% of Davidson's students belonged to one. Those who did not formed a residual category known as "GDI's" ("goddammed independents"), required to eat in the Student Union cafeteria throughout their college years. Junior Bob Denham, my host when I visited the campus back in April, advised me to participate in Rush Week, and explained that Davidson's fraternities were not residential—only dining and social clubs in a semicircle of new houses behind the dorms where the food was much better than in the Union. Student body president John Kuykendahl and he were members of Phi Delta Theta, prompting me to try for that house. When I learned how many "legacy" candidates were hoping to get in and did not, I realized how lucky I was to be invited to join one of the best fraternities on campus.

Conventional wisdom holds that fraternities are a monochromatic social environment. To the contrary, in my case Phi Delta Theta's enforced "brotherhood" constituted one of the most inclusive experiences of my life. I would never have hung around "Hog" Anderson otherwise; and "Hog" would surely have black-balled me if he had known that I was a teetotaler who held all four years to the dreary conviction that the social costs of drinking alcohol were not worth its pleasures (a sentiment especially unwelcome at weekend after-dance parties when everyone else was getting drunk) as well as an oboe player, which REALLY made me a weirdo! Soon after pledging Phi Delta Theta, I was invited by the brothers to celebrate my musical peculiarity with Randy Austin, a singing-and-banjo-picking fellow pledge, atop a dining room table for a rendition of "Columbus Stockade Blues." My first musical performance at Davidson College earned me the nickname, "Oboe Joe," as well as a jar of Jiffy peanut butter to eat on the spot—a precedent of "playing for my supper" that would continue in more sophisticated ways throughout my professional career.

Another of my fraternity pledge brothers was a lieutenant for the Billy Graham Crusade scheduled in the Charlotte Coliseum that September. Graham Allison transferred to Harvard following his sophomore year at Davidson, after which he won a Marshall scholarship, headed the John F. Kennedy School, authored many books, and advised several U.S. Presidents. Today he is considered one of the nation's leading authorities on nuclear weaponry. But back then, after he had invited several of us freshmen to attend the Billy Graham Crusade, someone got the idea to visit another evangelical rally later in the year. A newspaper photograph of an entourage of black Cadillacs arriving in Charlotte heralded Oklahoma faith healer A. A. Allen's upcoming revival meetings and inspired an upper-class fraternity brother's idea to send a few pledges in and put the reverend's healing powers to the test.

Four of us settled into our seats high up in the Coliseum. Three joined lustily in all the hymn-singing and watched with sacrilegious amusement as congregates danced themselves into a "speaking in tongues" frenzy. When Pastor Allen summoned the "halt and lame" to come forward and form a line for healing, the three of us with open eyes guided the fourth—our "blind" Phi Delt brother John Chiles—down the steep coliseum steps. "Keep 'em shut!" we whispered through clenched teeth, but John's eye-lids would not stop fluttering. Choking back suppressed laughter, we had barely joined the queue in front of A. A. Allen's makeshift pulpit when beefy bouncers spotted us. They yanked us roughly out of line and escorted us straight through the crowd to the Coliseum exit. It was not the religious experience we expected, but it may have been a "healing" after all. We didn't mock other peoples' religious observances after that!

Something more traumatic scarred my spring semester. Returning to Davidson College from Lenoir on a glorious Easter Sunday afternoon, I was dropped off by a friend in front of the Sealtest plant on US 21 just north of Charlotte. Hitch-hiking was commonplace among students in those days, so I just stuck my thumb out and waited. Soon a driver stopped to pick me up. His looks bothered me, but I had never preconceived how to say "Thanks, but no thanks" to someone unsavory who might offer me a ride. Social convention just sucked me onto the front seat of the car. I knew at once it was a mistake. The swarthy driver, all long arms and legs, twisted his torso and shifted his weight so he could stare at me as much as the road ahead. His left arm was draped awkwardly across the top of the steering wheel and his right dangled off the edge of the seat between us. Avoiding his glance, I admired the redbuds, azaleas and dogwood trees in bloom on my side of the car and tried to relax into the ride.

An imprecise gesture crossed the corner of my eye, making me turn reflexively towards it. Half a foot from my face and staring back at me like the eye of a Cyclops, was the barrel of a large caliber pistol! I heard "CLICK!" and thought I was dead! Instead, bullets fell from the open magazine and bounced off the seat into my lap. Picking one up, I feigned wonderment and said, "Wow! These are great! We're studying guns and bullets in ROTC right now!" My left hand was clutching a leather-bound book of poetry Dad had given me and my right gripped the passenger-side door handle tightly. I resolved to jump from the car if the guy slowed to turn onto a red clay track somewhere up the road. Holding up the leather volume, I lied hopefully that I was a per-ministerial student; but the driver's expression never changed. He leered at me between glances at the road ahead.

Suddenly he reached down again and snatched from

behind my feet the butt of a sawed-off shotgun. He opened the glove compartment and shotgun shells tumbled onto the floor. Then he told me to turn around and look at a dirty bedspread covering objects on the back seat as he boasted, "I have a radio up here that can track any police signal in the state!" By now my senses were white hot—so alert to the car's rhythm that I twitched at every turn of the wheel or touch of the brakes. Thankfully, the guy drove on for a while without incident.

As he approached the town limits of Davidson, he began to rant and curse his life in the military. I congratulated him meekly for serving, when he swerved suddenly and stopped with a jolt beside the curb northwest of campus. Incredulous that I was still in one piece and at the place I hoped to be, I opened the door and stepped onto the curb. A bony talon snared my left forearm and yanked me back onto the front seat of the car. Through grimy, yellow teeth the guy hissed into my face, "I just want to wish you all the luck in the world!" Then he gave me a push and sped away, leaving me with my heart pounding like timpani in the opening of Brahms' First Symphony. When I was able, I walked to the Phi Delt house to report what had happened. My own story sounded as incredible as a stranger's account of a bad dream; I could hardly believe it myself! I resolved never to hitchhike again.

The oboe I played during my freshman year belonged to Davidson College. Frank West had assured me it was a Lorée available to me as long as I wanted, but he didn't tell me it was an antique "ring-system" instrument with many fewer keys than the modern instrument I had used in the Lenoir High School Band. Davidson College's Wind Ensemble was equally disappointing. Old Shearer Hall, the former greystone college chapel that was being replaced by a new red-brick church (the Davidson College Presbyterian Church, or "DCPC" as it was called) on the southwest corner of the campus, was not yet demolished. Only its pews had been stripped away. Twelve bandsmen (three of whom played saxophone) showed up for our first Thursday evening rehearsal. We arranged our own chairs and music stands on the sloping wooden floor of the sanctuary and slogged our way through an arrangement of Tchaikovsky's "1812" Overture that sounded like hell. Walking back to the dorm afterward, I wondered if I had sacrificed my love of music upon the altar of a liberal education.

At the end of long rows of book stacks in the library, carrels were assigned to students for private study. They provided sanctuary from dorm room wrestling matches and noisy horseplay in the halls. One of my required freshman courses was a survey dubbed "the culture course" because of its emphasis upon esoteric names and dates and historical minutiae. The willowy professor who taught it liked to patrol in front of the class with a pointer held in his hand like a swagger stick, and he called me "Bo." The night before the spring term final exam in his course, he slipped quietly through the stacks to my carrel to ask how things were going.

"Why don't you take a study break and come over to the house?" he asked, pressing his privates uncomfortably against my shoulder. His hot breath was in my ear, "My wife is out of town this week, Bo. If you bring your pajamas, I will give you an 'A!'"

As soon as he was out of sight, I ran across campus to tell my roommate that I HAD to go to a professor's house.

"If I am not back in fifteen minutes, you must . . . you MUST come get me! Promise me," I begged him. "Don't ask why! Just do it!"

The professor lived an easy walk from campus. Nevertheless, my heart was pounding when I climbed the stairs onto his front porch and knocked on the screen door, which swung open immediately. Looking down at me, the professor asked, "Where are your pajamas, Bo?"

"I'm not that ambitious," I answered through clinched teeth, knees shaking.

"Well, come on in, anyway. Take a seat in the den and wait for me."

Motioning casually toward a chair, he went into the kitchen and sliced a piece of chocolate cake and poured me a glass of milk. We sat chatting awkwardly about European history in the den for a while—until he asked me what I thought about Marie Antoinette's sex life. That's when the room went out of focus and began to spin around me. "My God, he's drugged the milk!" I thought.

"I . . . I . . . I have to go now," I said, struggling to get to my feet, stammering and stumbling toward the door. "I have an important exam tomorrow!"

Thankfully the professor did not protest or intercept me. Instead, he insisted on driving me back to the campus, and once we were in the car, acting deflated and embarrassed, he muttered about learning some interesting things in the Navy. My grade on his exam the next day was an honest "A-minus."

Little brick modules with windows in them connected to each other like segments of a caterpillar and sat in two parallel strips at the front of the campus. Called "Oak Row" and "Elm Row," they were the original 1837 Davidson College dormitories—now office and rehearsal spaces used by the Music Department. The chairman was Donald Plott, a superb choral man with a beaming smile and luxuriant mane who conducted the Charlotte Oratorio Society as well as the Davidson College Male Chorus and Chapel Choir. As much as the Male Chorus was one of the glories of Davidson College, the Wind Ensemble was not. Poorly attended, it languished for two hours on Monday and Thursday evenings under the baton of its conductor, a ruddy fellow dubbed by his students "the little red mole," whom I often found sound asleep mid-afternoons at his desk in Elm Row. Under construction, the Cunningham Fine Arts Building would soon provide better facilities for music, art and theater, but the two caterpillars survived. A room was always available in one of them whenever I wanted to practice. A symbiotic relationship between academics and music now characterized my life at Davidson College, with concentration lost in one realm regenerated in the other. I never considered majoring in Music, however. The strength of Davidson's faculty and curriculum lay elsewhere.

Oboe reeds were a problem that worsened during my freshman year. John Kaufman had to cut my umbilical cord to the Lenoir High School Band in order to save John Mack's reeds for oboe students coming along behind me. Consequently, my only recourse was to write Moennig directly and beg him for help. He responded by mailing me some of the useless substitutes I had hated in high school, explaining that John Mack once again had not delivered his on time. With important off-campus professional gigs coming up, I was getting desperate by the time four John Mack reeds appeared in my mailbox. One of them won me second chair in the Charlotte Symphony—a position I held most of the four years I was at Davidson; another, first chair in a new chamber orchestra called The Charlotte Symphonette; and with still another, I made a recording of a Handel sonata that accompanied my application to Tanglewood in Lenox, Massachusetts.

Meeting John Mack

Above my top bunk at Transylvania Music Camp, I could see a wooden beam on which John Mack had boldly carved his name, giving evidence that he once slept there. (In fact, he spent four summers playing and teaching at Brevard.) Furthermore, John Mack's uncle, Professor Charles Eberhardt, had served as camp chaplain at Transylvania Music Camp for many years and once headed the Davidson College Religion Department. His father, Sy Mack, also an ordained Presbyterian minister, worked in New York City in the denomination's Office of Foreign Missions. Both had an exalted opinion of Davidson College, often referring to it as "Princeton of the South," and John Mack's wife, Anne Doane, was a violist well-known to and admired by many of the musicians with whom I freelanced. She was from Charlotte, where her mother still resided.

So here is the bottom line: the greatest reed-maker in America, upon whom I was utterly dependent from the first day I picked up an oboe; who could have come from

Timbuktu and had no affinity for me or my predicament whatsoever; and whom I knew only as the young first oboist of the New Orleans Philharmonic—this utter stranger—turned out to be practically my kinsman!

It was a miracle!

In the winter of my freshman year I initiated an intense correspondence with John Mack, sending my first letter to him c/o the New Orleans Philharmonic. His response to me, dated February 17, 1959 was thoughtful, eloquent and exhaustive—typed by him single-spaced, on both sides of a single piece of stationery. After a few preliminary comments relating to the risks of a career in music if I chose to pursue one, he wrote, "Now to get down to things of more immediate importance and interest to you, namely reeds. You are in the neighborhood of the three-thousandth person to write me for reeds, and your letter wins the prize, were there one, for appeal, though your hopes are quite frankly foundless . . . You should immediately begin to make your own reeds to avoid being dependent upon an outside source."

One week later he wrote again: "I must confess that your letters intrigue me, evidenced by the fact that they are being answered. If this keeps up much longer, I shall feel compelled to bill you for your lessons."

He included the name and address of a man in Long Island who could send me the supplies I needed to begin my own reed-making. Later in that letter, responding to my persistent questions about musical professionalism, he summed up his view of the creative challenges of playing an instrument in this way: "I recognize the enormity of the job of coming up with anything that, as a finished product, includes a tone both good and beautiful, good phrasing, an understanding of balance and the effects of acoustics on every element of performance, technique equal to the demands, completely reliable and adjustable intonation, and a viewpoint with real musical value. A person who can muster up enough of these requisites to do creditable work often finds that the strain, physical and mental and to the nervous system, precludes his continuance in the field. It takes guts."

On March 6, another missive arrived: "You are forcing me to extend myself literately in order to be able to rest easy after your letters. Your tenacity is hopeful." He suggested that I find a decent tape recorder and send him a sample of my playing.

Intent upon demonstrating to him that I had the requisite guts to be an oboe player, I ordered basic reed-making tools and materials from Irving Cohn as instructed, and went to work. Beginner's luck charmed my first attempt: the reed actually played! I practiced on it for an hour, packed it up and sent it to John Mack in New Orleans for a critique. When it came back to me a week later, it was marked with X's and O's indicating where Mack thought I should have scraped more or less. (I still have that reed.) But his note of congratulations was already ironic. In the weeks following that first lucky reed, I carved days of my college life into the waste basket trying to make another one that worked. Tests went unprepared and papers unwritten. In desperation, I whined that if John Mack left me destitute, I would surely flunk out of Davidson College or give up the oboe entirely.

Just then word came that my recording of the Handel Sonata had favorably impressed the Tanglewood admissions committee. Their letter offered me a generous scholarship for study at the renowned summer home of the Boston Symphony. I wrote John Mack at once, telling him the good news and assuring him that even though we had never met each other, he must not take the chance that I might misrepresent him in the land of his rival Ralph Gomberg. Now he would HAVE to violate his professional principles and send me some reeds to take to Tanglewood!

The ploy worked. A telegram arrived immediately, indicating that John Mack was playing the Moravian Music Festival with Thor Johnson in nearby Winston-Salem. It stated the date, place, and time of our encounter in June and said simply, "Meet me!" Bassoonist Wilfred Roberts accompanied me from Lenoir to the appointed spot on the Salem College campus. After searching all around, we found a note tacked to a dormitory door that explained that he would be delayed because of car repairs in Greensboro. His monstrous green Cadillac ("It's the image, m'boy!") was ailing. The note instructed me to await his return.

We met later that afternoon in an occasion that was supercharged for both of us. John Mack was only thirty years old but he seemed much more mature to me than that—a fully grown adult possessing great energy, charisma and authority. I think I must have appeared younger than eighteen to him—just a presumptuous kid pretending to be his protégé. I pulled out my oboe and stuck in a reed, ready to play for him; but before I could utter a note, Mack demanded, "Show me your teeth!"

"Hmmm, Bugs Bunny incisors," he mused. "Even if you are talented, with teeth like that don't count on becoming a professional oboist. Your upper lip isn't long enough to cover the top blade of the reed."

"Maybe on other people's reeds," I remember thinking, because when I played on his, people told me I sounded great whether I covered the top blade or not. Nevertheless, recalling photographs I had seen in *National Geographic* magazine, I tugged hard on my upper lip whenever I thought about it. Unknown to me and much more important in the long run was a mysterious genetic predisposition for the enamel on the inside of my upper teeth to erode, making my upper teeth vulnerable to midnight bruxing. By the time I encountered Marcel Tabuteau four years later, my front upper teeth had been ground down enough in my sleep to cover anybody's reed!

It was too late for a real lesson, so I played a couple of scales and read through a Barret melody. My first meeting with John Mack was very short; but in the way that mattered most to me, it was a triumph! Before I left, selecting each one very carefully, Mack pulled nine reeds from his own cases and handed them to me to take to Tanglewood.

"Don't you dare tell Ralph Gomberg where these came from!" he said.

Tanglewood: Summer of 1959

We were still living in the country when Dad took my brother on a trip to visit relatives in Ohio. At the time, he promised me a similar outing, but years passed without the right opportunity. Now in 1959, squaring the fraternal score, he proposed giving his new pink and grey Chevy a road test by driving me to Tanglewood—just the two of us.

We headed north through the Shenandoah Valley on the Skyline Drive, following a route our family had taken when we visited Washington, D.C. in 1947, and were halfway to the Berkshires before we detoured into downtown Philadelphia to find 15 South 21st Street. That is where Hans Moennig, a gnarly East German immigrant who squinted over and through his half-lens glasses and continually lit and re-lit his little pipe as he worked, replaced pads and tuned and adjusted flutes, clarinets, oboes, and bassoons for the finest woodwind players in America. Expecting us, he tweaked Davidson's antique oboe until he declared it "fit for Tanglewood," and charged almost nothing for his work. It really impressed Moennig that John Mack had given me some of his own reeds to take to Tanglewood, but as we were leaving he whispered, "Why in the world do you want to play the oboe? You're too smart for that!"

Dad and I skirted New York City on the ten-lane Garden State Parkway, taking the Taconic north into Massachusetts, and arrived in Lenox early in the evening. A Victorian rooming house with a vacancy sign out front invited us in for the night. Diner food and feather pillows had already ruined Dad's trip, but Massachusetts was the worst. Doctors at Duke Medical Center diagnosed Dad's emphysema the summer I was in Cincinnati, and the disease was now beginning to cause him real distress. Next morning, wheezing and eager to go home, Dad paid a few remaining fees for me and drove off, leaving me standing alone in front of Tanglewood's large Main Gate.

I expected New England to be deforested, overdeveloped and overcrowded, stripped of its natural beauty by the generations of colonists and farmers who settled here. I was wrong. Nature easily reclaimed former pastureland and absorbed old stone walls, and the verdant woodsy landscape looked a lot like Western North Carolina, except that the trees were taller, the grass greener and the flowers more colorful at this northern latitude. Tanglewood itself was awesome. Broad tree-canopied lawns surrounded an open-sided concert hall that could accommodate 5,000 people underneath its roof, with space for another 10,000 on blankets or in chairs out on the lawn. An acoustical shell that looked like the top half of a giant megaphone stretched upward from the stage to a very high ceiling. Out of its colossal mouth was regularly proclaimed "musical truth" by one of the finest symphony orchestras in the world!

Four other oboists were in my fellowship program at Tanglewood in 1959: Donald Hilts, on leave from the Air Force Band in Washington, D.C.; Adrian Gnam, an 18-year-old student of the French oboist Maurice Dandois at Cincinnati College-Conservatory (Adrian's father was a well-known artist who visited often from his home in Upstate New York); Peter Hedrick, a graduate of Oberlin Conservatory on his way to Yale to study with Robert Bloom who was my roommate at the Lenox School for Boys; and Donald Wells, a mid-career teacher from Ithaca College who was the oldest. (Another Tanglewood oboist, Dorothy Kidney, was in the Fromm contemporary music program.) All but one of them would intersect my life in surprising ways in the years to come.

When Peter Hedrick moved into our room, he unloaded what looked like a U-Haul trailer full of reed-making paraphernalia unknown to me and arrayed the stuff on a table in the corner—pre-gougers, gougers, splitters, shapers, mandrels, cane, thread, beeswax, etc., etc. And when he asked me about "Le Tombeau de Couperin" and "Marc Lifschey," I had no idea what he was talking about. The situation was so intimidating, I did not play a note in anyone's hearing during my first three days at Tanglewood. My bedraggled oboe case with its red Davidson College pennant decal stayed hidden under the bed.

Ralph Gomberg, Principal Oboist of the Boston Symphony, was only thirty-eight years old in 1959. Except in Boston he was somewhat less-celebrated than his older brother Harold, who held the same position in the New York Philharmonic. (Harold had the advantage of being a television star in Leonard Bernstein's popular New York Philharmonic "Young People's Concerts.") Both Gombergs were graduates of the Curtis Institute and students of the great Marcel Tabuteau. Our first meeting with Ralph at Tanglewood was at placement auditions, when he would hear us play and assign oboe parts for the first fellowship orchestra concert. Principal oboe on Tchaikovsky's 4th was the prize we all wanted.

I hung back before putting my oboe together—but was confident that John Mack's reeds would sound better than the ones I heard chirping all around me. (Oboists all warm up with unconscious patterns of notes that are as distinctive as bird calls.) When I finally started, everybody else stopped playing and even Ralph Gomberg turned to listen. The audition results awarded the big English horn solo in "The Swan of Tuonela" to Adrian Gnam, but Tchaikovsky's 4th and most of the other important oboe repertory for the rest of the summer went to me.

My greatest advantage in having John Mack's reeds was not only to exult in their inherent attributes of beautiful tone, stable pitch and eager response, but to have time actually to play on them. Peter Hedrick whittled away hours every day trying to construct reeds that were never as good as mine. And while he and the others scraped, I practiced scales, long tones and technical exercises for an hour after breakfast each morning and again for an hour after lunch. This productive routine was in addition to the daily demands of orchestra and chamber music rehearsals, etc.

Despite all of my hard work that summer, another oboist's long shadow hung over Tanglewood in 1959, dimming any distinction John Mack's reeds and I were able to achieve. Jimmy Caldwell, who had won Tanglewood's "Best Student Award" the year before, was still being talked about, partly because he was participating in the more prestigious Marlboro Music Festival nearby in Vermont. On the day Jimmy drove over to attend Tanglewood's final Saturday afternoon concert, I played a huge first oboe part in Mozart's majestic "Grand Partita." Following the performance and hoping for a favorable review from Jimmy, I ran to meet him; but he was politely noncommittal. Neither of us imagined how often our paths would cross again in the years ahead.

Musical greatness was all around me at Tanglewood. Soloists Rudolf Serkin and Isaac Stern were at the height of their careers. Charles Munch and Pierre Monteux conducted the student orchestra as well as the Boston Symphony, which rehearsed almost every day and performed concerts we could attend for free. Aaron Copland was in residence, and Leonard Bernstein visited regularly. Joseph Silverstein, Boston's brilliant future concertmaster, was still seated in the back of the second violin section, and Charles Dutoit was just one of Tanglewood's 1959 student conductors. Bassoonist Sherman Walt coached our chamber music groups.

Listening to a rehearsal of Tchaikovsky's Violin Concerto with Isaac Stern one morning, Ralph Gomberg astonished me by leaping from his chair in the center of the orchestra to play an insouciant little oboe solo in the last movement standing up! Stern and the mostly-male ensemble roared, requiring several minutes before everyone settled down again. Ralph's impulsive prank reflected his cocky, brash, fun-loving personality. He was an excellent oboist who never seemed to take himself TOO seriously.

That he also did not take his students too seriously was evidenced by his showing up only once for our scheduled Saturday morning master classes. On that particular occasion, he arrived sporting black-out dark glasses and a bad mood. Even though John Mack's reeds were better, I took extensive notes as he lectured on the fundamentals of reed-making. Ralph had continually postponed a private lesson he promised me at the beginning of the summer. To remind him about it, I used to practice his orchestral solos in a Manor House room next to the one where he coached chamber music. After playing through the Brahms Violin Concerto solo eight or nine times one afternoon, I heard the door creak open behind me. "Keep that up, Robinson!" Ralph exclaimed. "Maybe someday you will play it in . . . the Davidson Philharmonic!"

Wham! went the door.

Three programs a week made Tanglewood a busy place for members of the Boston Symphony, but compared to their subscription season in Boston's Symphony Hall, the weeks in the Berkshires constituted a summer vacation. By August the great instrumentalists of the Boston Symphony sometimes sounded competent rather than inspired; but a rehearsal of Robert Schumann's Second Symphony one morning changed things in a flash. Passages like torrents in a raging stream had drawn me from the great lawn into the shed, where the string players attacked their instruments with fury, bows flying, and fingers smoking—the intensity was almost unbearable. Then transcendence happened! The epiphany of Schumann's glorious third movement, some of the most sublime music ever written, suddenly sanctified the moment and transformed an ordinary rehearsal into a religious experience for most of the players—validating Erich Leinsdorf's quip that one need but scratch below the surface of the crustiest professional to find a seventeen-year-old still passionately in love with music. For me it was the "altar call" I had not obeyed as a teenager in the Methodist Church in Lenoir. Then and there I recommitted myself to music.

Unfortunately, the radiance of that moment would fade at Davidson College in the year to follow . . .

A well-dressed middle-aged man confronted me at the edge of the stage following one of our concerts. "Your tone is beautiful," he said. "It reminds me of the greatest oboist in America—ours in the Chicago Symphony!" That was Ray Still, a player I had never even heard of until then. "How anyone could sound better than John Mack!" I wondered.

Jack Holmes was Assistant Principal Oboe of the Boston Symphony. He asked me at lunch one day if I would go with him to look at "The Three Romances for Oboe and Piano" by Robert Schumann. Flattered, I followed him to the Manor House to find a room. As we approached the mansion, impressive oboe playing wafted down from a room above us. On the second-floor landing, Holmes suggested we use Copland's Studio, and he gestured gallantly for me to enter first. There, standing right in front of me, was Ralph Gomberg, waiting for me to show up for the long-promised private lesson I had completely forgotten! I closed Holmes out unseen behind me, and apologized loudly for being so late. An hour later, walking downstairs together, Ralph and I found Jack Holmes sitting in the foyer, still waiting to take me out for Schumann.

I don't remember anything Ralph Gomberg said that afternoon, but Jack Holmes completely changed my musical perspective.

"I have been listening to you all summer," he said. "You practice TOO MUCH! True artistry is more about 'how' than 'what'—more about the music than the notes. You should listen more carefully, especially to singers, to learn precisely what expression is made of."

It was remarkable advice, and the great soprano Montserrat Caballe happened to be singing with the Boston Symphony that night.

A slender young man with olive skin, black hair and a radiant smile found me backstage at the Shed following one of our last Fellowship Orchestra concerts.

"Gus Manos," I exclaimed when we were face to face! "What are you doing here?"

The idealistic freelance photographer I so admired at Transylvania Music Camp the previous summer told me that the Boston Symphony had hired him to produce a photographic essay about the members of the orchestra. What a coincidence! He insisted that I accompany him to a friends' gathering "next Sunday afternoon," and said he would pick me up. When we arrived at a picturesque

Victorian home hosting the party, I thought it odd that no women were present—only men skinny-dipping in a pool in a stream behind the house. They shouted for me to undress and join them; but as insistently as they invited, I declined. The situation reminded me vaguely of Cincinnati by the time Gus took me home that night.

I fell in love at Tanglewood—at least my nineteen-year-old self thought I did! Jeanne Ruviella, from Collingswood, New Jersey, was an exotic mix of Irish, French and Italian immigrants. She was a beauty who studied violin at Boston University; and even though she was already "pinned" to a graduate student oboe player, I pursued her relentlessly throughout the summer. My flirting was fruitless until her boyfriend came to visit one weekend; after which for some reason she warmed up to me. Foregoing a performance of Beethoven's Ninth one Sunday afternoon, we explored "Freundshaft" on our own in a stranger's front porch swing. When Jeanne invited me to go with her for a couple of days to her grandparents' charming Connecticut farmhouse—a home she said had once belonged to the famous watchmaker Seth Thomas—I was ecstatic! My parents said I could go but warned that the bus ride home would take twenty-four hours. At the farm Jeanne and I wandered about the place hand-in-hand and sat together under a blanket on the couch watching a television movie the first night, but (perhaps because of her grandparents) she was never really amorous again. I languished unrequited at the farm and traveled to North Carolina with my heart in my throat. For weeks afterwards, I lived only for letters from her that never arrived.

Summer postscript: James Pfohl asked me in early August if after Tanglewood, I would return to play second oboe in the Brevard Music Festival's concerts that followed Transylvania Music Camp. I could earn a little money and sit for two full weeks next to Julien Balogh, the flamboyant first oboist of the Miami Philharmonic. Eager for distraction from love sickness in Lenoir, I quickly agreed.

There is no question that I appreciated the great honor of being at Tanglewood with the Boston Symphony in the

Berkshires; but as soon as I returned to Brevard—home of "Service to Youth through Music" where my personal development epitomized Transylvania Music Camp's stated mission, I viewed Tanglewood differently—more as an institution "Serving Music through Youth," with its educational program secondary to the business of selling tickets to Boston Symphony concerts. (Ken Haas, the late Executive Director of the Boston Symphony, once told me that the fiscal health of his orchestra depended every year "upon the weather in the Berkshires.") Furthermore, I opined that the Tanglewood Orchestra functioned more as a laboratory for apprentice conductors, rehearsing movements or mere fragments of movements, than as a polished ensemble performing complete symphonic works for the public. My letter to Tanglewood administrator Harry Kraut complained about the "commercial compromises" I thought had undermined my Tanglewood experience. Dr. Pfohl was not displeased.

Julien Balogh was a larger-than-life oboe player, not unlike his Julliard teacher Harold Gomberg. As principal in the National Symphony Orchestra, he told me his salary was so low he had to work as a bank night watchman in Washington, D.C. just to pay the rent. Even two jobs could not sustain the lifestyle to which he was accustomed, growing up among wealthy jewelers in Miami. So, Julien left Washington, D.C. to take over one of his family's stores on the "Miracle Mile" in Coral Gables. He said he could finally afford then to be an oboe player! He performed with the Miami Philharmonic and taught oboe for many years at the University of Miami. His wife Sonny was a platinum blond whose hair fluttered like a halo around her head whenever they drove together into camp in an expensive Buick convertible. Julien was an oboe player whose strength of personality and musical authority were expressed in his blaring tone.

(Julien Balogh sold Mary Kay and my wife our wedding and engagement rings in 1970. When he died several years later, two pages in the Miami HERALD speculated that the cause of his death was cyanide poisoning laced into his morning coffee by one of his co-workers at the jewelry store. The case has never been solved.)

Davidson College: Sophomore Year
"Consternation"

Returning for my second year in college required another round of intellectual boot camp. It was a month before my brain re-learned how to absorb and process all the new information in Biology, Economics, Psychology, Romantic Poetry, and German. John Mack was so delighted by my success at Tanglewood that he assured me good reeds would continue to appear in my mailbox, but we both knew oboe playing would have to take a back seat to academics during my sophomore year.

Accompanied by my same first-year roommate, I moved into a newer second floor room in Belk Dormitory. It was the September Frisbee came to Davidson. Turning a corner onto Patterson Court, I almost stepped on one that rolled toward me. Fraternity brothers standing in a clot in front of the Phi Delt House yelled at the sight: "Whoa! Don't let 'Ob's' throw it!" "Hey, 'Ob's' can't throw it!" ("Oboe Joe" had morphed into a more abbreviated moniker). I picked up the plastic disc gingerly, as if fearing it would break—turning it this way and that and upside down, while howls crescendoed in front of me. "He doesn't know what it is!" "Somebody, go get it!" they yelled. Just then I coiled and uncoiled—stepped forward, slung my arm and snapped my wrist in just the right sequence, and sent that Frisbee whistling in a blur towards them. A cross wind caught it, lifting it high over their heads, and carried it across the Beta House a hundred yards away. The brothers' disbelief was sublime! Forget Hell Week; my rite of passage into brotherhood was accomplished in one colossal toss of a Frisbee. "Ob's" had become a man!

Wilfred Roberts, my bassoonist high school band friend, told me that he had accepted a scholarship to attend a college I had never heard of called Oberlin. He reported often that Oberlin's Conservatory was fantastic—not far from

Severance Hall and the mighty Cleveland Orchestra, with student groups better even than the ones he had played in at Brevard the previous summer. How ironic that his wonderful bassoon teacher at the Conservatory, Kenneth Moore, had been Davidson's Wind Ensemble conductor before joining Oberlin's faculty! I was jealous. Wilfred frequently urged me to transfer as soon as possible.

Henry Lilly was an irresistible eccentric, his collar "a world too wide" for his shrunk neck, his head as mottled as a pecan shell. He was slightly stooped, with arms that extended too far in front of his body, and he moved like a crab sideways along the platform in the front of our Romantic Poetry classroom. Often one hand pressed against the side of his forehead as if warming it might more easily hatch the next brilliant idea. When he introduced his favorite lake poets to us one morning, he fairly gurgled with anticipation, "Gentlemen! Today we are TRULY embarrassed by the riches of choice!" It was in his class I that I first perceived the fertile nexus that connects language and the arts—the rhythm, texture and forms of poetry, and the narrative potential of music. I wrote for Dr. Lilly my first admired term paper, one in which I elucidated the Romantic similarities of Lord Byron's "Don Juan" and Hector Berlioz's "Harold in Italy." Although I turned it in too late for an "A," whenever I saw Henry Lilly again—even years after graduation, he reminded me of "that marvelous essay" he thought should have been published.

Ebullient Charlie Ratliff was another of my new professors my sophomore year. The title of his course, "Introduction to Economics," implied usefulness my businessman father approved; and the subject, which addressed the eternal problem of reconciling limited natural resources with unlimited human appetites in a way that maximizes social well-being, increasingly intrigued me. Using the Socratic Method, Professor Ratliff shifted the burden of creative thought to his sleepy students. He was so upbeat and energetic, and his love of economics so contagious, he even made the umpteenth edition of our

Samuelson textbook come alive! I frequently left his class "on air" and began to think about economics as a potential major.

My parents didn't want me hitch-hiking anymore after what happened the previous spring, so at home in Lenoir one Saturday afternoon when Dad said, "Let's go find you a car!" I leapt from the couch. He claimed to know a good used car dealer—a man in Whitnel with a phone booth office and eight or ten cars all lined up in a row along NC 321. The dealer was probably one of Dad's life insurance customers who had already made a deal, because it took Dad only a few minutes to hand the man $150 in exchange for a black 1950 Chevrolet 2-door coupe. The car had a 3-speed manual gearshift with a lever mounted under the steering wheel and looked terrible, but I was thrilled to have wheels of my own. Now I could take myself to musical engagements and drive to and from home across the devolving rural landscape between Conover, North Carolina and Davidson that became the bottom of future Lake Norman.

The Chevy's maiden voyage from Davidson took me to South Carolina for a concert with the Greenville Symphony Orchestra. Between Charlotte and Greenville, Interstate 85 was under construction. Some sections of it were complete, but most of the time I had to drive on a two-lane road that ran parallel to it, and the trip required about three hours each way. After the concert at around midnight, driving home alone beneath heavy cloud cover, my headlights went out, casting me into complete darkness as the road surface changed beneath me. Supposing I had driven off the road on the right-hand side, I instinctively braked and steered hard to the left. The car bumped and bounced violently, making loud swishing and scraping noises until it stopped with a jolt in the middle of a corn field on the other side of the road. I was shaken but unhurt. "Blind luck" quite literally saved me from hitting a tree!

The vehicle that was supposed to rescue me from hitch-hiking put me once again on the side of a road with my thumb pointing north, this time in the middle of nowhere.

Thankfully, a Good Samaritan truck driver stopped to pick me up. He recognized my problem as a blown fuse, took me to the only filling station in the area still open at that time of night, and drove me back to my car. He replaced the fuse and together we pushed the Chevy out of the corn field.

Although it had a tendency to "throw a rod" under the hood when the gear shift locked up, the car behaved pretty well after that. However, coming out of the Davidson College campus eighteen months later, as I tried to slow down approaching Concord Road, my right foot sent the brake pedal to the floor with a thump! I sailed right across Concord Road and bounced onto the sidewalk on the other side, miraculously un-struck by on-coming traffic. The braking system's master cylinder was completely shot. And that is where the 1950 Chevrolet and I parted company. Mother spent some inheritance money of her own to buy me a new robin's-egg-blue English Vauxhall which I drove proudly until graduation.

In the spring of 1960, racing late to lunch, I landed on a walnut the wrong way and broke a bone in my right foot. It was puffing purple over the top of my shoe by the time I arrived at the infirmary for an X-ray. The ensuing days are memorable for some of the hardest work of my life before a plaster boot with a spike on the bottom replaced the crutches. The boot was so much fun I spun and hopped around on it until I tried jumping across a ditch that was a little too wide. The spike collapsed right through the bottom of the cast and broke my foot all over again. What a depressing mistake!

"Abnormal Psychology" was depressing also—even though its affable young professor, John Kelton, was married to a woman from Lenoir whose father was the County School Superintendent known to my parents. And Biology was not much better. I took that course only to complete my A.B. degree's science requirement. Memorizing all the requisite nomenclature didn't bother me, but, as it had in high school, the smell of formaldehyde in the lab gave me a headache.

Off-campus gigs my sophomore year earned me some spending money and bolstered my musical self-respect; but on-campus music-making remained meager and mediocre. I felt increasingly under-nourished, marginalized and under-appreciated by my classmates and fraternity brothers at Davidson. All of the many disappointments my sophomore year pushed me past a tipping point. Without telling anyone, I applied to transfer to Oberlin College.

Back at Brevard: Summer 1960

Ah, music and mountains, who could want more? At Brevard with a car, about to turn twenty, and playing first oboe in the Transylvania Symphony, morale improved immediately.

In fact, my recovery had begun a couple of weeks earlier—at another mountain setting called WILDACRES. Home to an annual retreat by the Charlotte Oratorio Singers, WILDACRES was a 1600-acre conference facility located just off the Blue Ridge Parkway southwest of Spruce Pine on a forested knob. From its porches, it offered glorious views of the mountains. The property and buildings had been purchased in 1936 by a Jewish businessman in Charlotte for the astonishing price of $6,500 from bankrupt Thomas Dixon, a writer whose racist novels glorified the Ku Klux Klan and inspired the movie *The Birth of a Nation.* In defiant repudiation of the property's previous owner, the Blumenthal family dedicated WILDACRES to racial and religious tolerance, the betterment of human relations, and to the arts. Here truly was an inspiring institutional expression of the compatibility of artistic excellence and social responsibility. Donald Plott— himself a magnetic role model for my aspirations—conducted the chorus and orchestra in rehearsals at WILDACRES that week of several of the most beautiful sinfonias and cantatas of J. S. Bach.

Two major orchestras at Brevard were configured differently. The Transylvania Symphony was larger, made up of the best students with faculty members assisting. Because Dr. Pfohl had established an ingenious network of National Music Club scholarships in dozens of affiliate communities, young instrumentalists were able to come from all over the Southeast to Transylvania Music Camp with scholarships, and competition among campers for ensemble placement was fierce. Three out of four principal woodwinds in the Transylvania Symphony that summer of 1960 were from the Lenoir High School Band—bassoonist Wilfred Roberts, flutist Katherine Menefee and myself! In the other orchestra—the BMC Orchestra led by the faculty in which students were subordinate, I played second oboe and sat next to my teacher.

Dr. Pfohl relaxed camp rules for me that summer. I no longer had an evening curfew or requirement to check in and out. With a car of my own, I was able to spend many Sunday mornings in Pisgah Forest on the Blue Ridge Parkway at a hidden overlook communing with the God of Creation. I swam under Looking Glass Falls and slipped down Sliding Rock after dark in my birthday suit. I played tennis and Frisbee and basked in Dr. Pfohl's continual approval.

Wilfred Roberts and I roomed together beneath the front porch of Dr. Pfohl's cabin in the woods. Our unpainted bedroom with its exposed ceiling beams was home to all kinds of spiders and bugs which we attacked regularly (but ineffectively) with cans of Raid. We shared a tiny bathroom. Many nights we lay in the steamy Southern darkness listening to a cacophony of cicadas and the sorrowful sounds of marital unhappiness in the bedroom above us.

"Jim, I will never understand you," wailed Louise Pfohl.

"Joe! Joe!" a man shouted at me following a Saturday night concert, as I was changing clothes backstage for a patrons' party at Dr. Pfohl's house. Gus Manos came rushing towards me.

"Wow, what are you doing here?" I asked incredulously. (The swimming party at Tanglewood made me wary.)

"I drove down here just to see YOU," he exclaimed, beaming. "I have a new Volkswagen camper and am spending a few nights in Pisgah Forest. There's a queen-sized mattress in the back. Come on! Come go with me!"

The old fear tightened in my throat. "Sorry, Gus, I am going to a party at Dr. Pfohl's house and can't do it."

He responded quickly, "Then I'll wait for you in the parking lot."

At around midnight when I returned to camp, Gus banged on the passenger's side car window and jumped in beside me. There was no more pretending.

"Hey, Joe, what are you afraid of? I want to show you something you'll like. Don't knock it until you've tried it!" And on and on . . .

He continued to ignore my demands that he get out of the car. Finally, my left leg, which had been depressing the clutch pedal, began to wobble, and the same sensation of being drugged as in that Davidson professor's home swept over me. It was all I could do to turn the ignition key and start driving away from Gus's VW.

"Okay, okay," he mumbled as we approached the stone gate. "Stop the car!" With that he jumped out and disappeared into the night, and I never saw Gus ("Costa") Manos again. He became one of the most celebrated photographers of his generation and my homophobia lasted for years.

Midsummer an official letter appeared in my mailbox on the lodge porch reminding me of my forgotten, pending application to Oberlin Conservatory. Excitedly I opened the letter and began to read:

"We regret to inform you . . ."

What? I could not believe my eyes! A Davidson College dean's list student with a John Mack-reed audition tape like THAT, and they rejected me? How was that possible?

"Only a dozen places for transfer students were available," the letter said, and I did not make the cut. (Twenty years later, Oberlin's president would invite me to apply for the position of dean of the conservatory!)

Reflecting on my impulse to transfer to Oberlin, I realized that it had grown in my estimation because of Wilfred Roberts' regular reports about the rich musical diet he enjoyed there. Wilfred had persuaded me that Oberlin was the best institution in America protecting and developing professional musical potential at the same time affording students an outstanding liberal arts education. I think he was probably right, but that letter slammed the door shut for me at Oberlin. Thank goodness the summer fun at Brevard made the pain of rejection pass quickly, and I was finally glad that I had not told my parents or anyone else about it. I had no choice but to downgrade my musical aspirations and make the best of life at Davidson.

Davidson College: Junior Year
"Vindication"

Senior David Edwards was my roommate my junior year. He was a pre-law English major from Winston-Salem who played trumpet. David collected classical LPs as avidly as I did and spent many weeks assisting Dr. Pfohl at Brevard and Donald Plott at WILDACRES. He was also president of the Davidson College Wind Ensemble.

Freed from compulsory physical education, military history, science and math, and religion—all core requirements—my electives now included Music History, Creative Writing, Shakespeare, Economic Thought and the History of Art. In addition, I took an English Honors seminar entitled "Modern Drama" in which I was the only student enrolled. My professor and I met once each week for three hours in his converted garage. There Dr. Lilly—wearing a green visor with his sleeves rolled up like an accountant, sat at a card table across from me assiduously taking notes as I read my assignment aloud—always a three-thousand-word critique of the play of the week. When I finished, we adjourned to the living room for Mrs. Lilly's tea and some delicious homemade cookies. Back in the garage our roles reversed, and Dr. Lilly, accompanied by loud postprandial rumblings, critiqued my critique as I suppressed laughter and jotted down notes.

Professor William Goodykoontz taught two other important English courses that year: Creative Writing and Shakespeare. In the first course, assignments alternated between narrative expression and formal criticism. Short stories, news items, features and poems, etc. were written by half the class and submitted for peer review by the other half. We were a tough and sometimes unkind group of judges. But Shakespeare was more challenging, because the Bard was so venerated at home by my parents. Many evenings, instead of watching television, Dad had pulled volumes of Shakespeare off the shelf, or quoted extensive favorite passages perfectly from memory. Fortunately, I did some of that in the oral portion of my final exam, reciting seventy-five lines without error; and in the written section, Professor Goodykoontz called my defense of Shakespeare as an essential component of higher learning before a hypothetical Davidson College Board of Trustees "brilliant." It was my term paper dealing with the various kinds of instruments and music used in the Globe Theatre—including several illustrations I drew free-hand, however, that impressed Professor Goodykoontz the most. To the great delight of my parents, my final grade in Shakespeare was "A-plus."

My junior year marked a resurgence of artistic activity beyond those Shakespeare illustrations, because I took a History of Art survey in the fall and Studio Art in the spring. Both courses were led by a visiting professor named Philip Moose, who loomed large among regional artists in the Southeast despite being diminutive, gentle and soft-spoken in the classroom. History of Art revealed the many dimensions of aesthetic kinship between visual art and music—color values, texture, rhythm, dramatic conflict, form, etc. Studio Art provided an opportunity to apply these insights in original paintings. I produced three major works in the spring semester—a still life in chalk, an oil painting, and a final, large pastel mountain landscape. These were exhibited in the foyer of Chambers Auditorium along with other classmates' paintings at the end of May. Louise Martin, wife of the Davidson College president, asked if she could have my oil painting on loan and hang it in her den. When she returned it several years later, it was chosen for exhibition at the Lincoln Center Art Show in New York City.

Organist Robert Lord joined the faculty from Yale that year, determined to make his History of Music a serious challenge. He demanded that we digest most of Grout's standard textbook in order to pass his course, and it was all I could do to earn a "B" in my first-ever music elective. He was an excellent organist with whom I performed frequently in services at the campus Presbyterian Church. Except during exam periods at the end of each semester, I practiced the oboe at least two hours every day.

Meanwhile off-campus musical opportunities proliferated. I rehearsed or performed somewhere three or four nights a week—second oboe in the Charlotte Symphony; first oboe in the Charlotte Symphonette and the Greenville Symphony, and increasingly as a soloist with a chamber orchestra at Queens College in Charlotte. My social life was unconventional for a fraternity man, but often a delightful by-product of so much activity away from the campus. In Greenville, I dated a beautiful singer I had met at Brevard—a future Miss South Carolina named Janet McGee; and at Queens, I pursued a torrid relationship with a violinist named Anita Cahoon.

The Philadelphia Orchestra came again to Charlotte on tour that spring, performing in the same Ovens Auditorium where Dennis Rash and I first heard it when we were in high school. To my astonishment, John DeLancie was not the first oboist. A younger fellow was—someone who looked familiar. It was Jimmy Caldwell, my presumed Tanglewood "rival," whose actual playing that night impressed me less than the fact that he was there at all—sitting at my age where Marcel Tabuteau had ruled the American oboe scene for four decades in the center of one of the greatest orchestras in the world! Backstage after the concert, Jimmy told me he was filling in for his teacher for the entire season—recordings and all, until DeLancie recovered from a heart attack.

"Can you go back to Curtis for another year after this?" I asked him.

He said he wasn't sure he would. He thought he might already have learned everything DeLancie had to teach him—most importantly, "how to distill the tone to its essence."

"What about reed-making?" I asked Jimmy, doubting that DeLancie's reeds could possibly be as good as John Mack's.

His answer surprised me: "DeLancie says the most important thing about reed-making is to keep a sharp knife!"

"What a simplistic notion," I thought at the time. Years later I wished I had asked him "How?"

In contrast to my sophomore year, 1960-61 at Davidson College was an exhilarating affirmation, and "Book of the Year" was its highlight. Sometime early in the summer of 1960 I agreed to try continuing a YMCA series initiated successfully the previous year when Vance Packard came to campus to discuss his book, *The Status Seekers*. For weeks, I researched best-sellers and canvassed publishers in search of the right book and author to maintain the Packard standard; but none of the lesser choices panned out.

Suddenly in mid-September the BIG ONE did! A letter arrived on the 18th from Leon Uris, whose novel *Exodus* was a best-seller being made into a movie by Otto Preminger. Uris wrote to me, "One of my greatest regrets in the past is that I have not had the time to fill the numerous requests for appearances in the colleges and universities. However, I find your invitation so tempting that I am unable to decline." He and I immediately set the dates of his campus visit for

February 22 and 23, 1961.

Dr. James Pfohl's example inspired and motivated my response to this extraordinary opportunity. When Leon Uris asked me to include his good friend Moshe Leshem, the Israeli Consul in Atlanta, I invited him immediately. Elaborate schedules were synchronized, and time lines developed in order for Uris and Leshem to make the most of their presence on campus. A gala banquet welcomed them when they arrived the first evening, and a question-and-answer luncheon next day introduced them to all the faculty and students. The two men participated in classes and ate in the fraternity houses and were generously accessible to everyone. But the main event was a discussion about Zionism led by my freshman advisor, Professor Max Polley, that included as panelists a prominent Jewish journalist named Harry Golden, a Charlotte rabbi, and two other Davidson College teachers. Open to the public, it was promoted and reported widely by all the regional media and broadcast live on WBT Radio in Charlotte. Chambers Auditorium was completely packed. A pro-Palestinian delegation from William and Mary College even stormed the stage and had to be escorted from the building!

In a letter dated February 27 and addressed to me, President D. Grier Martin wrote: "It seems to me that no event in the recent history of Davidson College has created more interest and excitement on the campus than the coming of Mr. Uris, Mr. Leshem and the widely varied assortment of other participants in the activities sponsored under this program."

In response to those events, a lead editorial in the college newspaper wore the banner headline: "TO JOE ROBINSON: THANKS."

My stock on campus soared! While it was gratifying to receive so much credit, my intention from the beginning had been to make the "Book of the Year" program secure for the future and to expand the college's service to a wider off-campus constituency.

To Joe Robinson: Thanks

In his remarks introducing this year's Book-of-the-Year program, Chairman Joe Robinson remarked: "In this program, I believe Davidson College has found a new and pertinent means of service to its community and alumni, as well as to its students. Making the college serve a vital educational purpose outside the limited scope of its own community is one of the most difficult, but most important of its functions. Tonight and in the future, Davidson hopes to better accomplish this community goal."

We whole heartedly agree with this statement (see last week's editorial "A Challenge to the College"). The Book-of-the-Year program certainly makes a vital contribution to this broad educational goal. Wednesday night, Davidson was no longer a sheltered cloister out in the sticks, but, rather, was a live, cosmopolitan, intellectual center, drawing visitors from near (Cornelius) and far (William and Mary).

With programs such as the Book-of-the-Year program and the Reynolds Lectures (which has yet to receive the publicity it deserves), Davidson College can begin to live up to its reputation. By promoting such programs and encouraging outside participation, Davidson will truly become an educational center, rather than just a secluded campus.

The benefits will touch not only the guests, but also the immediate college community itself. The numerous visitor-student discussions during the coffee hour Wednesday night added an exciting freshness to the campus atmosphere. The new ideas and fresh perspectives produced renewed vigor in student discussion. The biologist, wary of excessive interbreeding, introduces new strains to maintain vigor within various families. The same principle applies here.

As a program within this new, broad educational vision, the Book-of-the-Year was a great success. As with all programs which set a high ideal, it was not without its problems and shortcomings, but its success far overshadows these few points.

The success of the program is largely due to the sacrifice of time and energy of Chairman Joe Robinson and Faculty Advisor Max Polley. To them goes our warmest expression of appreciation.

T.B.C.

And my mid-year report card finally showed straight "A's."

Brevard Again

I was too old for Transylvania Music Camp in the summer of 1961, but Dr. Pfohl created a special niche for me. He labeled me "junior faculty," with responsibility to coach the youthful oboists in the Hilltopper Band and Orchestra. In my elevated status, there were no restrictions of any kind on my coming and going from camp.

An oboe teacher of real stature arrived at Brevard that summer. DeVere Moore, who had studied at Eastman and played professionally, was Professor of Oboe at Oberlin Conservatory. He would have been my teacher there if my application to Oberlin the previous summer had been accepted. How ironic that he was now my colleague at Brevard!

Short and powerfully rotund, DeVere Moore was a good-natured fellow who exhibited more than his share of machismo. He was also dogmatic. He required his students to practice in the half deep-knee-bent posture of a baseball catcher to "more firmly plant their tone." (I reckoned that approach might lead to hyper-developed thighs, but not much else.) Another of his exercises was more helpful. Playing glissandi between pitches demonstrated dramatically how much more resistant intervals are on the oboe than the notes themselves. A lifted key such as G, for instance, in the first millisecond expresses neither G nor A, but is a leaky pad inhibiting the reed's vibration. That resistance is the source of the dreaded "wah-wah" syndrome—the consequence of young oboists' biting their reeds between notes in order not to break their slurs. Blowing harder between the notes is a better way to connect them without changing one's horizontal line.

I played second oboe to DeVere in the BMC Orchestra. One Sunday afternoon during a run-out concert to Highlands, North Carolina, Pfohl struck his clip-on black bow tie with an unusually vigorous upbeat, which left it barely dangling on the left edge of his white dress shirt collar. Sweating copiously in the summer heat, he fumbled with his left hand trying to reattach the tie while struggling with his right to maintain a circular beat. All of this happened just ahead of an extended oboe solo in Tchaikovsky's *Capriccio Italien,* and DeVere Moore's chair was already shaking the woodwind risers before he began to play. The snorts and sputters of his suppressed laughter forced half the orchestra to duck in tears beneath their stands during the oboe solo. Tchaikovsky never sounded so funny!

The Transylvania Symphony also had a new student first oboist, sixteen-year-old Eric "Ricky" Barr from Columbus, Georgia. Ricky looked a lot like Art Garfunkel. Sitting taller than he really was at the center of the orchestra, he wore a wide-eyed, eager expression that made him appear continually startled. His father was the band director at Brevard, and his mother the camp's long-time Registrar. Ricky was a skinny kid with a skinny tone who boasted the fastest fingers and tongue in the state of Georgia! He followed DeVere Moore to Oberlin, after which he joined the Marine Band; played second oboe to me in Atlanta for a couple of years; and went on to a thirty-three-year career as the celebrated principal oboist of the Dallas Symphony.

I coached two unforgettable young women in the Hilltopper groups that summer. One was Jean Martin, daughter of Indiana University Professor Clyde Martin, co-author of the famous Kinsey Reports on human sexuality. She herself was one of the sexiest females I ever encountered. Eighteen years old, she played the oboe badly but swam in the lake like an otter and emerged on the dock with her short black hair glistening red and green and yellow highlights, her perfect, tawny skin beaded with water. The other girl was younger—a smoldering beauty from Atlanta named Jean Thomas. She had the most expressive brown eyes I had ever seen, but she was untouchable—the girlfriend of Dr. Pfohl's son David.

In my seventh year as an oboist, I finally acquired an instrument of my own. It was a pre-owned Lorée akin to the one I played in the Lenoir High School Band, complete with all of the auxiliary keys missing on the Davidson College instrument I had been using. DeVere Moore sold it to my dad for less than $400.

"Boys, I had a dream last night," Dr. Pfohl announced at a staff breakfast one morning. "I dreamed the Transylvania Symphony played at the White House for President Kennedy!"

A month later, it actually happened! That was the way James Christian Pfohl did things—any good idea was father of the deed. It helped that he maintained close contact with his "Davidson boys," continually seeking and fostering connections that facilitated his projects. In the case of the White House trip, a former Davidson College oboe player named Henry Hall Wilson, President Kennedy's special liaison to the House of Representatives who worked in the White House, was able to direct the idea to the First Lady's staff. Jackie Kennedy herself agreed to sponsor a series of concerts by young musicians for handicapped children and invited Brevard's Transylvania Symphony to perform first on the White House lawn.

I was one of the faculty coaches who came along as a chaperon on the trip that occurred just after the end of camp. We traveled by train and stayed together at the Mayflower Hotel. At a celebratory luncheon on the day of the concert, North Carolina Governor Terry Sanford congratulated the orchestra and pledged the power and authority of his office to create a school that would keep talented North Carolinians "at home" for their professional training. He actually fulfilled that promise a few years later when the first state-supported conservatory in America, the North Carolina School of the Arts (dubbed "the tippy-toe school") was miraculously approved by the state's rural legislature. Terry Sanford, who had seconded John F. Kennedy's nomination for President at the Democratic National Convention in San Francisco and was a close friend of Henry Hall Wilson, once played tuba for Dr. Pfohl at Brevard.

In a time of limited communication before cell phones, it was easy to misconnect. That happened when my brother and I set out together in early September to drive to Mobile, expecting to stay with a fraternity brother until John Mack returned to nearby New Orleans from Wisconsin. Unfortunately, when Ed and I arrived at John Harris' home no one was there. We sent Dad the following Western Union telegram: "John not home. Have only $4.00. Need money fast . . ." It was dated September 2, 1961. We also arrived late in New Orleans for my second meeting and first real oboe lesson with John Mack. When we found each other, he and James Yestadt were putting out on the eighteen green of the New Orleans Municipal Course, finishing a round of golf. A relative novice in love with the game, Mack exclaimed, "Golf and oboe, Laddie! Who could want more?"

Ed and I followed Mack to his modest home. Entering,

I caught sight of something incredible—one hundred John Mack oboe reeds all lined up on his living room couch waiting to be packed and shipped to Hans Moennig! In the little bedroom that served as his studio, when we actually got down to the business of oboe playing, as he listened to me Mack became increasingly annoyed and perplexed.

"You ARE touching the tip of the reed when you tongue, aren't you?" he asked abruptly."

"No," I responded naively. "Are you?"

It was as if I had fallen through the ice! The only other player John Mack ever heard of who touched the roof of his mouth instead of the reed when tonguing "Tee" or "Tah" on the oboe was John DeLancie when he first arrived at Curtis as a sixteen-year-old from California. (Many years later, John Mack would say that John DeLancie and I had "the best articulation in the business"—proving once again that converts are the most fanatical!)

Ed and I were in his car about to leave when John Mack stuck his head through the passenger-side window and said to me nose-to-nose, "Listen, Joe. I can't tell you how to fix your tonguing problem, but I can tell you that if you don't fix it, you may just as well forget becoming a professional oboe player!" (First it was my teeth; now my tongue!)

Driving back to North Carolina, I knew that John Mack thought I couldn't do anything about it. I also realized that his challenge—"Fix it, or else!"—was an ultimatum I would have to meet head-on. How I responded the next few weeks probably saved my career as well as our friendship.

When I started on saxophone, I folded my lower lip across my bottom teeth, forming a flat resting place for its wide single reed. (Some saxophonists use a "double embouchure," with their upper lip between their teeth and the top of the hard rubber mouthpiece, but I bit the mouthpiece with my teeth directly on top.) After converting to oboe, I continued using a saxophone embouchure—hence John Mack's concern about my inadequate "upper-lip function" and my inability to touch the tip of the oboe reed with the tip of my tongue. Just as with tennis, I had developed advanced skills on the oboe employing incorrect fundamentals. And as much as my forehand stroke was feeble when I tried the "handshake grip," my embouchure was feeble when I touched the reed the way I was supposed to. In addition to rearranging my lips, I had to teach my tongue to move forward and back inside my mouth instead of up and down.

Concerts were looming that required continued playing. How was I going to perform at a high level and start over at the same time? The solution was to radicalize my new embouchure and isolate it totally from the old, as if I had taken up another instrument altogether. In the beginning, if I held the reed with my lower lip out and my tongue forward for only five seconds at a time before breaking down, I played one hundred five second notes correctly every time I picked up the oboe. Monitoring my new position, I stood in front of a mirror and held notes only for as long as I saw them correctly sustained—twelve, fifteen, eventually twenty seconds. After doing that, I practiced, rehearsed, and concertized just as I had before. Like hybrid seed planted experimentally in a corner the garden upon which I did not depend for sustenance, my alternative approach gradually took root and began to grow. When it was fully developed, I was able to substitute it for the old approach, first in rehearsals and then in concerts, without any risk to my playing whatsoever. The complete transformation was accomplished within two months, and John Mack was VERY impressed!

Davidson College: Senior Year
"Celebration"

People asked me all the time how I liked Davidson College and what my major was. In response to the first question, I usually said, "It is killing me, but I love it!" If I counted an occasional nap in the afternoon as productive, there were many days during my middle college years when I actually did not waste any time at all. Dad's formula of two hours' study outside of class for every hour in worked for me. Only in my senior year did I settle on a major—actually "majors," because I was unable to choose between English and economics and chose them both. The most important course of the year was in neither area, however. It was a Philosophy survey taught by one of the giants of the faculty, Dr. George Abernethy, and I was wise to take it late.

Dr. Abernethy was one of those extraordinary people so serenely competent and self-assured they display no defensiveness whatsoever. He was brilliant. He was also sometimes acerbic, stinging slackers and the muddle-headed with quick rebukes and corrections. I actually dared to meet him in his office one afternoon and suggest that he use more pedagogical carrot and less stick! He tolerated my impudence with bemusement, rubbing his little gray mustache while I orated, and then he reached over next to me and pulled open a long filing cabinet drawer.

"This drawer, Mr. Robinson," he said, "is full of hundreds of letters of commendation from former students. One of yours may find its way in here someday. Stop whining and get tomorrow's paper in on time!"

Everyone knew that Dr. Abernethy graded handwritten pop quizzes and exhaustive reports relentlessly and worked harder than any of us. It surprised us to see him during "free time" scanning *The New York Times* in the library every day. Only one student in each of his classes ever earned an "A," setting the bar too high for the rest of us, and I was not one of those. But three letters praising him eventually did join the others in Dr. Abernethy's filing cabinet. His course was the most rigorous analytical training I ever received.

David Edwards was at Duke Law School by now. My new roommate was David Jordan, editor of the college newspaper, *The Davidsonian*, and an outstanding history major. He told me he enrolled in Professor Lord's History of Music class to prove that he could beat me in it. Soon after he had written brilliantly about the advent of Romanticism in Beethoven's Ninth Symphony, we were across the hall in a neighbor's room listening to the bass-baritone introduce the magnificent choral portion of the last movement. We sat on a bed transfixed until the end.

Walking back to our room, David commented, "That sounded nice—what was it?"

I was astonished. "Good grief, David—you just wrote about this music! Are you kidding me?" But David had no idea; he couldn't remember or replicate a single tune, not even from childhood.

"How can anyone write authoritatively about a composer's music without recognizing it?" I thought. But David did it. And that was the first time I realized how completely abstractions can form a conceptual superstructure representing and substituting for human beings' entire sensory experience. Tone-deaf David Jordan did indeed beat me in Professor Lord's class when he earned an "A."

In October, the Philadelphia Orchestra returned to North Carolina. Woodwind principals were scheduled to present a brief quintet recital and teach individual afternoon master classes at Duke University before performing with the orchestra that evening in Raleigh. Encouraged by a Davidson College professor's wife—herself a superb violinist who had graduated from Oberlin before attending the Curtis Institute—I drove three hours in a rainstorm to Durham to talk to John DeLancie about auditioning for Curtis. A half-hour break separated the quintet recital from the oboe master class—a perfect time for me to accost Mr. DeLancie backstage with my oboe in hand.

"How OLD are you?" he asked, brusquely interrupting my self-introduction.

"Twenty-one," I responded. "You're too old to attend THE Curtis!" he said.

"But . . . but . . . Elaine Richey told me that she came to study violin at Curtis after graduating from Oberlin . . ."

DeLancie turned on his heel and walked away, snapping over his shoulder as he went, "Go ahead and apply then. If you're lucky, I'll hear you play in the spring!"

In that moment I knew I could never study with him even if he accepted me as his student. The Curtis "high road" to my professional career was abruptly barricaded with a sign marked "CLOSED!"

The genial concertmaster of the Charlotte Symphony was James Weber, a merchant when he wasn't fiddling, and both of his sons were musical—Jim, the older one, majoring in Math at Davidson, played flute in the Wind Ensemble next to me, and David, thirteen years old was just beginning to play the oboe. At his father's request, I drove to Myers Park Methodist Church in Charlotte every Wednesday afternoon to teach David and his best friend, Daniel Werts. Those two boys were my first oboe students.

More should be said about the Charlotte Symphony, which was a consistent musical lifeline during my college years. Jim Pfohl no longer conducted it. He had been succeeded my freshman year by a pianist/conductor from Oberlin named Henry Janiec, who scavenged much of his own career—including the Charlotte Opera and the Brevard Music Center later on, from the carcasses of institutions Dr. Pfohl started but subsequently abandoned. (It was easier for Dr. Pfohl to create institutions than to administer them.). One might say that Henry had a "lean and hungry look." He was too circumspect and self-aware to lose himself fully in a performance, but he managed well and conducted with clarity. Often clenching a pipe stem between his teeth when he spoke, he talked out of the other side of his mouth with a voice that sounded like a muted trumpet. He even frowned when he laughed. Jim Pfohl's reach may have exceeded his grasp, but Henry Janiec's never did.

First oboe parts in the Charlotte Symphony were played by a school music teacher and youth orchestra conductor named David Serrins, a man of great amiability whose self-deprecating humor belied formidable natural talent and musical authority. He belittled himself and whined about his reeds, but enchanted everyone with his lissome playing. There were many other fine musicians in the Charlotte Symphony who worked "day jobs," wishing they could earn enough money to express their love of music full-time. Before the Ford Foundation grants of 1966, hundreds of symphony orchestras in the United States existed primarily to serve the musicians who played in them rather than people who wanted to hear their music. As an industry, the classical orchestra business has almost always been driven more by supply than by demand. John F. Kennedy's Presidential leadership helped change that by starting the so-called "Culture Boom" in the United States, with its credo articulated by Duke University graduate Nancy Hanks in her famous Rockefeller Brothers Fund Study of the Performing Arts in 1965—"The arts should be at the center and not the periphery of society and serve the many and not just the privileged few." Overnight, support for the arts became a civic obligation.

Frank West departed to take over the Music Department of St. Andrews College, a new Presbyterian school in Laurinburg, North Carolina, and Grier Williams replaced him as conductor of the Davidson College Wind Ensemble. The change was invigorating. Grier was an excellent trumpeter, conductor, and ensemble recruiter. He even re-orchestrated the accompaniment to Handel's G Minor Oboe Concerto for wind ensemble in order to feature me as soloist in concerts on a Florida tour. That tour, scheduled between semesters in mid-January, began at an Air Force base in Florida, where everyone bedded down on cots that were arranged in some kind of hangar or warehouse. A cold front came through during the night that kept us shivering. Next morning in the bus traveling to Cape Canaveral, site of the NASA's first orbiter missions, I could hardly swallow, and fever and chills were not far behind. At several concert locations on the tour after that, I entered campus infirmaries in the afternoon and left in the evening just long enough to appear as the Handel Concerto soloist. Performing from memory in those concerts, I floated in a pleasant feverish delirium; but by the end of the trip, my tongue was lemon-yellow, and I could barely speak.

Spring semester of my senior year was marred by recurring episodes of similar symptoms, with intermittent infirmary and hospital stays and cycles of antibiotics. At times I seemed to recover, but never regained enough strength not to sweat profusely at the slightest exertion.

Desperate diagnoses were being discussed by my doctors when a blood test finally confirmed mononucleosis.

Despite all of the illness and absenteeism, academic honors piled up—*Who's Who in American Colleges and Universities*, Omicron Delta Kappa (the national college honor leadership fraternity) and Phi Beta Kappa. I was a finalist both for a Fulbright Award to Germany and a Woodrow Wilson Teaching Fellowship in English. In January, I learned that I was an alternate for the Fulbright, which left little hope on that front; but in the spring, an interview for the Woodrow Wilson Fellowship came through in Greensboro.

The University of Virginia examiner tied me in knots by asking, "Would you say there is actually such a thing as a 'Christian' tragedy?" to which I responded too quickly

"Of course!" Then, remembering Jesus' redemptive sacrifice on the cross and suspecting it was a trick question, equivocated and muttered, "Well, maybe . . . er . . . no, I guess not!"

The professor fired back, "What about T. S. Eliot's *Murder in the Cathedral*?"

I had never read that one and couldn't think of anything meaningful to say about it. That's when my Woodrow Wilson Fellowship opportunity slipped down the drain!

Something I HAD recently read, however, left a deeper and more formative impression. Expressed by the American literary critic and philosopher Cleanth Brooks, it asserted that young adults should always take their stand in life at the point where their greatest relative abilities intersect the world's greatest need. Trusting my talent as an oboist and rationalizing the world's need for more art, I resolutely resolved to pursue a career in music one way or another!

Martin Bellar, conductor of the Charlotte Symphonette, programmed Mozart's Oboe Quartet (possibly the greatest piece of chamber music ever written for oboe) that season, and my performance of it yielded an excellent review as well as a tape sent along with my application to Yale University. The oboe teacher at Yale was Robert Bloom, Marcel Tabuteau's first great student, who played English horn in the Philadelphia

Orchestra before he even graduated from the Curtis Institute and was hand-picked by Arturo Toscanini for the first oboe chair in the NBC Symphony. Studying with Robert Bloom was a compromise John Mack reluctantly approved because there was no graduate school option for me in New Orleans; but we both knew that Bloom's reed-making skills were suspect. (Later John Mack learned that many of the reeds he had sent to Moennig over the years found their way secretly to Robert Bloom's desk in New Haven, sustaining his famous rival's playing as much as mine!) Maybe that's why Robert Bloom admired my Mozart performance enough to invite me to come to New Haven on full scholarship. I would still have to pay for living expenses, but I accepted the offer and made plans to enroll at Yale in pursuit of a Master of Music degree.

At about the same time, the New York Philharmonic came to perform one Sunday afternoon in Charlotte's Ovens Auditorium. Just before 3:00 p.m., a handsome orchestra administrator from Spartanburg (pronounced "Spaaaht . . . n . . . bu-ugh") South Carolina named Carlos Moseley walked onto the stage and addressed the audience. He explained that the instrument trucks had lost their way coming across the mountains from Chattanooga, and the concert would be delayed for an hour. What luck! I raced backstage in search of principal oboist Harold Gomberg, once again carrying my oboe and some John Mack reeds.

Harold was a more imposing man than his younger brother Ralph, although both of them were handsome, had jet black hair, large bright eyes, and commanding personalities. Cornered with time on his hands, Harold was pleasant enough until I told him about my reeds.

"Wow, let me see them!" he exclaimed. (John Mack and he had not spoken to each other for years after Harold flunked Mack for leaving Juilliard to study with Marcel Tabuteau at Curtis.)

Harold was practically drooling as he put his oboe together to try my reeds. Playing one after another of them, he was completely engrossed until he caught sight of something that "stopped him in his quacks!" Turning to see what startled him, I realized it was himself—reflected in a large mirror behind me! Completely transfixed now by his own image, Harold Gomberg laid his oboe on a chair and began to preen—turning his massive head this way and that, straightening one-by-one each of the little Caligula curls on his forehead. Satisfied at last, he stood up very tall and turned from the mirror. "Young man, I am going to LEAVE you now!" (It was obvious he already had . . .) Then he strode grandly away.

My Frisbee prowess at Davidson College was legendary by the time President D. Grier Martin, dressed in gym shorts and wearing track shoes, knocked on my dorm room door one sunny afternoon.

"Can you take a study break?" he asked, brandishing his own "professional model" Frisbee.

I jumped at the invitation and raced off to the soccer field with him for an unexpected workout. The college president who had pledged his kinship during the first week of my freshman year now demonstrated it with extraordinary enthusiasm and affection in one of the last weeks of my senior year.

"Spring Frolics" was the last of our annual dance weekends—a time when young women migrated to the campus from schools as far away as Atlanta. Many senior-year couples were already engaged when I drove into Davidson in a yellow Buick convertible with "Miss South Carolina" written across the side of it in gaudy black script. I took my own victory lap as Janet McGee and I cruised around campus. Her companionship was the ultimate social vindication for me at Davidson, and "Ob's" had never looked so good! Janet was a vivacious, talented, delightful girl from Atlanta my parents and their friends adored. And I would have adored her too if I could only have forgotten Jean Thomas's incredible brown eyes!

An auspicious telephone call came in mid-April from the Office of International Education in New York City. "Congratulations!" said the caller. "You have been awarded a Fulbright to Germany and will attend the University of Cologne next year."

Wow! My audacious experiment in "grantsmanship" had succeeded after all. Knowing that I could not apply for a German Fulbright to study English, I had improvised an improbable application under the rubric of economics, and proposed to investigate the nature and extent of German federal government support to the arts. With the National Endowment for the Arts in Washington, D.C. in its early planning stages and many foundations making grants for investigation of European prototypes, the topic turned out to be better than I imagined. Officials in Germany had struggled in the beginning to find a university that could accommodate my project—hence my "alternate" status, but at last they unearthed in Cologne a Professor Silberman, whose major book was entitled Die Soziologie der Musik. And my grant was approved.

The decision to bet my life on music was postponed yet again . . .

The Baccalaureate was a religious exclamation point marking the end of college life at Davidson. A Sunday morning church service that preceded afternoon graduation ceremonies, it pronounced a parting benediction upon the senior class. The Reverend John Oliver Nelson from Yale Divinity School was our guest preacher and his sermon was entitled "Simplicity beyond Complexity." He made the intriguing point that while Davidson College in the best liberal arts tradition had filled our heads with as much information about as many different subjects as possible, it was not so much knowledge as adherence to faith in five basic principles that would ultimately determine the quality of our lives. These were: 1) honesty, 2) fairness, 3) diligence, 4) gratitude and 5) service. The beautiful offertory I played in that service reinforced his message perfectly: written by Cesar Franck for oboe and organ, it was entitled simply *Piece V.*

Graduation day was a blur of activity. Move-out from dorm rooms was happening; relatives swarmed all over the campus; professors raced to line up in their academic regalia; and we seniors adjusted our mortarboard hats and tassels and zipped up our robes. It was blazing hot by the time Harlee Branch came forward to address us with a speech so insufferably long it ended the tradition of commencement addresses. (Harlee was President of the Southern Company in Atlanta and father of classmate Barry Branch.) The final G.P.A. ranking for the Class of '62 placed me sixth and a graduate *cum laude*. When my name was called, I strode proudly across the platform toward President Grier Martin and accepted my diploma. Davidson College student life ended for me with his firm handshake on May 27, 1962.

moderato assai

Summer 1962

Mother shook me awake early the next morning. "Joe," she said, "Some strange man is at the back door. He says you invited him to play golf with you today."

Good grief! It was John Mack! I had completely forgotten that he was coming from Charlotte to play the Boone Golf Club course I had been raving about. It was not yet 7:00 a.m. and luminescent white sheets draped every window of our house. I had never seen fog so thick. Throwing on a shirt and pants, I raced to the back door to greet John Mack and call the pro shop in Boone to see if we could play.

"Not until noon," the attendant told me, "and only then if the fog burns off completely."

There was nothing to do but prepare a big country breakfast and invite my parents to help welcome the man who was responsible more than any other for my disenchantment with Dad's insurance business! Fortunately, John Mack charmed us all. He promised me a facsimile copy of the Mozart Oboe Quartet from the Bibliotheque in Paris, but his visit that morning was an even better graduation present.

Between the end of college and anticipation of my year in Europe, the summer of 1962 passed mostly in a blur.

I met the challenge of preaching the Youth Sunday sermon at First Methodist Church with rectitude, borrowing generously from *The Cost of Discipleship* by Dietrich Bonhoeffer—a book I had critiqued in Professor Abernethy's Philosophy class. In my sermon, I equated Bonhoeffer's concept of "cheap grace" with the easy absolution most Lenoir church-goers found in their disregard for racial and economic injustice. My mother said it made her uncomfortable.

A new Advanced Division began at Brevard with college-age and graduate students housed off-campus in the dormitories of tiny Brevard College. I was named "Resident Advisor for Boys" with the unpleasant job of policing the male musicians' evening curfews. Struggling to make a reed one night, I tested it quietly but scraped away far too late. Around midnight someone looking red-eyed and frazzled knocked on my door and demanded, "Hey, if you're going to make so much noise past curfew, at least play something! Real music might put me to sleep, but that 'brack, brack, brack' is driving me CRAZY!"

Jean Thomas, my beautiful oboe protégé no longer attached to David Pfohl, improved the summer's romantic prospects exponentially, but a relapse of mononucleosis during the second week, forced me to leave Brevard and return to Lenoir for convalescence. Mother's cooking and armchair idleness revived me enough to go to WILDACRES for a week with the Oratorio Singers. I felt better back in the mountains. But apprehension mingling with excitement increased daily, and there were only thirty more of them before I would sail into the German unknown!

Foreign students called "Richardson scholars" were

assigned at Davidson to different fraternities. Fernando Rodas from Guatemala was at Phi Delta Theta my senior year, but he was so unassuming and shy, most of us hardly noticed him. A few others not as reserved as Fernando flaunted their distinctiveness and made no attempt to assimilate into the life of the college. They persuaded me to become as "German" as possible during my year abroad.

Mother and I scoured Lenoir for a steamer trunk and a winter coat heavy enough to keep me warm in the frigid winter weather we imagined lay ahead. A trunk with impressive brass fittings, which was otherwise just heavy pressed cardboard, looked big enough; and a coat like something from a 1920s movie—long and white with a fuzzy black lining and a non-descript faux-fur collar, certainly felt warm enough in Lenoir in August!

In addition to studying German, I practiced oboe every day. As president of the local Mozart Music Club, Mother scheduled a performance for me at a fund-raising musicale on September 2. Closing out that concert was a fine singer named Gerald Coffey, who had only recently become known to me as the "Wunderkind" my dad anointed to take over his insurance business once he realized I wasn't interested. Dad discovered Gerald in Collettesville, North Carolina (a trading post more than a town) ten miles or so west of Lenoir on Johns River, after trudging over plowed ground to sell his father a $5,000 life insurance policy. Gerald's "million-dollar smile" was so often extolled around our dinner table, it made me jealous. "How could I be so easily replaced in my father's favor?" I wondered.

(Fifty years later I would fall into Gerald's arms in Boca Raton as if he were a lost half-brother, and learn that he had decided to sell "tangible" rather than "intangible" stuff— Bernhardt furniture instead of Dad's life insurance, which he did successfully in Florida at the rate of about $30 million a year!)

A flat wooden cigar box lined with cotton arrived. Like newborns in a nursery, thirteen oboe reeds lay snuggled up next to each other in that box. John Mack had sent them to keep me alive musically during my year abroad. A 3-by-5 card was included. On it were the hand-written names of six or eight wholesalers whose oboe cane grew in the famous fields of the Var—the southeastern region of France which for generations produced the finest Arundo Donax (the largest species of grass) in the world. Mack promised to share with me any cane I could collect from them. That little card was going to be my ticket to oboe cane heaven!

Before leaving for Germany, I had one urgent piece of business—to see wondrous Jean Thomas at Converse College, where she was enrolling as a freshman Music and Religion major, and say goodbye to her. Mother loaned me her new Chevrolet Impala for the trip to Spartanburg, South Carolina. Somewhere between Morganton and Rutherfordton, an afternoon thundershower made the two-lane road so slick the Chevrolet's jerky power steering sent the car spinning off it like a hockey puck. It was the second time I careened out of control into a corn field—this time just slipping by a telephone pole that would have totaled the car and ended my story. Jean and I promised to stay in touch.

My European adventure began at the passenger train station in Hickory, North Carolina, on the evening of September 11. Mother cried a little, and Dad and I looked resolute if not very confident. I waved goodbye to my parents through the window of a sleeper car. During the overnight trip to New York City, reflecting on what Davidson College had meant to me, I reckoned my adventure of self-discovery there probably constituted a greater adventure than the one that awaited me in Germany. What a luxury it had been to incubate young adulthood in such a beneficent place! Plato's three-horse chariot—mind, body, spirit—was ideally balanced at Davidson, which had as its singular mission the healthful maturation of young men like myself.

Wearing my ridiculous snow-white winter coat in order not to carry it, I hailed a cab at Pennsylvania Station and told the driver to take me to the Taft Hotel. We circled it a few times before I found the courage to tell him to pull over, and then tipped him anyway. Next morning at Pier 88 on West 48th Street I boarded Norddeutscherlloyd's MS Berlin, a converted Swedish freighter reputed to be the slowest passenger ship on the North Atlantic. Ours would be an eleven-day crossing. Two other Fulbrighters preceded me into the tiny stateroom we shared, so I threw my coat onto the remaining unclaimed middle berth.

Life on board our old boat was luxurious in one respect—the food was endless! In the beginning, we ate five times a day, sampling everything on the breakfast menu and the midnight buffet, and even choosing the fish course in addition to a meat entrée at dinner. Rough seas soon enforced moderation. Our only scheduled activity was a German language class led each morning by a pretty blonde Julie Andrews look-alike named Gertraud. The rest of the time we walked the deck, read, or napped down below— activities that completely dissipated whatever was left of my mononucleosis. Salt air and boredom did the job. Near the end of the voyage I even felt well enough to entice Gertraud for some private "tutelage" under a blanket in one of the chairs on deck! Despite stopping most of one day for engine repairs mid-Atlantic, the MS Berlin docked at Bremerhaven right on schedule.

Germany/the Elligers

The German Fulbright Commission offered grantees two choices before enrollment in our various universities: we could stay a month with a German family in the "Experiment in International Living Program" or study German at the Goethe Institute in Goettingen. I chose to live with a family.

Arriving from Bremen at the train station in Muenster/ Westfalen late in the afternoon, I saw all of the Elligers waiting to greet me—Helmut, director of public transportation for the region; his wife Gerti, a decorated architect working with her brother Klaus; and their four children: Ulrike, 12; Martin, 8; Tillman, 6; and Klaus, almost 4. The three boys were lined up on the platform like Donald Duck's nephews, dressed in identical Lederhosen. They gawked at me as if at an alien while Ulrike stood warily apart. Helmut and Gerti were so exuberant in their welcome, "sensory overload" characterized my reaction during our meeting and the trip in Helmut's Mercedes to the Elliger's home at Propsteistrasse 52.

The Elliger Family

My place in the family became obvious at breakfast the very first morning. Trying in vain to communicate that no hot water issued from my shower upstairs, charades on all sides were required for me to understand that hot water heaters had to be turned on individually. The older children snickered and giggled while this was going on, but, three-year-old Klaus just stared wide-eyed at me from across the table, amazed by my linguistic ineptitude. His language skills were so much better than mine I realized that I would have to grow up all over again just to catch him. A German "second childhood" offered some interesting possibilities.

"Nobody knows me here," I thought. "I can become any kind of German I want!" (Credit or blame inertia, but, except for speaking a new language and learning to enjoy beer and wine, the "German" Joe Robinson never became anyone much different from the guy who boarded the train in Hickory.)

Brick with a tile roof and decorative shutters just like its neighbors up and down Propsteistrasse, the Elliger home exuded solid upper-middle-class well-being. Thanks to Gerti's ingenious designs, it was much larger and more functional than it appeared outside. Rooms revealed little of themselves without investigation. For instance, I never discovered Helmut and Gertis' bedroom off the stairway landing going up to the second floor and only learned much later that there was a bedroom up in the attic and a sauna and bedroom in addition to the wine cellar in the basement below. My bedroom was the middle one in a row of them on the second floor, between Ulrike's and the boys' on the same side of the hallway. A narrow balcony and wrought-iron railing that ran behind these rooms overlooked a spacious back garden where the children played.

From the foyer one stepped into a spacious, sunken living room. Helmut's Bechstein anchored it, surrounded by Scandinavian furniture that accommodated more people than one would suppose. Social gatherings, to which Helmut and Gerti always invited me, happened almost every night. In the beginning I impressed everyone with how well I tolerated my first glasses of wine. Since I had never been "high" before, I fought off the effects of alcohol enough to drink quite a lot without obvious effect. During my first month at the Elliger's home, twelve other visitors from all over the world came and went—friends from Italy, Finland, France, Africa, and a Jewish couple from Hollywood. I wondered if their inclusive lifestyle was atonement for the war.

The German word for "host" is Gastgeber (literally, "guest-giver") which described perfectly the extraordinary generosity of my host family. Helmut and Gerti Elliger were the most hospitable people I had ever met. And their generosity was not just in material things. It was expressed most of all in the quality of their connection to people, the all-embracing way they welcomed everyone. It was also revealed in a necessary expression of "tough love" towards me—the refusal to speak English at any time when I was with them, even though it would have been easier and more fun for them to do so. One obvious consequence of World War II at Propsteistrasse 52 was the number of single women who served the Elliger family. Irma lived in the home and ran the kitchen; Waltraud worked as maid and washerwoman. Many other "aunties"—widows rather than blood relatives— came and went continually.

In what otherwise could have been bedlam, characteristic German order steadied the family. A chauffeur picked up CEO Helmut every morning and delivered him from his office in time for supper. When the children left for school, Gerti went to work with her brother in his architectural firm nearby. Breakfast and the early evening meal were almost always the same—a soft-boiled egg eaten with a tiny spoon from a cup, brown bread, jam and tea in the morning; whole-corn black bread, Muenster cheese and (Helmut's favorite) home-made smoked "Wurst" in the evening. If Helmut drank beer, it was always two Dortmunder Union's from his cellar—the first one chug-a-lugged with "his teeth in it" as he would say; the second savored more slowly. In the beginning, I more often drank a tepid Coca Cola, also from the cellar instead of the fridge. Lunch at around 1:00 p.m. was the culinary highlight of the day, sometimes featuring "Rouladen" (my favorite), braised beef roll-ups filled with dill pickles, followed by "Quark" served in a bowl with cinnamon and brown sugar on top for dessert. The children came and went quietly, more often seen than heard, and were shepherded efficiently in management of their homework and other duties by Irma when Gerti was not at home.

Helmut could hardly wait to show me off, so he invited a violinist my age to perform the Bach Double Concerto with me in a little "Hauskonzert." That is how I met "die Tante

Hete" ("Aunt Hete"), a fulsome Teutonic blond who soon evinced interest in more than music. When Irma prepared a picnic lunch for us one day and sent us biking into the countryside, an historic antique chapel provided sanctuary for more than our morning prayers!

Muenster's Lord Mayor welcomed us Fulbrighters to a reception in the historic Rathaus, site of the signing of the Treaty of Westphalia that ended the Thirty Years War in 1648. The Lord Mayor forgave my late arrival by telling everyone that his own experiences in Rock Hill, South Carolina, had taught him that Southerners go at a slower pace! He seated me next to him during the banquet, after which he suggested we get together again—just for the two of us. That made me feel that my first adventure in high-level diplomacy had gone well enough. The occasion also gave us a chance to tour downtown Muenster and discover how beautifully its medieval facades and streets had been restored. (Lacking any heavy industry that supported the war effort, Muenster was not as badly damaged by Allied bombing as most other German cities.) Muenster was not only a major university city, but it was the primary commercial center in flat fertile farmland near Holland. Helmut drove us across the border one Saturday just to eat at a favorite Chinese restaurant that served fresh vegetables so good, he said, they were worth the trip.

The Liebrechts were aristocratic neighbors of Helmut and Gerti who agreed to take me with them on a trip to Switzerland. From the back of their large Mercedes, I leaned over the front seat as if I were a child again, struggling to understand adult conversation. Wherever I looked in Switzerland, I expected to see "Heidi" cavorting in the beautiful highland meadows. Alpine views in every direction were magnificent. We even drove into the middle of a flock of sheep one evening at twilight. In Basel, I ate fondue for the first time. At one five-star hotel, because reservations had not been made ahead of time for me, I was forced to sleep on a rollaway cot in the maids' linen closet.

It was time to travel to Cologne to matriculate at the

University and consult about my course of study. Just as important, I had to find a place to live. The train took me through Essen, famous for Krupp's Ironworks, and Duesseldorf, the "Paris of Germany" before the war, and across the Rhein into a railway station that adjoined the colossal Cologne Cathedral. I wondered how any social compact could possibly survive the 800 years it took to construct that church. Was it a miracle or Allied discretion that saved the Cathedral from ruinous bombing? From the train station, I took a streetcar to the university, gazing all along the way at a German industrial city still recovering from total destruction. Every third or fourth building bore heavy scars of war, and many lots cleared of rubble still sat vacant, looking like missing teeth in the urban landscape. Wherever new construction had been hastily built, it looked starkly utilitarian. Cologne in 1962 was not a pretty city.

Strap-hanging, middle-aged women, standing uncomfortably close to me on the streetcar that hot September morning, displayed their bushy armpits, while others sitting directly across from me revealed shaggy, unshaven legs. They also were not a pretty sight!

Enrollment in only one course each semester was required by the Fulbright Commission, and at the International Student Office, I learned that Professor Silbermann's course on the Sociology of Music would not be offered until the spring semester. Until then a class taught by Professor Rene Koenig, an anthropologist considered one of the best lecturers at the University, was highly recommended When I asked about housing, advisers said to check listings in the newspaper and find something for myself—a daunting prospect, to say the least!

Just then a young woman who had overheard the conversation stepped into the office. "Hey, I just sat beside somebody on the train this morning who told me a friend of hers works for a dentist across the street who is thinking about renting out one of his rooms. Want me to call her?"

What a Godsend! Within minutes I was knocking on the door of Dr. Dieter Hartmann's practice at Zulpicherstrasse

182, directly across from the main classroom building of the University.

The exchange rate in 1962 favored the US dollar over the German Mark four to one. That meant I had about 400 Deutsche Marks a month to spend, and Dr. Hartmann wanted only 90 for rent. He said it might take some time to furnish the empty back room—a couch that folded out into a bed, a table and a couple of chairs and a lamp; but I told him not to worry, the semester did not begin for another week. Fortunately, Dieter Hartmann was an orthodontist. No screaming children tried to flee in his offices. Instead, a couple of women sat casting and sculpting and grinding implants and dentures; and no one occupied the building after 5:00 p.m. Such a room was called "sturmfrei"—meaning it was free from the prying eyes and nagging complaints of a landlady and considered the most prized of all student accommodations in the city.

There were two minor problems, however: 1) the only WC was outside in the building's foyer and 2) there was no shower. Dr. Hartmann told me I would have to take the streetcar to a public facility in downtown Cologne whenever I needed a bath. Despite that inconvenience, I was elated with the results of my first venture alone in Germany and could hardly wait to tell the Elligers!

Helmut and Gerti were not church-goers, except perhaps at Easter. Nevertheless they were officially designated "evangelisch" and paid taxes to support Protestant ministers and churches, and they routinely gave thanks before each evening meal by holding hands around the table and reciting the Moravian blessing—"Come Lord Jesus, our guest to be, and bless these gifts bestowed by thee." One Sunday I pedaled off by myself to attend a service in a large church nearby, where I found a few old people scattered about in the sanctuary, huddled up in their winter coats. The sermon was so incomprehensible, and the church so near-dead, I never returned.

Helmut and Gerti personified another German word—"begeistert" (high spirited)! They were exuberant lovers of life. Helmut often clapped his hands in front of the house on crisp fall mornings, emitting puffy little clouds as he exclaimed, "Herrlich!" "Herrlich!" and Gerti was a dervish of kinetic happiness! Always busy with her hands, she taught classes in crafts at a nearby community college; and in the car, she would throw her head back and sing lustily as she drove. Helmut taught me the best way to arrange a restaurant celebration when he asked his favorite chef, Herr Dowling in Winterberg, to select and prepare lunch for us. Helmut told Dowling how much he was willing to spend and when we would return to eat—and then left everything else up to him. At the appointed time, Dowling himself welcomed and seated us, then presented each surprising dish with personal pleasure and pride. Shifting the creative responsibility for our particular meal onto the shoulders of the chef himself was a brilliant idea I have emulated many times ever since.

My language skills were improving daily, thanks to the discipline of reading a newspaper article before German class each morning and never speaking a word of English. Nevertheless, they were not good enough to make the alarming events of the Cuban missile crisis entirely clear to me. Helmut remained riveted to television news during much of late October when the showdown with Russia was being reported, and he kept trying to explain that the threat of imminent nuclear war was real. Fortunately, I never believed it.

("Where ignorance is bliss, 'tis folly to be wise!")

The Experiment in International Living Program ended for everyone but me the day we enrolled in our universities. In almost every sense short of legal adoption, I was now the Elligers' oldest "son." If I wanted to bring dirty laundry home to Muenster, invite friends to visit, or spend Christmas vacation with them—whatever, I was encouraged to do so. Our relationship grew and deepened continually throughout the year.

Cologne/ Fall Semester

In the German University system in 1962, students attended classes at their own discretion. There were no regular tests or exams for most courses—only a final cataclysm that determined pass or failure for the degree as a whole. Consequently, some German students spent their young adulthood moving from one university to another, or lingering in a fraternity before submitting themselves for their exhaustive final exams. I attended Professor Koenig's lectures faithfully at first, but soon relaxed into more typical absenteeism. It seemed to me enlightened on the part of the Fulbright Commission to require enrollment in only one course each semester, because it gave grantees freedom to experience bi-cultural living in depth. Perhaps it is not a fair analogy, but I considered Americans who sequestered themselves in German libraries doing nothing but research all day to be just as self-centered as those who only skied and drank beer!

Turning my little room at the back of Dr. Hartmann's dentist offices into a livable space required some outfitting, most importantly with a hotplate and the largest plastic tub I could find. It was a month or so after I moved in before Dr. Hartmann realized his electric bill had gone through the roof—a discovery that almost got me evicted. I had to confess to him that I had been filling my tub with hot water from a faucet next to one of his patient's chairs and scrunching up in my tub to take a bath. (The practice may not have been hygienic enough to keep me from seeking medical treatment for a nasty case of crab lice!) Without refrigeration in my room, I ate a lot of fruit, bread and cheese from a little grocery store around the corner, and lunched in the "Mensa" (the university cafeteria) where 50 cents bought one meal and 75 cents bought another with meat.

A series of orientation meetings soon took place in Bad Godesburg near Bonn, where I encountered the REAL oboist in our group—a young woman from Boston University named Dorothy Kidney. She had been a participant in the

Fromm New Music Project at Tanglewood in 1959. She was also assigned to Cologne, at the "Musikhochschule" (conservatory) where she studied with a famous teacher named Helmuth Huecke. David Effron was the other musical Fulbrighter, also assigned to Cologne. He was a pianist and conducting student from Indiana University who worked with singers at the Opera. (David and I would reconnect many years later when he became Artistic Director and Conductor of the Brevard Music Center.)

Affiliation with two groups enriched my life right away. The first was the "Evangelische Gemeinde" (the Protestant Student Association), and the other the University of Cologne Symphony Orchestra. In the first, I met an American from Michigan whose "cover" struck me as so implausible I openly and frequently accused him of being a spy. To "gag" me, his CIA handlers instructed him to tell me that he really was one! He was paid cash under a table in Bonn to report on American exchange students and members of a Russian trade mission down the street in Cologne. The "Evangelische Gemeinde" was led by a pastor who required no religious profession or affiliation from residents in its dormitory. The second was the university orchestra, led by Conductor Dr. Drux, who limped badly from injuries he received in the war. He welcomed me into his ensemble and gave me the first oboe chair next to a handsome flutist named Fritz Raber, a law student from Salzburg who became one of my best friends. Together Fritz and I assembled an international woodwind quintet that employed a horn player from England and two German students playing clarinet and bassoon respectively.

In late November, students from the "Evangelische Gemeinde" invited me to accompany them on a skiing trip to Austria. They had reserved their own railroad car and rooms in Bayrischzell, a quaint little ski resort northeast of Munich on the Austrian border. Helmut urged me to go and equipped me with some of his own outmoded gear—boots, insulated underwear, gloves and a hat, etc. We were a motley group— Turks, Palestinians, a Hungarian refugee, someone from Ghana and a few Germans in addition to me. As soon as our train arrived at twilight, our leader ran to check us into the hotel. She returned agitated and announced that a mistake had been made—not enough rooms had been reserved for everyone. Two of us would have to stay outside of town in a farmhouse that served as a bed and breakfast during ski season. An attractive guy from the Gaza Strip agreed to share a bedroom with me in a section of the barn that was attached to the farmhouse, just above cows that were already huddled for the night. On a dresser in the room were two large bowls, pitchers of water, and two towels. Searching for some common ground before retiring, I told my roommate about the "Book of the Year" event at Davidson College and how I had read *Exodus* and knew Leon Uris. What a mistake! The intractable passions of the Mideast exploded right in front of me.

"Why didn't you give the Jews California instead of my home town?" the guy yelled, his rant gaining momentum for at least half an hour before he wore himself out. After that during the rest of the trip he never spoke to me again.

It snowed overnight, adding to nearly three feet of the stuff already on the ground. The ski rental shop in Bayerischzell was out of equipment, so I had to take the train back down the valley to another town to rent some skis. The only ones left there were World War I vintage, too long for me and made of wood with leather bindings. I took them anyway. By the time I returned to Bayrischzell, the lifts in town were closed for the day. Ten of us who were skiing for the first time elected to try an Idiotenhuegel ("idiot hill") in the farmer's back pasture for our first run the next morning. Without a lift, we had to stairstep ourselves sideways up the hill, perspiring from the exertion despite frigid temperatures and discarding coats and sweaters along the way.

At last on top, we formed a line and waited for our leader to zoom straight down the hill, carving a "Bahn" (track) in the deep snow for us to follow. At the bottom, she turned smartly and waved her ski pole as a signal for us to follow. The Ghanaian in front of me had never before seen snow, but he was outfitted like a ski shop mannequin. As soon as he saw the signal, he pushed off with a whoop and disappeared over the crest of the hill.

"Los" (Go!), everyone shouted from behind me! I leaned forward and pushed hard, gathering speed quickly, until I was rocking back and forth with tears streaming from my eyes. I went airborne at the crest for one exhilarating moment, before looking down and seeing directly in front of me the student from Ghana crawling out of a hole in the snow. I crashed right in on top of him, snapping one of my wooden skis and badly spraining my ankle. Carried back to the farmhouse like a wounded warrior, I spent the rest of the week in front of a roaring fire drinking beer and lemonade. It was not an unpleasant end to my skiing career.

Helmut Elliger, as solicitous as my own father would have been, came to see me in Cologne and check out my living situation. (One difference was his insistence that we bar-hop, drinking schnapps and a beer at several "Stuben" in the neighborhood.) When I returned to Muenster mid-semester and went "kegelend" (bowling) with him, I joined his team for the club competition. My unsteady delivery late in the evening actually hit the mark and won the game for our side!

Helmut was wounded nine times in the war, with telltale bullet holes all over his body to prove it. He had fought on every front and was one of the last officers flown out of Stalingrad. By the time the war ended, he was a Wehrmacht Major with very few soldiers left to command. When I learned about his military experience, I expressed surprise and dismay that a man of such humane instincts and love of people could have been a great soldier. Helmut's response was instantaneous and irate.

"What other kind of soldier would you expect me to be?"

He had been valedictorian of his high school class, was an excellent athlete, and played Beethoven sonatas competently. All his life he did everything to the best of his ability. Like Gerti, he even served (BOMBSHELL!) as a leader in the Hitler Youth! Seventeen years after the revelation of the most heinous acts of public policy in modern history—Germany's systematic campaign to exterminate six million Jews, I found myself enthralled by an exemplary human being who was a product of the same culture that produced the Holocaust! I thought it impossible! But Reinhold Niebuhr's book, *Moral Man and Immoral Society,* came to mind and I realized that in 1962, all of Western Germany was being rebuilt by survivors who had grown up and participated to some degree in Nazism. I wondered if any Dietrich Bonhoeffers were still among them . . .

From its beginning in Muenster, the Experiment in International Living Program had been resisted by the Elligers. Helmut's favorite Gymnasium (high school) teacher finally persuaded them to participate, but Gerti agreed to do so only if they could have "the girl from the ranch" in Montana. She said they did not want "the boy from North Carolina." Their aversion to me was not personal (how could it be?). Instead, it was based on their revulsion for the way they felt black people had been mistreated in the South!

Eventually Helmut and I were able to speak frankly and at great length about these things. On at least two occasions, after talking all night, we walked into the backyard arm-in-arm to watch the sun come up. I considered Helmut Elliger to be one of the half dozen-or-so kindred spirits of my life! And he felt exactly the same way about me.

Berlin

Berlin, like Jerusalem, was a geopolitical "thalidomide child" of the war—distorted by its isolation in hostile territory and partitioned like a four-slice pizza pie. There were British, French, and American allied sectors west and south and a Russian sector mostly in the north. No place in the world put the reality of the Cold War in clearer focus than Berlin, with its sinister midtown scar expanding daily. The Berlin Wall was underestimated when it emerged like a rash overnight in August 1961. Eighteen months later, it was a bristling monstrosity that effectively tore the city apart. East

Germans died every day trying to run through it, climb over it, or dig under it. The only legal crossing point between the American and Russian sectors was known as "Checkpoint Charlie," under heavy military guard on both sides. Passing through it made me feel like an extra in a "James Bond" movie.

Mid-winter meetings brought us Fulbrighters to West Berlin for a week, introducing me to one of the most exciting cities in the world. Phoenix-like, Berlin was reemerging from the rubble of total devastation with incredible energy; and Communism and Capitalism competed on opposite sides of the wall for proof of each system's social and economic and political superiority. A day spent in East Berlin was enough to persuade me that it was no contest! Everything on the east side was drab, dull and gray, except for blood-red political slogans that screamed from billboards the lie of Communist superiority. Monotonous buildings of the same size and shape lined streets almost devoid of activity. Horse-drawn vehicles dodged the occasional near-empty street cars; and where there were pedestrians, they were hunkered down, bundled up, and smoking hard enough to make their cigarettes spark and crackle in the cold.

I found a music store selling Breitkopf und Haertel editions of Mozart and Beethoven serenades so inexpensive I gobbled up enough chamber music to last a lifetime. Prokofiev's *Romeo and Juliet* at the Opera Comique that night gave me opportunity to see the complete ballet for the first time. The rapturous music, the heart-breaking story and the hypnotic dancing were completely intoxicating. (Years later, Kurt Masur, by then my Music Director at the New York Philharmonic, would tell me he was conducting that very performance!) After the ballet with my head still reeling, I walked at midnight undisturbed down the center of Unter den Linden. In order to save fuel, East Berlin turned off all its street lights and the darkness was complete except for gaudy neon lights that were emblazoned and reflected in low-hanging winter clouds on the other side of the Brandenburg Gate. Suddenly a feeling of pride exploded within me. "Yes!

Yes!"—to color; to force of personality; to individualism; to acquisitive creativity!

"Yes!" to Capitalism.

The Kaiser Wilhelm Kirche on Kufurstendamm, itself a metaphor of old and new Berlin, had a dramatic modern geometric turret sanctuary erected inside the crater of its bombed-out nave. A beautiful blonde minister preached the sermon at the service I attended—the first female I ever saw in a pulpit. She reminded me that many professions formerly unavailable to women were now filled by them in post-war Germany. During thirty years of war, the country had lost almost two full generations of its young men. Within sight of the fearsome barbed-wire Wall, I toured the Berlin "Philharmonie," the gleaming new, acoustically-perfect home of the Berlin Philharmonic, and visited Berlin University and the stadium where black American Jesse Owens' personally repudiated the myth of Aryan superiority in the 1936 Olympics. At the nearby Egyptian Museum, the bust of "Queen Nefertiti" stopped me in my tracks. No other piece of sculpture ever knocked the breath right out of me like that!

Gertraud, my pretty German teacher from the boat, lived in Berlin and went with me to see *Pelleas and Melisande* at the Deutsche Oper. Considered Debussy's masterpiece, the opera dragged on so long without sub- or super-titles that Gertraud and I—who were seated in a score-reader's box in the back of the opera house, found ourselves more entertaining than the production on stage. Her kisses were a delightful way to say "Auf Wiedersehen" to Berlin!

Cologne/ Spring Semester

The holiday season at the Elligers had been a magical experience, especially Christmas Eve when the candles on the tree were lit and Kris Kringle came with presents for the children. Carols were sung; fragrant cakes and cookies baked. On one very cold winter night, when the Elliger household was filled with relatives and other guests, I was sent to the attic to sleep. A single bed was up there in the loft with no heat at all. I had just fashioned an igloo out of several down comforters when Hete appeared in the moonlight next to my bed. Letting her robe slip from her shoulders, she snuggled in beside me. I had never encountered the naked body of a young woman before, and mine over-reacted immediately! Born too soon for the sexual revolution and too intensely moralistic for unprotected sex, I lied that I was engaged to Jean Thomas and sent Hete sorrowing away.

Later my best Davidson College friend came from England to visit. Harrison Wellford was valedictorian of our class, rewarded for his outstanding achievements with a Marshall Scholarship that afforded him two years at Cambridge University. When he arrived in Muenster, true to form, the Elligers welcomed him warmly. We spent so much time together excitedly engaged in catch-up conversation, the reality of our German environment practically disappeared. It was the first English I had spoken with anyone in four months.

Back at the University of Cologne in the beginning of the spring semester, I attended the lectures of Professor Alphons Silbermann whose book, Die Soziologie der Musik, had made my Fulbright possible. They were such boring reiterations of what he had written, I soon stopped going to those also.

Downtown in Cologne one day, on an impulse, I walked into the "Musikhochschule" to ask if I could observe a student orchestra rehearsal.

"Did you bring your oboe with you?" asked the staff person who greeted me. "If you did, just go on in there and play with them."

Astonished, I thought how impossible it would be for me to waltz in off Broadway like that and join the Juilliard orchestra! I quickly soaked a reed and sat down in the first oboe chair. Instead of protesting my intrusion as I expected, the students welcomed me cheerfully. In an institution where instrumentalists prepared exclusively to become soloists or chamber musicians, orchestras were considered "necessary evils." (My wife told me it was the same at Juilliard when she attended in the late sixties.) For my part, I was thrilled to have an orchestra to play in, and that impromptu Musikhochschule rehearsal led to the invitation that soon arrived for me to play with the celebrated "Cologne Chamber Orchestra." My concert with the professionals included a delicious oboe solo by Handel that was the performance highlight of my year. My German audience had never heard a John Mack reed before!

John F. Kennedy visited that spring. Clutching little German and American flags in both hands, I ran with thousands of Germans through the streets of Cologne to see America's handsome young President cross the Rhein with Chancellor Konrad Adenauer ("Der Alte"), both of them standing in an open Mercedes convertible. I had never felt so patriotic! In West Berlin the next day, in one of the iconic moments of the Cold War, President Kennedy made his historic proclamation, "Ich bin ein Berliner!" It strategically and irrevocably threw down a gauntlet linking West Germany to the United States.

Concern about so many undergraduate deficiencies in music—especially in piano and theory—and how to pay for living expenses in New Haven discouraged me whenever I thought about attending Yale University. So, as a result, I applied to Northwestern University to see if I could win a larger fellowship. The same recording of the Mozart Oboe Quartet that impressed Robert Bloom persuaded Ray Still to accept me in Evanston; but Northwestern's fellowship, like Yale's, did not include a stipend for living expenses. Just then a letter from John Mack announced his intention to join the National Symphony as Principal Oboe in September. He told me to enroll in a master's degree program in the Washington, D.C. area that would allow us to work together at last. On a hunch, I wrote Emerson Head at the University of Maryland. He was the trumpet teacher at Transylvania Music Camp and conductor of the University of Maryland Symphony Orchestra. Emerson's reply informed me that there was indeed one graduate fellowship available in the

Music Department that also included money for room and board. Supported by his strong recommendation, he said I could win it if I applied at once. I did and was accepted.

In continual correspondence with my parents about everything important that happened since I left Lenoir, I urged Dad to visit Germany while he still had the lungs to do so. In the end, he declined because of emphysema. Despite not joining me, he agreed it was a good idea and the right time to buy a German car and ship it back to the United States. Helmut introduced me to a dealer in Muenster and helped negotiate my purchase of a new Volkswagen "Beetle" for $1,400. Shipping from Bremerhaven to New York mid-summer would cost another $600, but altogether it was a great bargain. In the meantime, I had wheels in Europe!

Intense correspondence developed throughout the winter between me and Jean Thomas, who was in her freshman year at Converse College in Spartanburg, South Carolina. If it is true that "absence makes the heart grow fonder," my year in Europe ramped up our relationship in a very serious way. She was the girl to whom I was feeling increasingly devoted. Another letter arrived that winter that would change the course of my life, although its significance was unknown at the time. Sent from Charlotte Symphony Concertmaster Jim Weber, it contained a check for $450 and a request for me to do him the favor if I were ever in Paris of buying his son David a new Lorée oboe directly from the factory. I added his check to John Mack's list of cane growers and drove to France straightaway.

Paris in springtime

A Fulbrighter from Harvard Law School named Bob Smith, who was studying philosophy at the University of Tuebingen, asked if I would take him to Madrid for a month of Spanish language study during spring break, and I agreed. We shared the maiden voyage of my blue VW Beetle, soon forsaking German and speaking English for the first time in months. Our itinerary took us south along the Rhein to Freiburg, where we viewed its magnificent red-rock cathedral, then to Basel and across Belgium into France. Approaching Paris, strong crosswinds buffeted my little rear-engine car so much I thought the steering mechanism was broken.

Friends in Paris expected Bob and Helmut had made reservations for me at a hotel near Place d'Etoile. After dropping Bob off at a convenient METRO station, I got caught up in the maelstrom of traffic spinning around the Arc de Triomphe, and only four circuits later was able to break free onto Rue Kleber. It was dark when I checked into Hotel Angleterre and even darker in the corridor leading to my little room. The concierge told me to share a toilet at the end of the hall.

Next morning the early March day was chilly but bright. I tucked my oboe under my arm and walked from the hotel to the American Drug Store, turned right and fairly skipped onto the Champs Elysee! It was the widest boulevard I had ever seen—so far across one side of it was barely visible at street level from the other. Gleaming white marble adorned the Paris cityscape like sequins on a wedding dress.

I needed to cash some traveler's checks, so I stepped into the first bank I came to and stood at the back of a queue. A gorgeous lithe brunette who actually shaved her legs (!) came through the door and took her place close behind me. After six months in Germany, I thought she was just about the most beautiful young woman I had ever seen.

"Wow! It must be true," I thought . . ."what they say about the French!"

At that moment, the girl reached into her handbag and pulled out her American passport!

"Vera LeCraw" from "Greensboro, North Carolina," it said.

"Golly, I'm from North Carolina, too!" I exclaimed, and the ice was broken.

Vera told me she was a student from Sweetbriar College spending her junior year in Paris at the Sorbonne. She even knew several of my Davidson College fraternity brothers.

Fortunately for me, the line moved slowly enough for Vera LeCraw to succumb to the strangest pick-up of her life by agreeing to accompany me as guide and translator on my mission to buy David Weber a brand new Lorée oboe!

Because I had no address for the factory and only the name "F. Lorée" stamped on the bell of my own instrument for reference, Vera suggested conferring with commercial people at the American Express office on Champs Elysee. She was sure someone there would know about the company. It turned out to be more complicated than that. No list of manufacturers in Paris or environs revealed the name "F. Lorée." A narrowed search of woodwind instrument makers also yielded nothing. Finally, working backwards from retail information, we discovered that patronymic succession had transmuted the company name over the years from "F. Lorée" to "Dubois." Lorée oboes were in fact made by "Instruments Dubois"—address, 4, Rue du Vert-Bois, near Place de l'Opéra.

It was lunchtime when we arrived in front of the ornate, resplendent Paris Opera. We ate a "croque monsieur" at a sidewalk café on Rue du Temple before walking to Rue du Vert-Bois in search of the oboe factory.

(Lorée oboes, reputed for decades to be the finest instruments in the world, nevertheless were plagued by the intractable problem that most of them cracked between the trill keys at the top of the upper joint during break-in. Insufficient aging of the grenadilla wood was generally thought to be the problem. How ironic, therefore, that Lorée oboes emanated from Rue du Vert-Bois—the "Street of Green Wood!")

We found number "4" imprinted at eye level next to a heavy iron gate. When I pushed hard against one side of it, chickens squawked and ran around the courtyard in front of us. On a list of upstairs tenants posted in the right-hand corner of the courtyard, one said "Instruments Dubois." Could this really be a factory?

The uneven wooden stairs, worn thin in the center by thousands of oboists' footsteps, creaked as we climbed them. On the second-floor landing, we confronted an office door that could have been Bob Cratchet's in Dicken's *A Christmas Carol,* and a little bell tinkled when we opened it. Inside, a dark anteroom exhibited as a museum might, antique prototype oboes standing like toy soldiers in glass cases. A receptionist greeted us warmly and invited us into a better-lit inner office, into which stepped a handsome gentleman she introduced as "Monsieur Robert de Gourdon," the man in charge. I could see that Vera's magic had its effect even before he said, "Bonjour!"

Batting her beautiful long eyelashes and speaking French that must have borne a Southern accent, Vera explained that I had come to buy a new oboe for a student of mine back home in America. Monsieur DeGourdon responded gallantly that no one had ever purchased an instrument directly from the company before—Lorée oboes could be bought only from franchised distributors. He would be happy to tell us where to go in Paris to find one. But Vera persisted and wheedled coyly.

"Please, Monsieur DeGourdon, couldn't Mr. Robinson just try a few instruments while he is here?"

A moment's hesitation . . . a perceptible crack in his resolve. (Later DeGourdon explained to me that a dispute involving a particular distributor in New York City had led to a law suit just then pending in the World Court at The Hague, and he was in fact just then reconsidering the company's policy against direct sales to customers.) Somewhat flushed, he stepped into a room behind and returned holding four oboe cases in his arms. Speaking in French to Vera, he asked her to direct me into an adjacent office to try the instruments while he showed her around the shop. Hundreds of oboists would follow me into that room, sampling one great oboe after another in a search for the elusive "perfect" instrument, but I was the first to do so.

On her tour, Vera learned from DeGourdon that the offices at 4, Rue du Vert-Bois, were a place for final adjustment of the oboes—packing, invoicing, and shipping to dealers around the world, and not the site of their manufacture. African blackwood itself (mostly grenadilla from Mozambique) was treated and aged elsewhere; and all the drilling and casting of keys happened in a workshop south of Paris. Setting the cork and bladder pads and assembling the nearly five hundred parts of each oboe were all accomplished by men and women working on a per unit basis in their homes away from the city. Oboe making was then, and still is, a cottage industry.

After about twenty minutes of testing the new instruments and comparing them with my own, I returned and asked Vera to tell Monsieur DeGourdon that these four oboes would not do—"Please ask him to bring others for me to try."

Stunned, our host took a step backward and told Vera that there were no other instruments. Unless . . . well, there might be one possibility . . . Marcel Tabuteau had recently come to Paris to purchase a new Lorée. He brought with him a list of specific modifications required to make him happy; but in some minor detail during early manufacture, Lorée had failed him, and he had gone across town to a competitor (Marigaux) to obtain the last oboe he would ever buy. DeGourdon told my pretty translator that I could have Tabuteau's Lorée if I could wait a few days for it to be finished. I nearly jumped out of my skin!

"Of course, I will!" I said to Vera. "Tell Mr. DeGourdon it's perfect! I will take Bob Smith to Barcelona and return to Paris one week from today."

Pleased, Monsieur DeGourdon suggested that I leave my own oboe with him for reconditioning while I was away. He said he would restore the wood, replace keys and pads, and make it like new again for $35!

In the afterglow of our agreement, while the paperwork for the transaction was being completed by Madame DeGourdon in another office, Robert and I were able to get better acquainted, thanks to Vera. Through her he told me that although Marcel Tabuteau was seventy-six years old, he was in reasonably good health and living in Nice.

"Don't hesitate to visit him," he explained. "He will be happy to see you." And he gave me Tabuteau's address: 111 Promenade des Anglais on the waterfront Nice's Bay of Angels. (John Mack had not done so, nor suggested a meeting with his teacher, because of recriminations Tabuteau promised if he found out that Mack had ever divulged any of his reed secrets to anyone!)

When I told DeGourdon that I was on a cane-hunting mission for John Mack, he wrote down the name of a favorite cane dealer in Paris.

"Go see Maurice Deriaz, "he said. "He is the same age as Marcel Tabuteau in a location you can find easily on Rue Pigalle. It is directly across from 'Moulin Rouge.' Tell him I sent you."

Vera and I parted company that afternoon with a promise to get together when I returned from Spain.

Next morning, I stood in the middle of one of the most famous night club districts in the world searching for the name "Deriaz" beside a dingy doorway. When I found it and touched the buzzer, a remarkable figure appeared. He looked like "the Michelin man"—completely bald, with a round head that melded seamlessly into massive sloping shoulders, and he shuffled as he walked.

"Bonjour!" I said in French, after which I admitted in French that I really did not speak French. I asked in English if he spoke English, and his answer in English was, "No I don't."

"Koennen Sie Deutsch?"

Bingo! He was born in Alsace-Lorraine and grew up speaking German, so we were in sync after that.

His shop was tall and well-lit, with colorful floor-to-ceiling circus posters covering its walls. Deriaz pointed proudly at them as I entered. The younger version of himself was at once recognizable in tights, lifting elephants and barbells, displaying rippling muscles in poses of ultimate strength. Maurice Deriaz had been the "Strongman of Europe" fifty-five years earlier, touring the continent with one circus after another! Now he padded around in frayed leather slippers selling oboe cane. Jabbering continually in German about the state of the world, he showed me around his shop—bins of tube cane gathered from secret suppliers in the Var here, drawers full of the stuff already gouged and shaped for sale there, etc. I explained that my purpose was to buy tube cane before it had been cut, so that my teacher John Mack—reputed to be the best oboe reed-maker in America, could prepare it to his own specifications and share it with me. Deriaz did not react at first, but soon led me into a glass-walled inner office where he carefully filled a box with a kilo (2.2 pounds) of 10.-10.5 mm golden tubes of cane. It had been a friendly encounter and genial negotiation. I shook his hand and thanked him warmly. As I left, I saw Madame Deriaz vigorously shaking her finger in her husband's face.

Nice

The trip with Bob Smith to Nice required only one day. We stopped to admire the wide tree-lined streets of Avignon and visit the magnificent Roman Theater of Orange, the best-preserved Roman amphitheater in all of Europe. Bob's guide book, the popular *Europe on $5 a Day*, disclosed an acceptable pension in Nice that took us in for the night. Somehow Helmut Elliger had transmitted the information to me in Paris that my VW needed a recall to tweak its oil pump, so I decided to get the car worked on the next afternoon. A mechanic told me his analysis would take about an hour . . . go wait somewhere. As I sat at an outdoor café drinking a beer in pleasant mid-afternoon sunshine, I debated whether to walk down to Promenade des Anglais and meet Marcel Tabuteau or not. Encountering the great man was an intimidating prospect; and my decision teetered in the balance until I remembered one of Capt. Harper's favorite admonitions to members of the Lenoir High School Band: "Strike while the iron is hot!" It was this advice that broke the tie, 51-to-49, prompting me to stand up, just put one foot in front of another, and walk uncertainly towards the bay.

On the fourth floor of his "Miramar" apartment building, it took another courageous impulse for me to push the buzzer. A suspicious lady peeked through the barely-opened door. Using the only French I knew, I lied quickly

"Je'suis ami de Marcel Tabuteau" and inserted the toe of my shoe into the crack. Alarmed, the woman made me understand that she was the housekeeper and the Tabuteaus were not at home. By then I was inside the apartment where I held her at bay long enough to locate a pencil and piece of paper and scribble the following note:

"Dear Mr. Tabuteau, I am an English major from Davidson College in Europe on a Fulbright, and I play the oboe. I have studied with Ralph Gomberg at Tanglewood and also with John Mack."

Confident that an older person in Lenoir would eat supper early and go to bed by 9:00 p.m., I added the following sentence: "I would like to return this evening at 8:00 just to shake your hand," after which the housekeeper practically swept me out into the hallway.

Bob Smith's tour book served as an effective guide once again, leading us to an excellent, inexpensive restaurant in the Old Quarter of Nice, where we stuffed ourselves before Bob asked if he could come along to meet the famous man I had been talking about.

"Of course," I said, glad for moral support and some company after dark.

We drove to 111 Promenade des Anglais together and climbed the stairs to Marcel Tabuteau's apartment, both gasping for breath.

This time the greatest oboe player and teacher of the first half of the twentieth century, smelling of Scotch and garlic and dressed in a white apron, opened the door himself. Behind him in the living room, I saw an elegant table set for three. Tabuteau had spent all afternoon cooking for me!

"So, you're the one!" he said exuberantly. "You don't LOOK like an oboe player!" Then noticing my companion behind me, he exclaimed, "Mon dieu, there are two of you!" and ran back into the kitchen to tell his wife.

Bob Smith and I looked at each other incredulously. Could we possibly eat again after the meal we had just consumed? We saw Madame Tabuteau scurry out of the kitchen with a fourth-place setting and another chair.

Tabuteau, who had come back to us at the doorway, said, "I am very sorry to disappoint you, but you are going to have to share your portion!"

That saved us.

The evening began with hilarity and high spirits, but things were dragging by 9:00 p.m., when dinner was still only half-eaten. Bob Smith had been a mostly mute observer and Madame Tabuteau a solicitous attendant; but any news of mine about oboists and the music world in the United States that interested Tabuteau had long since been told. "Morendo" describes the situation as Tabuteau's nose fell closer and closer to the sauce in his plate. I remembered just in time the list of cane growers John Mack had given me and pulled the 3-by-5 card from my shirt pocket.

Pushing it under Tabuteau's nose, I implored, "Will you look at these names, Mr. Tabuteau? John Mack told me if I ever visited the Var, I should buy some tube cane and send it to him."

The old man, lifting his head, took the list from my hand and held it out far enough to read.

"Why, this man has been dead for twenty years!" he roared. "And this one is making patio furniture! Ha, ha, ha . . . that Mack, he doesn't know ANYTHING!" Now fully awake, he told me that Americans were unwelcome in that part of France—especially ones who did not speak French. "Listen, young man, I hate to tell you . . . but you are NOT going to get any tube cane!"

"Well, I actually just bought a kilo of tube cane from Maurice Deriaz when I was in Paris," I told him.

Tabuteau nearly knocked his chair over jumping to his feet. "That's IMPOSSIBLE!" he roared. "No one ever got any tube cane from Deriaz!"

"Well I did. It's downstairs in the car."

Madame Tabuteau had already cleared the table, and Bob Smith settled safely in a living room chair with his Spanish primer in his lap when I returned with the cane. By now Tabuteau was wearing his workshop apron. Sending me into the kitchen for a glass of Scotch, he began furiously splitting and chopping the tubes into three-inch pieces, which he then tossed into a glass of hot water on his desk. In almost no time, he was planing them out with a machine in his lap called a gouging machine. Pulling out smooth strips of cane as they emerged from the knife, he held one up and exulted, "You see that? Cuts like butter!"

"Looks pretty good to me, Mr. Tabuteau!" I said, peering over his shoulder at the process for the first time.

The long-awaited Deriaz cane fulfilled its promise, because Tabuteau decided this must be a very good year for Arundo Donax. I was thrilled to see him so rejuvenated!

"Now will you take me cane-hunting for John Mack?" I wheedled.

Tabuteau replied that he had never done that for anyone—not even Harold Gomberg when he sailed over from Capri in his yacht the previous summer. He could not risk disclosing his secret cane sources in the Var to anyone. On the other hand . . . the doctor had just ordered him not to drive . . . and my new VW Beetle was sitting at the curb down below . . . and I wouldn't remember the sites we visited anyway. Relenting, he told me to come back early the next morning. We would go cane-hunting together after all.

Once again Bob Smith came along, reckoning this adventure was too weird to miss! In the living room before we left, Louise Tabuteau adjusted her husband's tie and pulled his hat down just so, and with obvious apprehension let him out for a day with the boys. Tabuteau rode shotgun and Bob clambered into the back. I drove west along the Cote d'Azur before turning inland away from the shore. Oboe cane was growing along embankments and in open areas everywhere. Spotting an inviting patch along the rural roadway, Tabuteau, shouted, "Stop!" Bob and I pushed our way into it to cut some tubes for future reference. Eventually we arrived at an open area where tall stalks of cane, stacked like tepees, were curing in the bright winter sunlight. A burly man ambled out of a shed to meet us, and Tabuteau told Bob and me to speak loudly to each other in German.

We visited four different farms that day—three before lunch and one afterward. Everywhere the charade was the same. Tabuteau introduced us as "his German exchange students," come to visit France in that era of the DeGaulle-Adenauer embrace across the Rhein. After haggling with the wholesalers over access and price, they would drag out a large bag of cane containing tubes almost as small as a pencil (oboe) and as large around as a coffee cup (baritone saxophone), bound for retailers in Paris. At each place, we were permitted to attack the sack for about ten minutes. Tabuteau, Bob, and I worked feverishly to pull out as many of the 10.5-millimeter-diameter tubes as possible. It was like going fishing!

On the way home, we made a curious diversion to Cogolin, a little town famous as much for the briar it produced for smokers' pipes as for its oboe cane. Tabuteau directed me to pull over in front of a particular pipe-maker's shop. He wanted to inquire about the brining solution the man used to cure his briar. Even after a lifetime of worrying about cracking oboes, Tabuteau suddenly had the notion that if boiling briars in brine kept pipes from cracking when tobacco was lit in them, perhaps the same solution would keep grenadilla from cracking when oboists' hot breath was blown into it. The cauldron I saw smelled like hot wine vinegar.

Tabuteau was napping in the car when I shook him awake for this photograph on the Riviera beach.

He posed happily, in such a jolly mood that he insisted I stay and help him cook spaghetti.

"You actually got into the kitchen, Laddie?" John Mack asked incredulously when I told him later about meeting Tabuteau.

Bob Smith departed before dinner that evening, leaving Tabuteau at the stove to continue his convivial ways with me— relating one orchestra story after another and whopping me backhand in the stomach with every anecdotal punchline. His favorite anecdote was about standing at the rail on the first-class deck of the Queen Mary when Serge Koussevitzky

(Music Director of the Boston Symphony) approached him and asked, "What are you doing on MY deck, Tabuteau?"

"Why Maestro," said Tabuteau, "I always travel to and from France first-class on this deck."

Tabuteau on the Riviera beach.

"Is that so? Well, Tabuteau, let me tell you something" he continued, "I have the greatest oboe player in the world in Boston (Fernand Gillet, nephew of Tabuteau's teacher at the Paris Conservatoire), and I pay him $30,000 a year!"

The pain of that comment was like a thorn in Tabuteau's liver throughout the following season, until Koussevitsy brought the Boston Symphony to Philadelphia for a concert in the Academy of Music. Tabuteau told me that at intermission he barged into Koussevitsky's dressing room backstage, exclaiming:

"Maestro, your orchestra is playing very well tonight, and you are conducting brilliantly. And after intermission you are playing Tchaikovsky's Fourth Symphony (with its famous oboe solo), and . . . and, I AM GOING HOME! Haw,

haw, haw, haw, haw!"

Tabuteau considered his comment to Koussevitsky an utimate squelch—truly a double-whapper!

Without my oboe, Tabuteau viewed me more as an amusing grandson than a student.

"Listen," he said to me at one point after dinner, "You REMIND ME OF MYSELF when I was a young man!"

That extravagant compliment prompted a preposterous idea, but I asked him anyway, "Mr. Tabuteau, could I return this summer and take a few lessons from you? I have several weeks free after school in Germany before going back to the United States." My words hung in the air for a few awkward moments. (I didn't know that he had turned students away for years, ever since he was forced out of the Philadelphia Orchestra by its policy of mandatory retirement at age 65.)

"Well, maybe we can work that out," he answered finally.

"I can't pay you anything," I said. (OOF!—my turn for a tummy-whopper!)

"Then just bring me a bottle of Scotch," he said. "Good stuff—Johnny Walker Black Label!"

Amazing! In a year of career limbo, a chance meeting just to say "Hello" to Marcel Tabuteau turned into the promise of lessons that would more than compensate for the conservatory training I never received!

Barcelona

The new part for my oil pump arrived in time for replacement in Nice on Saturday, the day Bob Smith and I were to drive across Southern France to Barcelona. I was walking along the beach, waiting for the work to be finished, when an attractive young man dressed in a suit approached me and asked if I spoke English. When I said I did, he told me his wallet had been stolen and he needed $30 to pay his hotel bill and take a bus back home to Monte Carlo. On the weekend, no banks or agencies were open that could help him. Would I please "loan" him the money? My Christian ethic fought against my common sense—"if a man asks for a coat, give him your shirt also," etc. The fellow was in need and begging for assistance; so, I told him I would see what I could do after I found out what my car repair was going to cost. We walked together to the repair shop, chatting like friends. He said he was from Switzerland working for a company in Monte Carlo. As soon as Bob heard what was going on, he pulled me around a corner and blasted me for being stupid and gullible.

"Fools and their money are quickly parted," he reminded me, quoting some Scripture of his own. Thus bolstered, I confronted the needy fellow and told him I was sorry to waste his time. I couldn't help him. His recriminations in reaction seared like acid rain! Bob and I hardly spoke to each other the rest of the afternoon.

We spent the night in Marseille and followed coastal routes around the Pyrenees into Spain the next morning. I dropped Bob off at the University of Madrid and checked into a modest hotel. During the one day allocated for sight-seeing, I drove to Montserrat ("the serrated mountain") and took a cable car to the top. Benedictine monks had constructed a monastery in and around massive sandstone formations near a grotto where visions of the Virgin Mary were reportedly witnessed in A.D. 880. A destination for Christian pilgrims ever since and site of the conversion experience of Ignatius Loyola—founder of the Jesuit Order, as well as of a famous "Black Madonna," Montserrat was the most exotically religious place I had ever seen. I turned from spectacular views of a countryside bathed in brilliant sunshine into the dark, cavernous space of the Basilica, where incense burned my nostrils and mystical incantations from the Montserrat Boy Choir made my hair stand on end. It was the first Roman Catholic mass I ever observed, and the experience was one of profound religious introversion. How different from the Cologne Cathedral, where souls expanded and soared upward towards its clerestory depiction of Heaven!

Next morning, I asked the hotel concierge if there was

a more direct inland route across the Pyrenees into France. He showed me on a map where to go and sent me off optimistically just before noon, headed for Toulouse. Despite a gas gauge that read half-empty, I felt sure I would find a station somewhere along the way. It was an international connector, after all. Driving almost due north and soon beyond the outskirts of Barcelona, all signs of human habitation disappeared. The two-lane road narrowed as it climbed higher and higher on the Spanish side of the Pyrenees. I had never worried about driving in the mountains of North Carolina, but the absence of guard rails and any vegetation beyond the shoulder unnerved me. Sheer drops increased with every switch-back, and my gas gauge now sagged below empty. I was in a panic by the time I crossed the crest and coasted several remaining miles down to a filling station in Andorra. The ascent back up the Pyrenees into France was just as harrowing for a different reason. At the top on that side, I found myself driving among skiers through snow banks higher than my car. Snow increasingly covered the road's surface, and I had no chains. At last I descended into desolate countryside on the French side and sighed in relief. On the outskirts of Toulouse, however, no rooms were available at any roadside inn, and I was forced to sleep in my little blue VW overnight.

Next morning, like a homing pigeon, I headed straight for Paris where a long nap at Hotel Angleterre revived me. Vera LeCraw did not accompany me when I collected my oboes at the Lorée shop, but a French oboist called "Monsieur Corn" acted as translator at an occasion that felt like a celebration. Everyone was delighted by my miraculous encounter with Marcel Tabuteau and the importance of the tube cane from Maurice Deriaz. Robert DeGourdon announced that he had made a reservation for lunch at one of his favorite restaurants, where his two children were to join us. Anne, who was about eighteen and crowned with the same glorious mane as her mother, reminded me of a red-headed Jackie Kennedy, and her freckle-faced fourteen-year-old brother Alain of Dennis the Menace! I ordered unforgettable trout amandine, and left the DeGourdon's feeling like a member of the family.

My own oboe looked brand new following its restoration by the Lorée workmen, and David Weber's "Tabuteau" oboe was already packed for shipment to his dad in Charlotte. It never occurred to me to swap the two instruments, as Tabuteau himself might have done; but I realized I ought to request a copy of David's new instrument for myself. Such an opportunity might never come again. The order was duly noted, and Robert DeGourdon said my new oboe would be ready in about a month. It was a wonderful instrument I tried but never kept. Yielding to entreaties from Jean Thomas, I sent it to her instead.

Vera and I had a REAL date that evening—dinner followed by a performance of *The Tales of Hoffmann* at the Opera Comique. We were seated in a prominent box in the balcony, where I enjoyed the attention Vera attracted almost as much as the opera. She was stunning!

After the performance, she begged me to walk with her to the famous chapel at Montmartre—"the most romantic place in Paris, with wonderful views of the city." A light rain began falling before we were halfway there. "Isn't this wonderful?" Vera purred, taking my arm and snuggling close to me. "Don't you think we should take a cab?" I muttered. "Oh, NO!" she insisted, and we walked on. The rain intensified little by little for the next hour, increasing my irritation with every cold drop. I had to get up early the next morning to drive to Germany. At last, when I could no longer stand walking in the rain—even in Paris in the springtime with a beautiful young woman, I hailed a cab and told Vera I was getting in whether she came or not. She did climb in and sit petulantly beside me, but by the time we reached her apartment, any hope of romance had been thoroughly washed away. I never saw or heard from Vera LeCraw again!

Back in Cologne

In many ways, the rest of the university semester in Cologne was denouement. My friendship intensified with Karoly Vali, a Hungarian medical student who had escaped from his home country hidden in a hay wagon in 1956, the year of the Hungarian uprising against the Soviet Union. "Korchi" and I played Frisbee and hung out a lot together. We sometimes double-dated, taking girls on picnics to the beautiful Moesel River Valley. At the "Amerika Haus" in Cologne, I met and pursued a blond attendant who personified Teutonic beauty and at age twenty-five had never been kissed. Her fearsome father (she was an only child) had competed in the high jump in the 1936 Olympics. He told me he watched drunken thugs trample his father to death in a Warsaw bar before the war, a brutal act justifying in his mind the German invasion of Poland. Despite working for NATO as an electrical lineman, he was a bitter and unreconstructed survivor of the Nazi era. Besides her father, Nolle had another guardian—a Siamese "attack cat" that pounced onto my shoulder from atop a book case the first time I entered her apartment. I think Nolle would have returned to the United States with me except for Jean Thomas.

Fritz Raber encouraged me to visit his parents in Salzburg, which I did during a week-long trip the middle of June. He had warned me about persistent clouds and rain in the Austrian Alps at that time of year, but the weather turned out to be glorious. I could have been an advance cameraman for *The Sound of Music* because almost every scene in the movie looked familiar to me, from the opening with Julie Andrews cavorting in a meadow above the town to the Schloss where she became the von Trapp children's governess. Walking one Sunday morning through a cathedral forest above Salzburg, thinking that amid such spectacular beauty as the overlooks revealed it was no wonder Mozart composed the music he wrote, I came upon a bust of the young genius set inconspicuously in a clearing at the very spot where, in a little cabin, he had composed *The Magic Flute*.

A conviction grew in me throughout the year that

nothing like Transylvania Music Camp existed for aspiring young musicians in Germany. I wrote to Dr. Pfohl, proposing scholarships at Brevard for German participants who would then return to their home communities as soloists with the Transylvania Symphony. The idea generated dozens of letters in many directions, before landing in tentative form at "Jeunesse Musicales," an offshoot of UNESCO in France. (The principle of "cultural sharing" rather than "cultural display" embodied in it eventually contributed to formulation of the American-Russian Youth Orchestra at Oberlin near the end of the Cold War.) Thinking nostalgically about my happy days at Brevard and sitting on a park bench in Cologne on June 10, I wrote a little essay entitled "The Spirit of Transylvania," which Dr. Pfohl read tearfully to campers at the Opening Night ceremony I could not attend.

The Spirit Of Transylvania

You sit in the cool dampness of the mountain evening and a "thousand-noted symphony of night things" plays all around you. To Transylvanians who are hearing it for the first time it may seem as loud and harsh as the smell of creosote in the wooden buildings. To old-timers who are trying to wrap themselves in the strange familiarity of last summer's friendships, it breaks through like an occasional chill and reminds them of their own first night at camp, and of the challenges which face them anew. It is the evening song of the mountains — the voice of the Spirit of the place in which you will live during the coming weeks. Listen, because many of you will not hear it so clearly again.

Life at Transylvania will change for you into patterns of social activity unconscious of their environment. Into eating, rehearsing, playing and sleeping; into paths from cabins to the dining hall, lake and auditorium. It will become hot morning sun off the parking lot, jokes in the cabin after taps, jealousy during sectionals, and sleepy afternoons in Heck Hall; concerts when you'd rather practice, practice when you'd rather swim, swimming when you'd rather sleep, and sleep when you'd rather talk about somebody special you sat beside at Vespers. It will be sweet-smelling sidewalks after rain in Brevard, breakfast at Berrie's on Sunday, softball against the faculty, and whispered prayers before the concerts— all the taken-for-granted threads of living at this summer music camp in Western North Carolina.

Then, one morning when you come down early for breakfast, you may look up at a startling blue sky and wonder why you hadn't noticed it before. Or walking home late after a concert, you may hear again the sounds you hear tonight, and feel suddenly and strangely alone. In those moments you will know that there is something more to living here than the orderly routine of encounters with your fellow campers.

Transylvania is a time of wonder at the miracle of being, and of awe before the infinitude of the universe — of curiosity about the truth of things and urgency about every fretting moment. It is a time, too, of gratitude for the unconditional and indescribably beautiful gifts of God — for the love of parents, the richness of your national heritage, and for the inspiration of mountains and great music. It is a time for discovering the truth in the beauty of nature.

This truth, which spoke to Brahms during his morning walks through the Vienna woods, gave Beethoven courage for living, and inspired Mozart in the cathedral forest on a hill above Salzburg; and this same truth — which has stirred the souls of sensitive men in *every* generation — is present with unusual strength in this beautiful place tonight. It trembles in the darkness around you, and can be found in any lonely corner of these mountains if you will only stop to let it speak to you. It can give your music meaning, and lift you out of the narrowness of petty thoughts and petty living. So, give it a chance this summer to speak to you. Dare to be still and to listen, to look and to wonder, and to be grateful that you are here. You will have opened your hearts then to the most beautiful of life's adventures.

The sounds you hear tonight are the evening song of the mountains. They are sounds of the Spirit of Transylvania. Listen, because many of you will not hear them so clearly again.

Joe Robinson, Former Camper
Cologne, June 10, 1963

Like a barrel on the Niagara River, my life's pace quickened as I moved towards disengagement from the Elligers and Germany. Arrangements had to be made to ship my car and steamer trunk to Cherbourg and thence to Brooklyn, as well as to travel back to France on the train and locate a place to stay in Nice. I waited until the very last day in Cologne to close my bank account at DeutscheBank, where I met a fellow Fulbrighter named David Effron standing in line to do the same thing.

Everything now focused on my upcoming second encounter with Marcel Tabuteau—this time with an oboe in my hand!

Lessons with the Master

The overnight train from Cologne to Nice took almost two days, and it was late afternoon by the time I arrived exhausted with my heavy suitcase at the hotel Tabuteau had recommended. I ate a bite and went to bed early. At first it was just a premonition, reminding me of the trains Thomas Wolf wrote about that inspired his yearning for distant places. But something inexorable and threatening was in the crescendo of that sound, which grew at a geometric rate. Framed pictures on the walls began to jiggle and the dresser to dance; and finally, the bed with me in it actually to bounce. The roar of the train was deafening. Staggering to the open window, I realized I was close enough to spit down upon box cars as they sped by below. The hotel stood at the top of a long rise that originated in the center of town a couple of miles away. Sleepless and shaken, I checked out the next morning.

The rigors of the previous night made me even more nervous when I arrived with a bottle of Johnny Walker Black Label at 111 Promenade des Anglais the next afternoon. My complaints about the trains outside my hotel window prompted Tabuteau to contact friends at the International Summer Academy and ask if they would permit me to live in their mansion-dormitory. When he returned thumbs up and assured me that I would not be run over by another train (at least, not by a REAL one), he placed a music stand in front of me in the living room and commanded, "Now unpack and let's see what kind of oboe player you are!"

The dreaded moment was at hand. My mouth was so dry I could hardly wet a reed, and I trembled as I twisted the joints of my oboe together. Marcel Tabuteau was, after all, the greatest player and teacher of the first half of the twentieth century—for me the absolute god of the oboe! When he exited the room to retrieve his own instrument, I took a few deep breaths and walked around the living room, trying to pull myself together. Since he had prescribed no particular music for my audition, when he returned, Tabuteau said simply, "Play something!"

I don't remember the first notes. Hyper-consciousness dulled my senses instead of sharpening them (or perhaps it was hyper-SELF-consciousness), because some other guy, sounding distant and not very good, was in that room playing the oboe. Across from me, Tabuteau's smile broke the spell.

"Not bad," he exclaimed, picking up his own instrument. "You know this passage from *Scheherazade*?" and he began playing the famous second movement solo for me.

Now my awareness snapped like a rubber band inside out, and I was transfixed by the wondrous sound that filled the room. I had never heard an oboe tone like that! Years later I would liken it to Crater Lake—fathomlessly deep, yet sparkling on the surface. His tone became the "Holy Grail of Oboe-dom" for me. My search for it consumed a lifetime.

In the apartment, my fears now gradually subsided. Back in September I had ranked John Mack's reeds from worst to best—practicing on thirteen, rehearsing on twelve, and performing on eleven. Throughout the year I ratcheted up the list as each practice reed wore out. An adjusted pipe cleaner drawn through them from time to time (as if "brushing their teeth") extended their life enough to preserve the three best reeds un-played until July. No wonder Tabuteau muttered from time to time, "Sounds better than I expected . . . better than I expected!" He was also feeding out line.

Like John Mack, he asked me to show him my teeth, which I did with a chimpanzee grin that won approval. My top incisors apparently were no longer a problem. What Tabuteau complained about instead was the way I blew against the reed.

"Why are you pressing down to make your air come up?" he asked. "Don't you know your lungs are trapped inside a bony cage, and the only doorway is underneath?" I had learned that much about anatomy in sophomore Biology and nodded in agreement. "Then why don't you do this to get the air to come up?" (He simulated a self-inflicted Heimlich maneuver, pulling his stomach up and in forcefully.) His chest sprang up in rebound and air came whistling out through his tightly pursed lips.

"Control of the wind is the most important element for oboe players—akin to control of the bow for string players," he said. "Conservatories are full of violinists who know what to do with their left hands. The soloists standing out front know how to use their bow, and it is exactly the same for wind players! Oboists must know when and where to take a breath and how to deliver the wind from their lungs to the tip of the reed."

During two hours together, things gradually relaxed into a kind of jam session. At one point, Tabuteau explained why he agreed to teach me after turning away so many other would-be students. It was because he felt he had one piece of unfinished business before playing his own "potential audition with St. Peter"—and that was to produce a method book. The note I left for him in his apartment back in March, revealing that I was an oboe-playing English major, inspired his thought that God might just have sent him a scribe!

Two young men came from Oberlin to see Tabuteau the week before I arrived. They were Don Baker (later Principal Oboe of the Dallas and Detroit Symphony Orchestras) and David Dutton (eventually Professor of Oboe at the University of Oregon and a Baroque oboe specialist), both on their way to study at the Mozarteum in Salzburg for a year. The Marigaux oboe Tabuteau purchased when he left

Lorée in a huff the previous spring turned out to be a dud; and Tabuteau thought David Dutton's instrument a jewel by comparison. Tabuteau confided to me with conspiratorial pleasure that he persuaded David to accept the Marigaux in exchange for David's Lorée by "playing this note flat, and that note sharp! Ha, ha, ha!" He said, I told him, "Young man, I hate to disappoint you, but you have a LEMON!'" (The story surprised and worried me a bit.)

Describing something similar at a later meeting, he recounted how a lady from the United States rushed to him after one of his concerts with Pablo Casals in Prades and said that she had heard all of his famous students back home and they were excellent—but not as good as he was.

"Of course not, madam," was his reply. "That's because I taught them all they know, but I did not teach them all I know! Ha, ha, ha, ha, ha!" Noting my similar reaction of dismay then, he added, "What? You think I was going to feed the dog to come around and bite me?" In the early years of orchestral formation in America, conductors did indeed exercise arbitrary and whimsical control over musicians' lives and careers. One could not be too careful!

Suddenly Tabuteau jumped to his feet.

"Time to go!" he announced. (Laila Storch has written in her fascinating biography of Tabuteau that he was probably in a hurry to get to the casino.) "See you tomorrow."

My blood sugar must have plummeted after so much adrenalin, because I felt let down as I left the apartment. "If this is Mecca for oboe players," I thought, "it didn't amount to much!" Tabuteau's demonstrations amazed me to be sure, but he had not explained specifically how to play a single phrase.

"What are your **real** secrets?" I wondered. "Aren't there any silver bullets in your gun?"

Thanking him as I walked out, I beseeched, "Mr. Tabuteau, could I bring the Mozart Oboe Quartet next time?" Because I was scheduled to play it in October, I thought the piece might prompt him to do some REAL coaching—'faster here, slower there, louder or softer, etc.'"

His eyes narrowed to slits as he purred in response, "Yes, yes. Good idea . . . bring Mozart . . . come early!"

The Riviera was gleaming when Louise Tabuteau opened the door to their apartment the next morning. "He's out on the balcony gouging cane," she said. And indeed, he was—in a chair facing the bay, hunched over with a tattered towel stretched tightly across his lap. On top of it was the brass planing tool that traveled back and forth flipping thin yellow ribbons of cane onto the floor.

"Good morning, Mr. Tabuteau!" I greeted cheerfully, as I stepped from the living room into bright sunlight. No answer . . . "How are you today?" I asked. Still no answer, so I thought, "Hmm, must have had a bad night . . . "

The silence thickened as I waited. In a flash Tabuteau pivoted halfway around and growled over his right shoulder, "Robinson! You are a very SICK oboe player!!!" Then he turned back to the clickety-clack, clickety-clack gouging of the piece of cane in his lap, pushing down and away hard at the end, brushing away tiny filaments of residue and finally holding it aloft in triumph. I waited, struggling to digest the implications of his surprising comment. Now swiveling to confront me directly, he spoke in a more conciliatory tone these words that sounded just as ominous, "I think I know the CURE, **but you're not going to like it!**"

I have often described my next impulse as the "most macho moment" of my life! A check-list of academic assets flashed through my mind—Davidson College *cum laude*, Phi Beta Kappa, sixth in my class, a Fulbright Award to Germany, etc. I had a safety net! "If he destroys me as an oboe player by his standards," I thought, "I will happily continue playing the way I have."

"Mr. Tabuteau," I boasted, "I can TAKE it!"

"NOOO," he roared. "I'll TAKE IT!" And he snatched my oboe and the Oboe Quartet from my hands and plopped them down on the back corner of his reed desk. With a pen knife, he scraped open the end of a tube of oboe cane just wide enough for my reed to fit into it and handed it across to me, saying, "Here is your instrument! Now you play on this!"

Sculpting Tone

And so, the cure began, a million miles from Mozart, with peeps a chick might make, on a 10 mm. tube of oboe cane with a reed stuck into it—"1,2,3,4,5,4,3,2,1." For several days, people passing by the courtyard of the International Summer Academy of Nice must have thought it was the "loony bin"—a young man sitting topless under a palm tree, chirping on something for hours on end!

If the conceptual challenge of the first part of Tabuteau's "cure" was simple—just express the dynamic potential of the noise-maker from as soft as possible to as loud as possible without changing its pitch, mastering it was another story. Blowing harder to play louder made the pitch go up; blowing slower to play softer made it go down. Even though opening and closing the reed were a way to compensate for the faster and slower wind speed (because opening the reed made the pitch go down and closing it by biting made it go up), the precise exchange of these elements was very tricky.

Years later John Mack showed me an "X diagram" Tabuteau used at Curtis to explain the exchange of blowing and biting along the dynamic continuum from *pp* to *ff*. One arrow pointed from southwest to northeast representing the work of blowing (from nothing to something), while the other pointed from southeast to northwest representing the work of biting the reed (from jaw agape to teeth together). The softest notes were accomplished by nine parts biting and one part blowing, and the loudest ones just the opposite. John Mack called this continual exchange of blowing and biting along the dynamic scale "carburetion" required to keep the pitch constant. Describing wind support, Tabuteau preached "Work to play; relax to breathe!" by which he meant that one need not inhale to prepare to play but begin as with speech from a posture of complete relaxation. ("Oboists are always suffocating from a surplus of air!" he often warned.) And describing jaw mobility, he said "When playing loud, one's jaw should resemble a trout's coming up for a bug"—meaning that one's teeth should be as far apart as lips permit.

Tabuteau preferred numbers to letters because they conveyed a clearer sense of dynamic proportion between levels of sound—e.g.,"4 is to 3, as 3 is to 2, as 2 is to 1", etc. He insisted that "2s" and "3s" and "4s" on both sides of the center not only sound the same but be produced in exactly the same way. And along the entire continuum of dynamic change from softest to loudest, despite the extreme volatility of "a reed adjusted on a tube of cane," the pitch should not bend sharp or flat.

Tabuteau was not happy with my progress on the tube. He told me 1-to-5 was kindergarten stuff at Curtis, where dynamic scaling might go as high as 12. He said my pronouncement of "1" was never soft enough, never sure enough, and not as clear as the tone of "3" or "4. If you want to increase your dynamic range," he kept insisting, "learn to play softer!" This required biting the reed down to a pin hole opening, with lips stretched tightly enough over my teeth not to smother the tone (hence the need for straight teeth). For some reason, the descending side of my pyramid exhibited more physical tension than the ascending side, and my pitch level was never constant enough to satisfy him.

Painfully in this way, by insisting on perfect execution without ever explaining precisely how each level was to be achieved, Tabuteau allowed me to discover for myself the bedrock relationship between blowing faster or slower on the one hand, and chewing to open or close the reed on the other. Exchanging these two variables in a controlled way preserves tone quality and intonation all along the dynamic continuum, making it possible for oboists to express the single most important creative potential in the interpretive art of music—**sculpting the tone through time**.

Up to this point I was playing only one fingered note, which Tabuteau himself often did when preparing his interpretations. In fact, he is the only instrumentalist I have ever known who sculpted phrases on a monotone as if "painting by numbers," adding the pitches themselves only when the **form** of the phrase was complete. Dynamic scaling is more difficult when multiple pitches are introduced because each note adds its own unique instrumental resonance and timbre to the line; and high notes generally sound louder than lower ones.

* * *

Meanwhile, my life as an interloper at the International Summer Academy developed happily. Streetcars shuttled me from Tabuteau's apartment at the edge of the bay to the International Summer Academy high above it, where I masqueraded as a German exchange student in order to enter more easily into the Academy's musical activities. When it was set up outside in the gardens, I played first oboe in the student orchestra and frequently attended master classes that convened there. The best of these were led by an emerging superstar of the flute world—Jean-Pierre Rampal. (When I praised him, Tabuteau dismissed Rampal with a sweep of his arm, snorting, "Why that man is overrated—he has no articulation!")

Breakfasts of café au lait, fresh croissants and raspberry jam were served every morning under olive trees on the other side of the mansion, not far from an outdoor pavilion where I heard Pierre Pierlot perform the Mozart Oboe Concerto one Saturday night. Most other meals were eaten in a comfortable dining room inside.

Sleeping arrangements, sometimes surreptitiously and tantalizingly co-ed, provided young men with single beds lined up barracks-style on both sides of a very large upstairs room. The balcony at the far end of the room faced south toward the bay, overlooking the mansion's gardens and half of Nice. I stood at its railing one night at midnight when a full moon made the Mediterranean limestone so incandescent I could have read a newspaper in its glow. Warm currents carried the sweet fragrance of flowers up to me from down below. The scene was so magically romantic, it reminded me of Lord Byron's description of ship-wrecked Don Juan on a deserted tropical beach when he opened his eyes and beheld his bewitching Haidee. In that moment, my heart ached from loneliness—experiencing such transcendent, hypnotic beauty with no one to confirm or preserve it by sharing. I withdrew to my dormitory bed and dreamed of Jean Thomas.

Inflection

A second stage of my "cure" began when Tabuteau announced that there could be no more rectangular notes in my dynamic pyramid.

"From now on," he said, "every note must have **inflection**!" (By which he meant must have an inclination up or down, faster or slower, forward or back!) That required me to play in 4/4 time: "down" on 1, "up" on 2, "down" on 3, "up" on 4, "down" on 5, and so on. (Actually, in 4/4, three other expressions of inflection exist at the same time—down, down, up, up; down, up, up, up; and down, down, down, up.) Upbeats preparatory to downbeats were already well-known to me, so I easily imagined "up" and "down" as the result of "splitting the diamond" of a long-tone crescendo-diminuendo—"up" being the crescendo side and "down" the diminuendo. But as with everything Tabuteau revealed, there were always more sophisticated permutations of the idea. For example, he often described "up" as "smoke rising into air," suggesting that an "up" unflection was more a matter of suspension than of loudness per se. Playing violin as a young man had convinced Tabuteau that the up-down motion of the bow simulated the necessary human business of inhaling and exhaling, with its inherent alternation of tension and release. He determined that oboe playing must replicate the process "in order to sound alive."

There are many overlapping layers of "up and down" in music, with larger diamonds continually subsuming and enveloping smaller ones. Inflection slopes extending "up" far enough constitute "the interrogative mode" (musical questions), while groups of notes starting loud and falling away on the other side constitute the "declarative mode" (musical answers). ("Answers" always begin a bit louder than the end of the "questions.") Tabuteau believed the length of these extensions was limited only by the imagination, discipline and skill of the player expressing them; and longer extensions are absolutely more sophisticated than shorter ones.

Syncopated notes are displaced "down" inflections. Except for these, all last beats in each measure are pronounced "up" in preparation for the downbeats that follow. Performance that does not use inflection to reveal the time signature in the melody is musical nonsense!

Gradually I came to understand that every note, every articulated group and every phrase has inflections within it. The infinite potential of this dimension of the interpretive art—generating audible tension and relaxation in the "skin" of the music, as it were, revealed a whole world of creative opportunity that I did not know exists in music!

Whenever Tabuteau introduced a new interpretive technique, he demonstrated its application, often using examples taken our first week together from *Scheherazade.* He played the big second movement solo again, and using just two variables, "dynamic" and "inflection," spelled out his interpretive intention in the following way: in terms of dynamics for the first phrases, "1,1,2; 2,2,3; 3,3,4; 3–1,1,2; 2,2,3,3,2;" and in terms of inflection, "down, up, up; down, up, up; down, up, up; down—down, up, up; down, up, up, up, down." Whenever he played precisely what he had just described "to prove I am square with what I say!" my jaw dropped in amazement. And when he re-molded his sculpture and reversed his inflections, fashioning a totally different character from the same notes, my jaw dropped again!

During breakfast in Tallahassee one morning in the summer of 1996, following my performance of the Vaughan-Williams Oboe Concerto at the International Double Reed Convention at Florida State University, bassoonist Sol Schoenbach, who performed as a young man with Marcel Tabuteau in the Philadelphia Orchestra, told me that Tabuteau was not the author of the "number system" of musical phrasing. His teacher at the Paris Conservatoire, Georges Gillet—a mathematical genius who had memorized the entire timetable of the French National Railroad when he worked for them—deserves most of the credit for conceiving phrase shapes numerically. Schoenbach added that there is also an excellent description of this approach by Camille Saint-Saens in his forward to an edition of Mozart's Piano Sonatas.

Tabuteau defended his fierce analysis of music by saying, "I would rather play the way I **think** than the way I feel!"

Many performers have found this assertion antithetical to their own emotional experience of music, but Tabuteau's insistence upon intelligent preparation and thorough understanding of phrasing formed the basis for his consummate musical artistry. While all music may be empowered by the spontaneous outpouring of strong feeling, great musical **art** becomes "classical" only when it rewards scrutiny and withstands the test of time.

(Later on, Tabuteau added an ironic postscript, "Listen . . . when you perform, do not get the best of the music; let the music get the best of you!" proving that he was a Romantic at heart after all.)

Marcel Tabuteau and I enjoyed great conviviality back in March when we met, palling around in the cane fields and cooking spaghetti together in his kitchen; and my first impressions of him were generally confirmed throughout the summer. From the beginning, he struck me as the virile, vibrant residue of a truly extraordinary man—someone who as a twenty-year-old in New York City exhibited physical strength impressive enough to attract professional boxing promoters, and someone who possessed intimidating intellect and authority as well as a comprehensive and irresistible zest for life. I believed he could have been CEO of any major corporation!

Madame Tabuteau was an omnipresent, quietly attentive servant, always busy in the background who intruded upon our interactions only once—the morning she zipped up his wind breaker and gently pulled his hat down on his head, before letting her great man out for cane-hunting.

(When I read about Tabuteau's death on January 6, 1966, in *The New York Times*, I wrote to Louise Tabuteau to express my shock and offer condolence, saying that I was sure she must feel her loss more keenly "for having chosen to tend a bonfire of a man.")

Color

"Do not misunderstand me . . . " Tabuteau said, starting a new lesson. "By the numbers, I do not mean 'loudness' or 'thickness'—rather a scaling of color!"

("Are you kidding?" I thought in dismay.)

I had spent a whole week chewing and blowing sculpted lines of sound only to be told that the numbers meant something other than dynamic shape! Of course, what Tabuteau really meant was that a secondary number system exists alongside dynamic shaping which is occasionally coincident with it. This second number system measures the changes of tonal hue from dark to bright and back again—"1,2,3,4,5,4,3,2,1."

"Notes are like gemstones," Tabuteau said. Good ones are pure and free of blemish. As with sapphires and diamonds, they come in many beautiful hues; and when they are expertly formed, faceted and polished, they all reflect light from the center. Notes that retain the same hue may be expanded and shrunk, or they may change chameleon-like from one color to another. It is this color potential that enables the oboe to sound like a flute one moment and a French horn the next.

Extolling this potential of his instrument in the November 25, 1944 edition of *MUSICAL AMERICA*, Tabuteau wrote, "Of all the orchestral instruments the oboe is nearest to the human voice in expressive power. It has an enormous range of emotional suggestion and nuance. It can be witty, melancholy, subtly humorous, appealing, sparkling, all within the space of a few measures of music. A fine oboist can produce as many as fifty different tone colors on one note, just as a singer may vary the colorings of the voice in an infinite number of ways. Therefore the oboist must think vocally. A beautiful tone emission is supremely important to him, and he must phrase with the subtlest sort of artistry. The oboist has no shield. His instrument has no coloratura, no purely technical bravura with which to dazzle the listener. Its penetrating tone and intensity of effect leave the player completely exposed. He must have the asset of musicality, for his role in the orchestra calls for the utmost in sensitivity and command of mood."

(Contemporary players can thank Swiss oboist Heinz Holliger for bringing "technical bravura" back to the oboe.)

So here was where some treasure was buried, and secrets revealed! But the "cure" was just beginning!

Changing color on the oboe requires changing the reed's position in one's lips, the physical action of which is easier than blowing or biting. One simply pushes the reed farther in the mouth to play brighter (uncovering the cane inside) and pulls it out to play darker (covering with one's lips all but the very tip of the cane). The reed can slip freely across the lips or cling to them. In the first case, the oboist plays "slide trombone" with the instrument, moving it in and out with the right hand; and in the second, says "ooh," "ah," "ee," "ah," "ooh" with the reed remaining stuck in place on the lips and the oboe following along. The brightest possible placement is with lips on the thread, and the darkest is at the very end of the reed. Some players lift and lower their upper lip on the top blade of the reed, as if raising and lowering a shade, to change color.

Depending upon construction of the reed itself, a more obvious consequence of these adjustments than changing color can be wildly-changing intonation. Moving in makes the air column shorter and the pitch go up, while playing on the very tip of the reed elongates the air column and makes the pitch go down. One must continually compensate with the speed of the wind to maintain volume and preserve constant pitch when moving along the color continuum. These compensations involve subtly changing the amount of pressure in the oboist's mouth.

The most unnatural thing about oboe playing is the internalized **pressure** resulting from the reed's tiny opening relative to the amount of wind needed to make it vibrate. This internalized pressure causes oboists' veins to bulge, necks to swell, and faces to turn beet red while playing. Because of this disfigurement, only one oboist I ever heard of ("Miss Georgia" a few years ago) ever made it into the Miss America Pageant! And more than one physician observing me in performance expressed concern that my blood pressure must be going through the roof.

"Responsive" reeds have a lower vibration threshold than "unresponsive" ones, making them easier to play. That is why responsiveness—along with a pleasant tone and stable pitch—is one of the three horses needed to pull every good reed's chariot. But regardless of the level of responsiveness—whether easy or resistant, the pressure in the player's mouth must vary while playing higher-lower, darker-brighter, etc.—something oboists face as an inevitable fact of performance life.

As Tabuteau insisted, "It is the gradation of . . . pressure which the student must develop to the highest degree."

Robert Sprenkle, Tabuteau's contemporary, was Professor of Oboe at the Eastman School of Music in Rochester, New York before Richard Killmer. Sprenkle seldom studied with Tabuteau, but he valued gradation of pressure enough to ask a colleague at the University's Medical School to devise a gauge for measuring it. By inserting a thin piece of surgical tubing into the corner of his students' mouths, a dial indicator could be observed at the other end revealing ounces of pressure per square inch as his students played the oboe. This visual evidence of changing pressure was more revealing than sensory perception alone, perhaps because having more nerve endings in our mouths would make it difficult to chew our food in there!

When I played for him, Tabuteau used a different physical frame of reference—an expanded little pouch beneath my jawbone—to observe the degree of air compression in my mouth. Complaining that mine deflated with every movement of my tongue (another evidence of my "sickness" as an oboe player), he pointed out that his remained continually inflated. Throughout a demonstration of the oboe solo which opens Robert Schumann's *Piano Concerto*, I observed that his "pressure pouch" never moved, regardless whether he played louder or softer, higher or lower—and not even during silences between the notes!

One of Tabuteau's greatest contributions to the art of oboe playing was the invention of a reed that converted "extensive" vibration into "intensive" vibration, that transformed the nasal sound of the oboe from something that inspired Prokofiev to assign it to the duck in *Peter and the Wolf,* into something more akin to the human voice. This transformation has been widely mischaracterized as tonal "darkness." In fact, "more focused," "more centered," or "more vertical" would be better descriptions of it. Unlike most of his progeny in the *American School of Oboe Playing,* Tabuteau did not eschew "brightness." He eschewed "spreadness." Obsession with the "darkest" possible tone has entrapped most American oboists (whose reeds themselves are too "bright") on only one side of the color spectrum, where they play exclusively at the very tip of the reed and over-blow to correct for pitch. Another of the glories of the John Mack reeds I had when I studied with Tabuteau is that I was able to play upon them in a bright way without "spreading" the tone.

John Mack, hoping to enter the Curtis Institute of Music at age sixteen, first auditioned for Marcel Tabuteau in a New York City hotel room. During that encounter, Tabuteau held his oboe out in front of him at arm's length and said, "You see, Mack, the oboe is shaped like a cone—small at the top, large at the bottom." Turning it upside down, he continued, "As long as you play it, you must make it sound otherwise!" Using a different analogy, he told me that his tone was like a ping pong ball on a fountain of water. "When the pressure goes up, the ball goes up; when the pressure goes down; the ball goes down—and it is spinning all the while!" Because the oboe has the acoustical properties of a closed pipe—akin to that of a flute or saxophone, it is naturally flat in the high register. There are two other possible remedies: (1) moving the reed in and out, or (2) chewing the reed open and closed; but Tabuteau's preferred means of correcting high register flatness involved blowing harder and generating more pressure going up and blowing slower and generating less pressure coming down. (Years later at Marlboro, Pablo Casals would insist, "When the melody goes up, play more; and when the melody goes down, play less!")

As the weeks wore on, my lessons at 111 Promenade des Anglais became less frequent and more difficult. I suffered from "information overload"—no more able to express what Tabuteau demanded on the oboe than I could have explained myself to him in French. In practical terms, "Tabuteau" was becoming an increasingly difficult musical language! No longer the jolly raconteur, my mentor poked and jabbed at me sarcastically, exhibiting increasing irritation and impatience.

"Don't be so STUPID!!" he bellowed, making me think sometimes that he was about to throw me over the balcony railing. Don't you understand ANYTHING?"

Sensing my growing frustration and resentment, one day he justified his Old School pedagogy with this analogy: "Robinson, consider all the little mollusks in the sea: how they writhe and squirm from the invading grains of sand. A few of them make pearls. Now it is up to you to make a pearl. I am not going to withhold the irritant!" after which he resumed grinding me under his heel.

Hoping to recover from a particularly rough session one afternoon, I strolled along Promenade des Anglais onto a wide boardwalk near the beach. A familiar figure came into view. He was conversing earnestly with an older gentleman, and I recognized him at once as that nice Swiss fellow I had so cruelly refused to help when he begged me for money back in March.

Rushing over to him now freed from guilt, I exclaimed, "My friend, I see that you still have not found your way back home to Monaco!"

He bristled and feigned non-recognition, then turned and disappeared into the crowd.

Melodic Intervals

Working with DeVere Moore at Brevard in the summer of 1961 helped me understand the degree to which intervals on the oboe are more resistant than the notes themselves, and why chewing between notes (the "wah-wah syndrome") is not the right way to deal with this problem. Now Tabuteau elucidated further the need to "fill the gap" between notes by accelerating the wind in proportion to the size of each interval.

"Like a horse approaching a hurdle," he said, "I play 'down, up, up, up' on the low note, and when I land on the high note, I don't have to do anything. The work has already been done. And when I play from a high note to a low one, I do exactly the same thing. I play 'down' on the high note and 'up, up, up, down' on the low one."

I prefer a roller coaster analogy to the equestrian one. The roller coaster gathers speed rolling down in order to go up on the other side. The farther down it plunges, the higher up it can soar. Playing legato from a low note to a higher one requires increasing wind velocity in the low note in proportion to the size of its upward reach. John Mack called this action in the lower note "travel." Like loops that get bigger but begin and end at the same point, this "inner work of melodic intervals" does not so much express the second note as anticipate it. In fact, the higher note of an upward interval begins softly and only then is fully revealed. This technique bevels the edge of an upward slur, as a singer would, and takes away the accent from the front of the louder, higher note.

Tabuteau himself described a downward slur as a car approaching a precipice.

"Don't put on the brakes and zig-zag your way down. Accelerate right over the edge!"

Watching the final scene of *Thelma and Louise* a few years later, I shouted aloud in the movie theater, "Tabuteau's downward slur!" Like their car, the player's wind should rush right across the edge of a descending interval, filling the gap between the higher and lower notes. I have never heard any other oboist play intervals with as much buttery connectedness as Marcel Tabuteau. Some of them almost replicated the glissando effect of violinists, and his mastery of intervals' "inner work" was a lifetime achievement. No dimension of the interpretive art has been more fascinating and rewarding since my "cure" in Nice than to **play intervals instead of notes.**

Articulation

Articulation is to music what diction is to speech. Oboe players use their tongues and/or wind to create the consonants and accents that clarify musical expression. Especially as a Frenchman, Tabuteau valued clear musical diction. Although it is possible to initiate notes with puffs of wind, Tabuteau insisted that every note begin with the tongue touching the tip of the reed. "Down inflections" were always to be expressed "strictly Tee or Tah . . . no Fa, no Ga, no Pa, no Ma!" Perceiving that low notes sound longer than high ones, he also insisted that two-octave articulated scales begin soft and short on the bottom and evolve into loud and long at the top. The length of each note was to be determined by the length of time the tip of the tongue touched the tip of the reed, impeding its vibration. "Tongue with your tongue" was a Tabuteau commandment carved in stone! Just as a loaf of sliced bread reveals its contour with alternate slices removed, a musical phrase can retain its shape whether tongued or slurred. Tonguing is independent of the blowing and chewing that sculpt the sound and the shifts of placement and pressure that color it.

Explosive tonguing can motivate the wind and exaggerate the consonant effect, and this capacity may be helpful in double-tonguing; but in fact, "tonguing with your tongue" means touching the tip of the reed with just enough contact to inhibit its vibration—a gesture so subtle, regardless of the dynamic level, that two taste buds can do the job! Such delicate articulation is more like defining vowels than exploding consonants. When John Mack discovered my inability to touch the end of the reed with the tip of my tongue in New Orleans two years earlier, he told me he had heard of only one other oboist who had the same problem—John DeLancie when he came to the Curtis Institute from California as a sixteen-year-old. Years later he would say that John DeLancie and I had the clearest articulation of all of Tabuteau's students, proving once again that converts are the most fanatical! DeLancie's famous recording of the Francaix *Flower Clock* is a consummate example of his ability to tongue with his tongue.

I used to believe that un-tongued notes (the ones under slur marks) were legato; but Tabuteau made it clear that there is much more to legato than simply not tonguing. Legato notes are disparate un-tongued pitches that must be unified, sculpted, and inflected like long tones. There is also much more to articulation than tonguing or not tonguing. Familiar note groupings such as four sixteenth notes, two slurred and two tongued, for instance, express nuances that begin on the first tongued 16th note, and NOT the first slurred 16th note. To spell this out, Tabuteau took a pencil and wrote in my notebook, "Tuh, Tuh, Tee-uh;" "up, up dow-own;" "1, 2, 3, 2"—all of which are implied by the articulation itself. Sequences of these nuances may be strung together like pearls of different sizes on a necklace—e.g., 1,2,3,2; 2,3,4,3; 3,4,5,4, etc. In a similar way, triplets—two slurred and one tongued—imply nuances that begin on the single tongued note and are played as "Tuh, Tee-uh;" "up, dow-own;" "1, 2, 1.," Tabuteau told me his students at Curtis spent a year just working on articulated patterns and nuances.

A corollary to "tongue with your tongue" is "finger with your fingers," implying that disparate pitches are subordinate to the nuances of which they are a part. Playing golf with John Mack some years later, I asked him, "What was the most important thing you learned from Tabuteau?" to which he responded without hesitation, "To put the notes on the wind!" Pitches ride the wind the way a surfboard rides a wave! The sculpted phrase is paramount. Blowing and chewing must not be compromised by the activity of one's fingers! Then Mack added a surprising second answer:

"And to play the life of each note"—meaning not to sacrifice the potential of any single note for the sake of the whole phrase!" For someone so recently enthralled by liberal arts at Davidson College, I was astonished to see the universal paradox in human experience of reconciling collective and individual values expressed in oboe playing as much as in economics, political systems, religion or philosophy. Musical notes must be subordinated to the phrase without sacrificing their unique individual potential.

Resting on the balcony one afternoon after a lesson, I asked Tabuteau if there was any "best time" in his career, thinking I might rush out and buy those recordings. He reflected for a few moments and answered, "Yes, when Arturo Toscanini came to conduct the Philadelphia Orchestra in Pension Concerts in the late 40s and early 50s. The most cerebral maestro engaging the greatest Romantic orchestra . . . the results were electrifying!" Then, contemplating the whole of his career—more than sixty years and thousands of concerts, he said, "There were a few good notes." (I thought that was the most humble thing I ever heard.) And then he turned and looked straight at me and said again, "There were a few good notes . . . **and they are still ringing!**" The hair stood up on the back of my neck. Tabuteau had just spoken the most outrageous affirmation of music I had ever heard—that Truth (with a capital "T") exists in music! It was an epiphany that changed my life, and I thought, "Where do I sign?"

Perhaps the most intriguing idea frequently repeated by Marcel Tabuteau when I studied with him, however, was "the logical inevitability of a phrase," an idea that pointed to an inherent potential in each uniquely sculpted nuance and gesture to sound "right"—somehow to be self-justifying. In the same November 25, 1944 *Musical America* article cited previously, Tabuteau elaborated upon this idea: "The production of a single tone involves the subtlest sense of proportion. To illustrate this, one might make a diagram symbolizing the course of one tone, in the form of an arc. Out of silence, the most perfect state of music in which everything is implicit, the tone begins. It grows in intensity, the vibrations of the reed increase, until it reaches its highest point. Then it recedes according to the same scale of intensity until it dies away in silence. If it is perfectly produced by the player, the listener will sense its symmetry even though he may not be conscious of how the effect has been produced."

David McGill, former Principal Bassoon of the Cleveland Orchestra and Chicago Symphony, spent thirteen years compiling information from taped interviews and other sources about Marcel Tabuteau's life and work. His marvelous book, entitled *Sound in Motion*, published by Indiana University Press at about the same time as Laila Storch's biography of Tabuteau, is the method book Tabuteau hoped I would write; and in it Tabuteau's perspectives on the creative dimensions of the interpretive art of music are more fully elucidated than anywhere else. David's title itself, "Sound in Motion," hints at the essential element making phrases "logically inevitable." It is **inertia.**

Whenever Tabuteau wrote down preferred numbers for musical phrases, they always over-ran the middle. Instead of 1,2,3,4–4,3,2,1, he would describe the same notes, 1,1,2,3–4,4,3,2. Crescendos and diminuendos develop late because of inertia, sculpting ideal phrase shapes that are not diamonds, as they appear to be on pages of the music, but little fish—like Pepperidge Farm fish crackers! That is why Rafael Kubelik, a favorite guest conductor, always said within twenty minutes of any rehearsal with the New York Philharmonic, "Dear friends, remember that in a four-bar phrase, the third bar is most important!" The perceptible shape of an oboist's phrase is called "the line," and it depends ultimately upon the rate of flow of the wind through the reed. If the wind's movement successfully obeys the law of inertia—like a golf swing that starts slow, speeds up, and follows through, the phrase can be said to be (as Tabuteau said it MUST be) "logically inevitable!"

Great classical musicians have always been obsessed with **line.** When Tanglewood celebrated its 50th anniversary in 1990, Leonard Bernstein was asked for a testimonial quote that could be printed on the front of its fund-raising brochure. Since Lenny had attended the first conducting seminar at Tanglewood in 1940 and maintained an affectionate connection with the Berkshire home of the Boston Symphony throughout his career, he eagerly agreed. What he wrote and what was printed, however, must surely have confounded people who read the quote: "Tanglewood was important in my life," he said, "because it is there that Koussevitsky taught me the meaning of **the true line!**"

There is absolute value in extending the line. It is probably the single most important measure of a musical artist's interpretative sophistication. George Szell often reminded John Mack that a four-bar phrase was worth MORE than two two-bar phrases, and Casals described melody as a "succession of rainbows." A single tone, tracing an arc in a logically inevitable way, becomes a life metaphor from which music derives much of its expressive power.

Reeds

One morning I arrived to a remarkable greeting, "Good morning, Robinson. I made a reed for you last night!" I couldn't wait to try it, but when I did, I felt as if someone's hand was on my head, holding me under water in the swimming pool! I could not play the left-hand octave notes high enough to be in tune. Tabuteau quickly recovered the reed from me with an expression that said "Baby!" and never returned it. In all our time together, he tried my reeds only once or twice without questioning their source. I never had to tell him that John Mack had made them.

In our time together, Tabuteau made only a few pithy pronouncements about reeds. They were:
1. "Scrape flat surfaces instead of slopes;"
2. "Keep the reed 'stiff and sharp' as you make it;"
3. "The finished reed must 'speak' easily and crow 'C';"
4. "The gouge is everything."

But what he **said** about making reeds was not as significant as what he revealed by working on them in front of me. A shoe box on his desk sat filled with ground-up gouging machine blades, evidence that his first remedy if he didn't like his cane or reeds over the years, was to take the blade out and change its curve. (John Mack told me he saw Tabuteau do this six times in one night.) Certainly his knife technique did not look very sophisticated! I watched him just thin and clip the tip of the reed, take a little bark off the heart and back, and play. From "blank" to Brahms in only a couple of minutes!

The shape of his reeds looked different also—almost parallel for the top two-thirds of the reed's length, tapering gently into the thread at the bottom. It made me think of Sophia Loren's calf—substantial but elegant! Although he took back that reed he had made for me, he did give me several pieces of shaped cane to keep. His reeds' openings were more diamond-shaped than round, encouraging quick response; and the ones he finished were a couple of millimeters longer than John Mack's. (Mack would say later that Tabuteau, ten years after retirement and playing alone on his balcony instead of in an orchestra, was "off the track" and playing flat himself!) His reeds nevertheless permitted him to play with that amazing "Crater Lake" tone in all the subtle ways his "cure" had revealed to me were possible.

Leaving Europe

On the morning I was to take the train from Nice to Cherbourg and board the *T. S. Bremen* for my six-day crossing to New York City, I stopped at 111 Promenade des Anglais to say goodbye. The Tabuteau apartment was jumping! Laila Storch and her little daughter Aloysia had just arrived for a visit. Laila was so dear to Tabuteau that I felt like an intruder at a family reunion until Tabuteau grabbed my arm and pulled me out onto the balcony.

"Listen to this!" he whispered. Twisting off his oboe's top joint and replacing it with Laila's, he played a few passages and asked excitedly, "What do you think? Sounds pretty good, eh?" He continued exchanging and comparing the two top joints like that until he convinced himself that Laila's top joint combined with his bottom and bell created the perfect oboe! An impending moral dilemma was coming, so I remained noncommittal.

Standing in the doorway on my way out and hoping for some final bit of approbation, I begged, "Mr.Tabuteau, isn't my embouchure better now?"

"It's all right for that note," he said. "If you want the notes to sound the same, you must play them differently!"

My heart sank within me. It took many years for me to understand that one's instrumental security depends ultimately and entirely upon **flexibility**.

Tabuteau had sketched on note paper a few exercises for me to practice—most of them huge upward and downward slurs, patterns of articulation, or groups of inflected notes. But the very last words Tabuteau spoke to me were these: "Get out of your throat and blow toward your nose!"

The trip to Cherbourg was numbing. I got in trouble with the train's conductor when he found me sitting in the aisle of a first-class car; but mostly it was a time of semi-consciousness. So many bewildering ideas about oboe minutia swirling around, mixed with unclear premonitions of life next year in the States. At least I knew I finally would be studying music full-time with my hero, John Mack!

CIA "operative" Mike Cameron was waiting for me when I arrived in Cherbourg. He had come there all the way from Cologne to see me board my ship. He had so ingratiated himself to the Elligers, he actually spent several days with them at their summer home in the mountains. He told me he would be returning soon to Alma, Michigan, where he expected our friendship to continue for many more years (which it did). Although several other Fulbrighters were booked on the *Bremen*, the return voyage was simply a means to an end rather than an end in itself. I was forced to practice oboe in the ship's boiler room where it was so loud I could hardly hear myself—which was just as well because I felt completely incompetent at the time!

Thick fog veiled Battery Park the morning we passed

under the Verrazano Bridge. Standing at the front of the ship's upper deck, I strained for a first glimpse of the famous skyline, when suddenly the breath-taking spectacle of lower Manhattan emerged in front of me—a colossal man-made mountain of steel, glass, and stone! It filled me with pride to be an American. A year earlier I had sailed past it in the opposite direction, having no idea what awaited me in Europe. Now as the fog morphed into a deep blue September sky over New York City, I felt sure of my future. People had asked continually when I was in school, "What are you going to do with your life?"—to which I always responded, "I am at Davidson College to try to figure that out!" Calling myself "President of the Undecideds' Club," I clung for years to the edge of my high nest with its intoxicating 360-degree view of limitless possibilities. Now the two great quests of young adulthood seemed accomplished: my course was fixed on a career in music, and I held within my heart the girl I believed I was going to marry!

When we disembarked, Davidson College roommate David Edwards greeted me and accompanied me to his apartment in the city. Next day we went together to pick up my car and steamer trunk at the Brooklyn Navy Yard, where despite intimidating circumstances, everything went smoothly. Franklyn Noll, first clarinet in the Lenoir High School Band and my date at her senior prom, was also in New York City. She invited David and me to watch a belly-dancer in a club she liked and reminded me that we had practiced more than band music during a couple of private section rehearsals her senior year! It surprised and annoyed me that I was continuing to translate everything I said from German into English.

Back in Lenoir, my parents told me that my brother had a wife. His bride, who came from a tobacco farm "down east," joined us for a Sunday lunch that was memorable for her bad manners and my mother's simmering indignation. Ed mostly stared at his plate. Somehow soon after that, their shotgun wedding was annulled. Ed's "ex-wife" went on to deliver her baby, attend medical school, and have a successful life.

scherzo capriccioso

Maryland Master's

Finally, a full-time commitment to the oboe was at hand!

An impressive new brick building for the Music Department was under construction on the campus of the University of Maryland in the fall of 1963, but offices, classrooms, practice and rehearsal spaces were still in World War II Quonset huts down the hill. Emerson Head greeted me when I arrived and introduced me to the departmental secretary, Mrs. Thom, as well as to the head of the department, Dr. Homer Ulrich. I would need to find a place to live; meet with my graduate advisor, clarinetist Norman Heim; and take a theory placement test. There was no reason to test my piano skills because I had none.

Discussions in the office about housing prompted a

suggestion from Mrs. Thom: "Why don't you rent a room in my house near the campus? I have a piano you can use and a private bath." The price was right, so as soon as my new landlady was off duty, she took me to see the modest ranch house she owned in College Park and I unloaded some of my gear. She said her teenage son lived there also.

Heim explained the extent to which I would need remedial work in the areas of music I had neglected as an undergraduate, and he proposed courses for the fall semester that included Beginning Piano, Theory, Conducting, Form and Analysis, History of the Opera, Oboe and Orchestra. My theory placement test was so bad, everyone disbelieved the score. "We decided you had a bad night before the test and advanced you to Sophomore Theory."

Heim continued, "Please contact Bruce Morrison, our new oboe teacher, as soon as possible to schedule your lessons with him."

"What new teacher?" I asked incredulously. "No oboe teacher was listed on the faculty when I applied. I came here to study with John Mack!"

Between the time I applied for my fellowship in March and arrived for the fall semester in September, a new oboe teacher had indeed joined the faculty. He was a former Assistant Principal Oboe of the Houston Symphony, a nice fellow with a tiny tone who assured me that he would cooperate with John Mack in overseeing my instrumental development. I wondered how John Mack would feel about that!

Mack lived in Arlington, Virginia, 180 degrees around the Beltway from College Park, Maryland, and the one-way trip on a good day took forty-five minutes. John and his wife Andy had just adopted their second child, an infant girl named Cecie. It was clear that with a new home, new job, and new daughter, there was little chance he could sustain a regular schedule of private lessons. (Years later he would say how much he regretted our not meeting more often.) Whenever we did get together, we had a great time and actually worked hard sometimes on Ferling and Barret. But without obligation or the incentive of payment from any institution (or me), we usually just took off and played golf.

Thirty-or-so undergraduates (mostly female) were already seated in her theory class when prim Miss O'Connell introduced me to everyone: "Class," she said, "this is Mr. Robinson—our one graduate fellow in Music. We hope he won't be embarrassed by our slow pace!"

Red-faced, I chose a back corner of the room and slunk down into my chair. The dreadful time arrived soon enough when all of us had to come forward and play a series of piano chords indicated only by Roman numerals with little numbers attached to their legs. Known as "Keyboard Harmony," the exercise was child's play for students with moderate piano skills. One after another, they hit the bench, pounded out seven chords, and bounced off again. When my turn came, I squirmed in agony trying to find middle C and finger the tonic chord in first inversion! Recurring nightmares about the experience have haunted me ever since.

That incident confirmed the urgency of my acquiring greater keyboard facility, but I spent so much time thumping out theory exercises instead of practicing seriously on the piano that I was barely able to learn the first Bach minuet. Assignments in Form and Analysis, a course I shared with military service bandsmen from places like Juilliard and Eastman, piled up; along with extensive reading in Grout's textbook on *A Short History of Opera*. Term papers were also ongoing onerous obligations. Was Dad right? Had I lost the capacity for academic rigor during my self-indulgent year in Germany? With only two orchestra rehearsals a week and one concert scheduled for the entire semester, the oboe was a neglected priority. This master of music idea was beginning quickly to feel like a mistake!

And living at Mrs. Thom's house did not help. My tiny bedroom behind the living room scarcely shielded my oboe playing from the others in the house. Especially when guests were present, I was too self-conscious to make reeds or practice in there, and I worked at the piano only when no one else was at home. The worst part was the pathological relationship between Mrs. Thom and her son, both of whom who yelled and screamed at each other and slammed doors whenever they were together.

Thankfully, an ecstatic weekend in October compensated for all of my disappointments. Jean Thomas came to visit. She spent two nights with Linda and Emerson Head—time enough for some magical moments shared in the Nation's Capital—sitting alone in the President's Box during a dress rehearsal of the National Symphony Orchestra in Constitution Hall and eating dinner with John Mack and his wife at Blackie's, a famous seafood restaurant on the Potomac. On a perfect fall Saturday afternoon (October 19, 1973), we watched the University of Maryland football team beat favored Air Force 21–14 on a spectacular touchdown pass in the last minute of the game. We kissed like a couple of movie stars on the moonlit steps of the Lincoln Memorial; and, just before boarding her train home, Jean accepted my fraternity pin as a symbol of our devotion. In those days being pinned was the next thing to becoming engaged. I was profoundly in love!

The next few weeks persuaded me that my "in-love-ness" was **insanity**. No amount of rational thought mitigated my suffering. I could hardly breathe and lost my appetite. Of course, Jean could not transfer from Converse College, where she was so happy and successful, and enroll at Maryland to be with me. But how could I live without her? I knew also that my disenchantments at Maryland, where I was playing the oboe less than I had in high school, was contributing to romantic overreaction. But how could I regain my balance? I had other symptoms as well—sleeplessness, distraction, and obsession. Physical things—people, places, school assignments—everything else around me ceased to exist and became ephemeral. The only reality was Jean, and I longed to be with her day and night.

Two extraordinary (one might say "neurotic") ideas came into focus. The first was phobic—a sense of panic if I lost her. So great a light dogged by so deep a shadow, like "love-death" in *Tristan and Isolde*! And the second was religious: "Thou shalt have no other gods before me!" which sounds wacky, but proved compelling. I decided my love for Jean was idolatry— one of the gravest of sins for which my suffering was a just punishment. Only penance could save me.

Jean and I had planned to meet two weeks hence. I was going to drive to Spartanburg and spend two days with her at Converse College; but, like Abraham when called upon to sacrifice Isaac, I decided to place that most precious prospect in the offering plate! Jean would surely understand . . . after all, she was a Religion major who had sought to comfort me with a book by Catherine Marshall and some prayers of Harry Emerson Fosdick. Instead, to my surprise, she was upset with me for canceling our reunion. My "self-denial" was selfish, she said. And in retrospect, I realize she probably was right. I never considered how much sacrificing our weekend might hurt her also.

The University of Maryland's College Park campus was deserted on fall weekends whenever the football team played elsewhere, as they did that sunny Saturday in early November when my "penance" began. I could **not** have been more miserable. Because concentration was impossible, I slammed shut my history of music textbook and wandered aimlessly through the stacks of the University library in the Humanities section for a while. My eye fell upon only one author's name: "Woodrow Wilson"—the most famous Davidson College student who became president of Princeton University, Governor of New Jersey and President of the United States. His book was a collection of essays which opened when I pulled it from the shelf to a chapter entitled, "When a Young Man Comes to Himself." I couldn't believe my eyes! It described Woodrow Wilson's painful transition from undergraduate to graduate status, with words that seemed to speak precisely to my own predicament! Whether "manna" or not, I interpreted that essay as divine intervention and copied copious sections of it into the inside covers of my opera history textbook, after which my misery somewhat abated.

During intermission of a National Symphony Orchestra concert the previous Thursday, Wyche Fowler, my Davidson College classmate and fraternity brother now an Army 2nd Lieutenant serving in Intelligence at the Pentagon, and I had literally bumped into each other. We agreed on the spot to get together at his Alexandria apartment Sunday night to catch up on everything. So, during the evening that followed my library "revelation,"—with a glass of scotch in hand in front of a roaring fireplace—I poured out my heart to Wyche, explaining all the disappointments at Maryland and most of all, my romantic distress. He sympathized about Jean and understood that I would need a student deferment not to be drafted (the Vietnam War was really heating up). And he knew that I was not interested in getting a PhD.

"Wait a minute!" he exclaimed suddenly. "I think I have just the thing for you!"

Returning quickly from his bedroom, he handed me a brochure that described the richest social science fellowship in America—a two-year masters degree requiring fluency in a modern language and sending its students overseas during the middle summer of the program. It came from the School of Public and International Affairs at Princeton University—the **Woodrow Wilson School**!

Considering the manner of its discovery and the price I paid to get it, my application to the Woodrow Wilson School was bound to be accepted. I had no doubt whatsoever. President Kennedy and "Camelot" had already inspired me, and I believed that every responsible citizen should know more about politics and public administration than I did. The Woodrow Wilson School might even re-energize my study of government support of the arts and send me back to Germany for some **real** research on the subject. Cultural Affairs in the Foreign Service or arts administration could also become acceptable career choices, and a Princeton degree would be a perfect academic capstone. After the penance I had just paid, how could it not be all right with the Man Upstairs? Unfortunately, it would never be all right again with Jean.

I felt healthier and more in balance about our relationship as Jean and I planned meeting in Lenoir over the Thanksgiving break, and I could hardly wait to tell her face-to-face about my new direction.

Early on Friday afternoon, November 22, walking across campus I heard someone scream from a dormitory window above me, "President Kennedy has been shot!" At a memorial service for the dead President in the University Chapel the following Sunday, Rev. William E. Smith spoke unforgettable words of grief and consolation entitled "How Slender is the Thread of Life." Although eloquent, they barely lessened the pall that was cast over everything. Cold rainy weather matched the mood of the country in Lenoir, where Jean and I sat with my parents on Monday, watching the official State Funeral on television. The next day we drove to Granite Falls to visit Mother's brother, hoping that Uncle Martin and Aunt Dorothy and their adorable five children might brighten our spirits; instead, back home that night, Jean told me she was leaving to go to Atlanta "tomorrow!"

"I promised someone I would be at home for Thanksgiving," she explained.

"Someone who?" I stammered in disbelief.

"Oh, he's just a high school friend who said he was

coming back from college to see me, and I told him, 'Okay.' I'm sorry. I really have to go."

"But we're pinned!" I cried. "You . . . you . . . can't just go off to see another guy!"

My protests that evening fell into a hole that opened inside me and died there, along with true love. I felt as if I had been shot myself! Jean Thomas did indeed depart the next morning with a cousin who drove her to Atlanta, and I never saw her again in my lifetime but once. The last letter she ever wrote to me announced her engagement to the boy she went home that Thanksgiving to meet.

Besides being lovesick, my existential dilemma at the University of Maryland was that I had shoved off against my parents' wishes in a career canoe that was taking on serious water! Instead of playing the oboe fulltime, I was enmeshed in a world of abstractions and theories about music which my tone-deaf college roommate could have handled more easily than I. What is more, I didn't care why composer Hans Leo Hassler left Germany to study in Italy or that the Vaughan Williams Oboe Concerto was composed in the Dorian mode. I wanted to play the oboe, and Wagner's *Overture to Die Meistersinger,* Handel's *Royal Fireworks Music,* a Schumann symphony in orchestra and the jury requirement of Malcolm Arnold's *Sonatina* comprised my entire performance menu that fall semester of 1963. Ironically, it was a musical diet less nourishing even than the one at Davidson College.

No wonder I disengaged so easily from my life's dream in the Music Department at the University of Maryland and turned to go in another direction!

Civil Rights 1964

I met all my academic commitments in College Park by the end of the semester and earned good grades in everything except piano, and was now totally preoccupied with going to Princeton. The School of International Service at American University offered remedial courses in foreign affairs and political science that could help prepare me. If I took those and also enrolled in one course at Wesley Theological Seminary, I could live during the spring semester in the Seminary's brand-new dormitory across the parking lot from American University. The arrangement could not have been more convenient.

Bill Smith, the Methodist minister who had preached so impressively at President Kennedy's memorial service two months earlier, was now Vice President of the Seminary. He arranged my residence at Wesley and begged me to consider going into the ministry.

"Ten years ago," he said, "the Christian Ministry attracted the best and brightest. Not anymore."

I told him I would think about it. My teacher at the seminary was a Southern Baptist professor from Mississippi who held a handful of advanced science degrees. His course, "The History of Theology," was much more interesting to me than the ones in international relations I was taking at American University—something that should have been a warning about the curriculum that awaited me at the Woodrow Wilson School.

"How Slender is the Thread ... " could also have described my oboe playing in the spring of 1964. Except for occasional visits to see John Mack, there was little musical stimulus or activity in my life, and any thoughts of a professional career had vanished completely. Despite my disillusionment, John Mack never gave up on me. He supplied the reeds I practiced on and welcomed me whenever I found time to visit. I was even with him in Arlington when two momentous telephone calls came—the first from an attorney telling him that his mother-in-law's estate was settled, to which he exclaimed incredulously, "Joe, I am a wealthy man—a wealthy man!" and the second when George Szell invited him to become Principal Oboe of The Cleveland Orchestra.

The Civil Rights Movement was more on our minds at Wesley Theological Seminary that spring than the Vietnam War. President Lyndon Johnson had used public outrage over JFK's assassination for leverage in passing "The Civil Rights Act of 1964," which he signed into law on July 2. It gave the federal government power to redress racial discrimination in specified kinds of public places. My parents were fair-minded people who preached tolerance and lived peaceably; but they were afraid of the changes in the status quo being provoked by the demonstrations and societal upheavals in the South. Dad denounced Martin Luther King, Jr. as an opportunist, demagogue and trouble maker; and my mother, objecting to my friendship with a young black man down the hall at the Seminary, said, "Don't you dare bring that boy home with you!"

Segregated communities in the South in 1950 existed in two dimensions, like objects and their shadows. It is no wonder black people in Lenoir were sometimes called "spooks!" On our side of town, they were almost invisible—no Negro children in my neighborhood or scout troop; in my classrooms or Sunday School classes or Little League teams or summer camps or tennis courts in the park. Their parents did not shop at Triplett's or eat in the drug stores and restaurants uptown in Lenoir. Instead, they lived "on their side" in a place called "Freedman" or "West End," or in red clay enclaves scattered around Caldwell County. At the movies on Saturday mornings, I saw Negroes lined up in an alleyway waiting to climb the stairs to "their" seats in the balcony of the Center Theater and wondered about "coloreds only" water fountains and rest rooms in the lobby. Sometimes I noticed Negro children huddled around mail boxes at the end of unpaved rural roads waiting for "their" school buses. But my young life intertwined with black people in a **real** way only when our maid Priscilla came to live with us after Mother returned to teaching.

We took "Jim Crow" laws for granted in my world, experiencing them in terms of inertia and benign neglect rather than malice. People said all the time, "They like it that way," or "That's just the way it is." When Ed and I asked if we could invite two black boys we had played with in a barn while our parents played bridge to come spend the night, we were told by Dad, **"No way, you can't do that!"** as if it were a law of Moses! The finality in his tone resealed the hole in the wall that had opened for those boys—and we never saw them again.

Priscilla (who had no other name as far as Ed and I knew) was a handsome woman in large dimension, but not fat. Dad built a special room for her in an unfinished part of the basement where she had her own toilet. Upstairs she fixed breakfast for all of us and cleaned up while Mother got Ed and me ready for school; and she hugged us on the way out. Her warm smile and the smell of freshly-baked peanut butter cookies often welcomed us to a cleaner house when we returned. Mother drove her home to Friedman mid-afternoons, unless there was a formal dinner party at our house in the evening. On those occasions, Priscilla donned a white uniform that strained at its seams and responded from the kitchen to the tinkling of a little glass bell Mother kept at her end of the table.

"Yessum, you rang?"

I was in junior high school still living in the country, when I walked into the kitchen for breakfast one morning and saw Priscilla rocking frantically back and forth in a chair.

"Oh, Miz Robinson, Lawd ha' mercy! Lawd ha' mercy!" she wailed.

Mother hovered over her imploring, "What's wrong with you, Priscilla?" Then . . . "Good heavens, Priscilla, are you in **labor**?"

And indeed she was! She was the least-obviously-pregnant woman anyone had ever seen, but she delivered her first healthy baby that very morning. It is a cliché to say it; but, while she lived with us, Priscilla was a member of our family. I must have kissed her black face hundreds of times growing up. Predictably, however, after she moved to New York City and exchanged a few letters with Mother, she disappeared completely.

George Mason Miller III was the only child of black parents in Mooresville, North Carolina. A Gary Coleman look-alike, he was four years younger and a foot shorter than me; and his ancient grandmother actually **was** a slave—

something that conferred special status upon the Miller family on his side of town. George's mother was a teacher and his father principal of a segregated school; and George, as he frequently reminded me, was not allowed to apply to Davidson College twenty miles down the road.

Nevertheless, George was a celebrity—the first national winner of a television game show sponsored by General Mills and hosted by Bert Parks called "Giant Step." By correctly naming all five islands of the Japanese mainland, he won a free undergraduate education at Columbia University. When I met George, he was doing graduate work in "Black History" at American University, suffering from academic advancement beyond his years. He eventually earned a PhD under John Hope Franklin at the University of Chicago, but he was now under relentless pressure to represent "his people" and be "great." His potential and others' expectations of him immobilized him. Perhaps that is why he was such a procrastinator. As George's "big brother," my first experiment in race relations was to counsel, encourage, and motivate him. Together with Wyche Fowler, we integrated the Georgetown Presbyterian Church one Sunday morning, prompting more than a few parishioners to rise from their pews and hit the doors as they stormed out.

A winsome, rambunctious M.Div. student (I will call her "Jenny") sometimes joined George and me at lunch in the seminary refectory. She was the most attractive young black woman I had ever seen, and she accused me continually of being a "phony liberal."

"When are you going to take me out?" she would ask. "Are you afraid of me?"

Of course, I was afraid of her—even of being seen with her; and she teased and taunted me about it for weeks. Just going on a date with her became my personal battleground in the Civil Rights struggle. One day when she suggested, "At least come over to my place and my mother will cook us Sunday dinner. There can't be any harm in that!" I surprised us both by accepting.

Jenny's family lived in one of the many nondescript brick

towers comprising a low-income housing project north of the Capitol. My new blue VW Beetle looked as incongruous parked out front as I did walking into the building. The day was sunny and bright outside, but the stairwell inside was dank and smelly. We climbed five or six flights to her parents' apartment, passing residents at every landing who gawked at me and grunted greeting to Jenny.

In the apartment, Jenny's parents were welcoming but wary. The heavy aroma of fried food pervaded the place, which was stifling despite wide open windows in the living room. My discomfort must have been contagious, because conversation was forced by everyone all afternoon. Except to explain how Jenny and I met at the Seminary, there wasn't much to talk about. During our meal and following it, neighbors, cousins, and friends dropped in to gawk at the integration spectacle—some of them clearly as disapproving as my mother would have been! It was a huge relief for me to return home safely before dark that evening; and Jenny and I never dated again.

Wyche Fowler called it "cheating on the Hatch Act" to befriend and assist Congressman Charles Weltner, his Representative from the Georgia Fifth District (Weltner cast the deciding vote for the Voting Rights Bill of 1965). In Wyche's company, dining in the Senate Office Building and partying with young staffers in Georgetown, etc., I became infatuated with Washington, D.C., its beauty, power and energy.

Six months after leaving Nice, the abrasions inflicted by Marcel Tabuteau had begun to heal, perhaps even to prompt a "pearl" to grow. I knew for sure that Tabuteau had transformed my view of the creative possibilities of the interpretive art of music. They are infinite. That is why he said one could never outlive the musical potential of a Brahms solo. In the spring of 1964, trying to ensure that his amazing pedagogy would be recorded, I contacted Arthur Hauser at Presser Publishing and officials at the Yale Living Library. I also suggested a residency for Tabuteau at the newly established North Carolina School of the Arts. In several letters we exchanged in 1964, Tabuteau wrote that he and his wife had discovered Winston-Salem on a map and noted with pleasure its proximity to Philadelphia. He urged me to return to Nice to work on his "codicil," and for $25, sent me 100 pieces of cane he gouged himself. "You have no idea how much work this cost me," he said. (And I didn't, of course.) Meanwhile, Wayne Rapier, Tabuteau's last oboe student at Curtis, sent him a tape recorder from Oberlin with which Tabuteau memorialized my lessons almost verbatim.

A letter came from James Pfohl that spring inviting me to be Public Relations Director of the Brevard Music Center. Dr. Pfohl said I would write promotional pieces, feature stories, news releases, radio and television spots, and produce and edit the season program book—even solicit the ads to pay for it all! He promised me an assistant, a secretary, and a new little chamber orchestra to play in called "The Brevard Sinfonietta." I was delighted and accepted at once!

Brevard: Summer 1964

Settling into a productive routine in the BMC Press Office took some time. A journalism major from Syracuse University who was to be my assistant objected to my style and quickly over-played her hand with Dr. Pfohl who fired her the end of the first week. After that there were just two of us to handle all of the work.

By offering room and board and a darkroom—including unlimited developing supplies and film, Dr. Pfohl for years had lured top young photographers from places like the Rochester Institute of Technology to Brevard without paying them a salary; and Brevard kept all of their prints. File cabinet drawers in the Press Office were full of first-rate photographs as a result. Using a stopwatch, I learned how many words filled the 20-second public service announcements for radio and television stations in the area; and the weekly announcements about up-coming concerts and guest artists became routine. Laying out and editing the season's commemorative program book was the most difficult part of the job. Bill Workman's former girlfriend, Flo Denny, came to help. She also recruited sponsors and sold ads for me. When Dr. Pfohl told me to go to Atlanta to meet the printer, I flew in a commercial airliner for the first time. My nose stayed pressed to the window during the flight as I marveled at the world passing beneath me.

1964 was a time of dramatic change at Brevard. Dr. Pfohl dreamed for years of a performance space better than a converted wooden gymnasium—for a real auditorium west of the lake in the softball field. Architectural drawings were produced and plans made to break ground in June, but excavators hit five gushing mountain springs where the stage and fly story were supposed to go. Engineers had to rotate the building 180 degrees, which required pilings to be driven in to support the building's weight in its new direction. Pounding noises were continuous throughout the summer; and with each "bang" of the pile driver, the auditorium's price went up. So did Dr. Pfohl's anxiety and blood pressure.

Bessie Whittington Pfohl, the director's mother, fell gravely ill that summer, giving Dr. Pfohl a way out of his financial dilemma: if she died, he could name the building for her and tax all of the Moravian faithful to pay for it! Because of that, ambivalence was the tone of the summer. When Dr. Pfohl reported from time to time that his mother had taken a turn for the worse, he would weep sorrowfully from one eye and hopefully from the other. The crisis dragged on and on. And when an important prospective donor invited Dr. Pfohl to visit him in Winston-Salem and spend the night at his home he asked me to tag along. We were lavishly hosted in the exclusive Hanes family compound by R. Philip Hanes, a national leader of the emerging arts council movement. Unfortunately, I remember the occasion more for Dr. Pfohl's exuberant bedroom flatulence than for his success with our prospective donor!

The BMC Sinfonietta gave Dr. Pfohl opportunity to acquire guest-conducting credits with colleagues from other orchestras. One of these was Guy Fraser Harrison, a lovable Brit who was Music Director of the Oklahoma City Symphony

Orchestra. We nicknamed him "Old Horse Face," because of the excessive folds of flesh that exaggerated his expressions. He programmed the *Marosszek Dances* by Zoltan Kodaly, a composition with an extravagant, extended oboe solo I never had a chance to play again. Another guest conductor was James Yestadt, John Mack's friend whom I had met putting on the 18th green of the New Orleans Municipal Golf Course in 1961 and who was Music Director of the Mobile Symphony Orchestra. Without knowing it, my performance of a charming piece for oboe and strings written by Converse College viola professor John McLean with Yestadt conducting was actually an audition for my first professional orchestra job. It was also the first time I ever used a reed I actually made myself. Later in the summer, when he visited Brevard and heard a recording of that McLean piece, John Mack exclaimed, "Wow, Joe! You **can** still play the oboe!"

Dr. Pfohl had survived many administrative crises throughout his career. But daily B-12 shots were required to get him through the 20-hour summer days of 1964, when financial pressures finally overwhelmed him. A faculty insurrection led by concertmaster Emil Raab that threatened an important evening concert prompted Brevard Music Center trustees to vote no confidence in their founder/director. They agreed that affiliation with a more established institution was the only way to guarantee support and save the Center. Dr. Pfohl "froze" in his bed one morning soon after that, unable to get up and dress himself—a condition described in those days as "having a nervous breakdown," and it took months for him to recover. Only after he was released from the hospital did he learn that control of his music center had been ceded to Converse College in Spartanburg, South Carolina. Henry Janiec was now in charge.

The Woodrow Wilson School

"Princeton"—just the name was intimidating! Driving west from Route 1 towards its Gothic spires on a sunny autumnal afternoon, a lump tightened in my throat. Could

I possibly measure up to the academic challenges of that august institution? Twelve months earlier I had been sure of both my career and my life's partner. But not anymore. I hoped the Woodrow Wilson School would lead me to a new profession—e.g., Cultural Affairs in the Foreign Service or an executive position as an arts manager. No romantic prospects were on the horizon.

Woodrow Wilson lost an argument about where to locate Princeton's resident Graduate College to his Dean of Faculty, Andrew Fleming West, who was rewarded with geographical separation of older students from Princeton undergraduates and a seat of honor in memoriam at the front of the Graduate College courtyard. Dean West sits there today—a bronze Buddha requiring (according to legend) the arrival of a virgin to arise from his chair. The dormitory space I shared with my roommate, a brilliant Wesleyan graduate named Alan Brewster, featured a wood-burning fireplace and two separate bedrooms. The dining hall (think "Hogwarts") was grand and ornate. Black academic robes, mostly handed down by former students in tatters, were required dress for evening meals, at which a Latin blessing was sometimes intoned by George Will, then a student of the Classics.

Within weeks I knew that my blue VW and I would have to part company; parking was too remote on campus and nearly impossible on Nassau Street. Dealing with it made me late for classes and cost a lot of money. As soon as possible, I drove the car to North Carolina and exchanged it for a bicycle.

The Woodrow Wilson School's address on Washington Road revealed an impressive brick building repositioned several hundred feet behind its original location. People told me it was moved back on railroad tracks to make room for its neighboring travertine marble replacement, a magnificent Yamasaki "Parthenon"—Princeton's new temple to public service. A huge gift in 1961 from A&P grocery chain heir, Charles Robertson, endowed the new building and funded the generous fellowships that were granted to my classmates and me. Mr. Robertson's stated purpose was to provide enhanced training for men and women aspiring to careers in the Foreign Service, elective office, or government agencies and bureaucracies. It was incumbent upon the school's administrators to identify a discreet body of esoteric knowledge, develop a new curriculum, and hire specialized faculty to comply with his mandate—in effect, to invent a totally new profession! Compared with other departments at Princeton, the Woodrow Wilson School was embarrassingly rich, and the MPA (Master of Public Affairs) degree program was, like the Yamasaki Building itself, a work in progress.

My first assignment was to meet my academic adviser, an ambitious young labor economist named William G. Bowen (later President of Princeton University and the Mellon Foundations) whose task it was to guide me towards either international or domestic affairs and help me select appropriate courses. What a coincidence! He was just then collaborating with a Princeton art historian, Professor William Baumol, on the most comprehensive study ever done of the economics of the performing arts in America. I could hardly wait to tell Professor Bowen that I was an oboe player eager to learn more about his project.

But his reaction was, "How in the world did you get in here?"—then to tell me that his only contribution to the whole tiresome arts business had been to organize and analyze the data. When I inquired if I could be helpful in some way, he said, "I'm afraid you don't possess any of the statistical skills we need right now."

At our opening plenary session, we were welcomed with gravitas by Dean Marver Bernstein, who aimed his remarkably resonant bass voice left and right toward alternate corners of the room's ceiling. It was the first of many similar performances introducing and sustaining a leitmotif of pomposity at the Woodrow Wilson School. And no wonder! Euphoria was the mood of everybody championing public service in those days. Almost twenty years of post-war economic consumerism had disenchanted college graduates of my generation, many of whom now disdained business careers in favor of non-profit organizations and the professions. Our idealistic consensus was articulated succinctly by John F. Kennedy in his inaugural address when he said, "Ask not what your country can do for you; ask what you can do for your country!" The Woodrow Wilson School was one of a number of similar institutions enjoying unprecedented public favor.

If "the best and brightest" were not entering seminaries in 1964, some of them undoubtedly were among my thirty-one classmates in the Woodrow Wilson School—valedictorians, student body presidents, mid-career up-and-comers, etc. They were a formidable group! And the faculty equally so. Ambassador George Kennan, a superstar of the Cold War era, taught the seminar I took entitled Diplomatic History of the 20th Century. Other first-year courses included: Economic Analysis (which morphed into "econometrics" for which calculus was requisite); American Political Process (in which I discovered the unique genius of the American Constitution to be "rules of the game" rather than an immutable substantive credo); Law & Public Policy (dealing with administrative process and conflict resolution); and Variations in Societies, taught by a colorful sociologist named Marion Levy.

A distinctive pedagogical element at the Woodrow Wilson School was the "Policy Conference," which engaged everyone in consideration of the same important public policy issue. For the fall semester, the seminar was entitled "Policies & Politics of Transportation" in which we analyzed and discussed the potential for a fourth regional airport in the New York City area. Assuming different advocate roles each of us argued for or against the idea in a mock Congressional hearing at the end of the term. I was a poorly-informed and unpersuasive spokesman for the American Institute of Architects.

Our curriculum at the school was arrayed like dishes at an opulent buffet. No one cared or asked whether we liked the menu—nor should they have. Sophomoric indecisiveness such as mine about one's career was as out of place at the

Woodrow Wilson School as it would have been in a medical
school or law school; and administrators reminded me
continually that a hundred noses were pressed to the
windows outside for every one of us seated at the banquet
inside. "Gorge and go!" was the official mantra, so I loosened
my belt and dug in with pretended gusto. Unfortunately,
academic indigestion was already roiling inside me.

Because fluency in a modern language was a requirement
for admission to the Woodrow Wilson School, I assumed my
German would be useful during the overseas component of
our MPA curriculum. What a surprise to learn that we were
all going to Central America!

On July 29, 1965, President Lyndon Johnson had signed
into law a $35 million aid package for the five countries
of Central America (Guatemala, Nicaragua, Honduras, El
Salvador and Costa Rica) under the Alliance for Progress—a
bill providing loans to facilitate creation of a common market
for the isthmus. It was a development Johnson called at the
signing ceremony "one of the most exciting in the world."
Unfortunately, only six of us who participated in the spring
semester Policy Conference and conducted on-site summer
research in Central America read and spoke Spanish. A
twelve-week crash course was instituted to bring everyone
else up to speed.

A Professor Lopez soon arrived from Columbia, South
America, to lead the Central American Policy Seminar. He
oversaw our study of the political and economic history of
the five countries of the region, including treaties, protocols
and agencies that had relevance for our general topic, and
invited each of us near the end of the term to select a research
project for the summer. I proposed exploring ways in which
the arts might contribute to an enhanced sense of Central
American regional identity. When Professor Bowen heard
about the idea, he called me into his office and scoffed, "Joe,
there are **no arts** in Central America! You will study labor
unions in Guatemala!" Mine was the only summer project
dictated in this way.

Meanwhile, beyond the walls of the Woodrow Wilson

School, a breeze was stirring that warmed the ashes of my forsaken musical career. It was John Mack's hot breath!

If my favorite oboist, mentor, and benefactor had surprising connections to Davidson College, the Brevard Music Center and Charlotte, North Carolina, they were nothing compared to his roots in New Jersey. John Mack was born and grew up in nearby Somerville where his father still resided, and his wife Andy was a graduate of Princeton's Westminster Choir College up the road. A letter from Mack preceding my arrival in Princeton introduced me to conductor Nicholas Harsanyi as "an oboe player incognito," one pretending to pursue foreign affairs at the Woodrow Wilson School. "Put him to good use!" it said.

Harsanyi was a former violist and Eugene Ormandy look-alike from Hungary who conducted the Princeton University Orchestra; the local Princeton Symphony; the Princeton Chamber Orchestra (made up of New York free-lancers); the Madison (New Jersey) Symphony, and about four others. His wife, Janice, a frequent soprano soloist with the Philadelphia Orchestra, was a childhood friend of John Mack's. She once told me how jealous she was that he won the New Jersey State Science Fair when they were in high school together.

The Princeton University Orchestra was the least interesting and most neglected of Harsanyi's ensembles, even though it met regularly throughout the academic year on Monday and Thursday evenings. Counting instrumentalists from Westminster Choir College, there were usually only 25 or 30 players at rehearsals; and John Mack's introduction and reeds made me a shoo-in for first chair oboe. Sensing some leverage, I made Harsanyi the following offer: "I will attend Princeton University Orchestra rehearsals faithfully if you permit me to play **for free** in your professional Princeton Chamber Orchestra." I knew it was a deal the Hungarian maestro could not resist! Soon he and his personnel manager, bass player David Walters, circumvented 802 union restrictions and the Chamber Orchestra's own contract by construing my participation as "educational" and invited me to join.

In my first professional concert with the Princeton Chamber Orchestra, I played second oboe to the Dorian Wind Quintet's oboist Charles Kuskin, who greeted me at a rehearsal break with, "Hey, not bad . . . **down in the parts!"** After that I played first oboe.

Other important musical opportunities arose off campus—Bach arias performed in the home of Walter Scheide, founding patron of the Bach Aria Group, for instance. But it was a particular encounter at a Princeton University Orchestra dress rehearsal that revived my hopes of a career in music. Student Concertmaster Nicholas Birchby was scheduled to appear as soloist in the end-of-semester concert, and he was rehearsing Saint-Saens' beautiful *Third Violin Concerto*. Our accompanying ensemble had more than doubled overnight, thanks to an influx of "ringers" from Juilliard and Curtis.

One of them introduced himself to me during the rehearsal break as bassoonist Tony Checchia and said: "I haven't heard an oboe tone like that since Marcel Tabuteau left Philadelphia."

"It's John Mack's reed," I confessed, blushing at the compliment.

"John Mack doesn't sound like that!" was his reply.

Coming from a Curtis graduate, husband of the great soprano, Benita Valente, and future manager of Marlboro Music, his startling affirmation was a rock upon which I believed I might once again build a musical future. A music-starved refuge from the University of Maryland, who had washed ashore on the steps of the Woodrow Wilson School of Public and International Affairs in Princeton, was now performing more often and more successfully than ever!

The same spring concert included Aaron Copland's *A Lincoln Portrait* for which a narrator is required. Harsanyi asked Princeton President Harold Goleen to do the job, but his political intentions backfired. Goleen, recognizing what a charade the Princeton University Orchestra had become with its dozens of outsiders swelling into a real ensemble only at concert time, replaced Harsanyi as conductor with future Eastman President Robert Freeman.

Marc Lifschey was someone I had never heard of before my Tanglewood roommate Peter Hedrick proclaimed him the finest oboist in the land. Now toward the end of March, the Cleveland Orchestra was coming to Princeton's McCarter Theater, and I hoped to hear Lifschey perform live in a concert for the first time. I had to wait anxiously at the back of a line to obtain a turn-back ticket, before hurrying into the lobby. A slip of paper that fell from the program book handed to me by a welcoming usher announced "Tonight's Principal Oboist is Mr. Adrian Gnam." IMPOSSIBLE! Surely this Adrian Gnam is an uncle of the duckling I knew at Tanglewood. Running to the edge of the stage, I stood there in disbelief, staring into the orchestra, awaiting the arrival of the guest principal oboist. Presently the young man I knew from the summer of 1959 did indeed stride onto the stage with a reed dangling from his lips., and Adrian Gnam took his seat at the center of the mighty Cleveland Orchestra.

Afterwards, in a restaurant on Nassau Street, Adrian told me the story of his incredible good fortune. He was studying at Juilliard when George Szell, Music Director of the Cleveland Orchestra, called his teacher Harold Gomberg to request a recommendation. Marc Lifschey had stormed out of a recording session and had be replaced immediately. Did Gomberg have a student who could do the job? Szell said he would come to New York to hear whomever Gomberg recommended. According to Adrian, Gomberg handed him his best reed and sent him off to Szell's hotel room for a private audition so successful the great conductor offered Adrian a two-year contract on the spot! Adrian told me he would perform one additional concert in the area before leaving with Cleveland for an eleven-week tour of Europe and the Soviet Union. The next day I went to hear him play in Carnegie Hall and feared his Gomberg reed sounded tired already.

Despite the increasing alienation I was feeling at the Woodrow Wilson School, 1965 was probably the apex of governmental interest in and support for the arts in America.

The National Endowment was established that year, giving concrete expression to Duke University graduate Nancy Hanks' resounding affirmation written for the Rockefeller Brothers Fund Report, that "the arts are not for a privileged few but for the many, that their place is not on the periphery of society but at its center, that they are not just a form of recreation but are of central importance to our well-being and happiness."

Van Cliburn's historic victory at the Tchaikovsky Competition in Moscow in 1958 had already given impetus to cultural exchanges funded by the Office of Cultural Presentations at the U.S. Department of State, which climaxed in 1965 with the Cleveland Orchestra's eleven-week tour— the most extensive to date. Lincoln Center opened in New York City, and later in 1965 ground was broken for the John F. Kennedy Center for the Performing Arts in Washington, D.C. R. Philip Hanes, Jr., whom I had met with Dr. Pfohl the previous summer, was a major national advocate for the emerging Arts Council Movement. The Education Act of 1965 included for the first time a Title III provision allocating $75 million for arts enrichment in the nation's schools. And in Winston-Salem, the first state-supported performing arts school in America opened its doors—itself a classic case study in state politics that fulfilled the promise Governor Terry Sanford made to members of the Transylvania Symphony at the Mayflower Hotel in the summer of 1961. I was coming of age just as the arts fermentation known as America's "Culture Boom" crested—a phenomenon that persuaded me ultimately to bet my life on its promises.

In mid-December a final letter arrived from Marcel Tabuteau. Written in his own florid hand, it promised that I "would join the club of [his] star pupils" if I returned to Nice to "help him with his codicil!" Three weeks later *The New York Times* announced Tabuteau's death from a heart attack. Another important letter arrived at about the same time, offering me a position as President Grier Martin's Special Assistant at Davidson College. Despite the compliment, I knew I would lose my graduate school deferment if I accepted his invitation.

The Woolworth Music Building was on the other side of Washington Road down from the Woodrow Wilson School, commodious and convenient, but uncommonly quiet. (Hardly any music-making happened in the building.) I made an appointment to meet with the chairman of the Music Department and asked if he would help me organize some chamber music for instrumentalists on campus. Dr. Arthur Mendel, a notable J. S. Bach scholar whose companions on the faculty included composers Roger Sessions, Milton Babbitt and Edward Cone, sniffed grumpily. "Mr. Robinson, this **not** a service department! For that you go to the gymnasium! At Princeton," he said, "we nurture the most important musical experience—the experience in the mind of the composer."

I was in the building one afternoon, when a knock on the door of my practice room interrupted hours of unsuccessful reed-making. (Earlier that spring I had scraped an entire sunny Saturday into the waste basket—stopping only at 4:30 for a hamburger on Nassau Street and pedaling gloomily back to the Graduate College at midnight without a single reed that would play.) The freckled smile filling the doorway belonged to S. Frederick Starr, a PhD candidate from Cincinnati studying Russian history with Professor James Billington, future head of the Library of Congress. Fred told me he played the clarinet (I remember thinking, "I bet you do!") and suggested cheerfully that we meet for chamber music sometime. Before I knew it, six others and he and I were performing Mozart serenades atop the steps of the Yamasaki Building! Like James Christian Pfohl, Fred Starr was a man for whom a good idea was always father of the deed! He became my lifelong friend and one of the most important men of our generation.

Insubordination

I made a good faith effort at researching labor unions in Guatemala before my arrival in Central America, spending three days at the Department of Labor in Washington, D.C.

and corresponding with numerous embassy officials in Central America. Two unsavory choices quickly presented themselves—either ingest and disgorge "boiler plate" that represented the official government position on unions in Guatemala or risk being shot by Communists who were organizing and arming finca workers in the jungle near Puerto Barrios. I was disinclined to go to the jungle.

As soon as all of us Woodie Wilsonites gathered in Guatemala, we began an orientation week at a spectacular resort in Antigua, not far from the capital city. Bougainvillea, canna lilies, palms and banana trees surrounded the swimming pool and hotel courtyard; and through the open windows of an upstairs conference room, we could see a perfect Walt Disney volcano. Pastel stucco buildings with orange tile roofs jostled each other on unpaved streets stretching away from the cathedral in the center of town. Barefoot native women on their knees, weaving technicolor fabrics or cane baskets for sale near the resort, were omnipresent. So were the lazy black flies that buzzed around us during our sessions in the conference room.

Those sessions were led by cabinet ministers and agency heads from the five Central American countries, under the general supervision of an affable project field director named Jose "Pepe" Monsanto, who hosted and introduced them. Students whose topics were being addressed by the relevant experts sat directly across from them at the center of a wide conference table. There they either comprehended or pretended to comprehend what was being said—depending on whether their Spanish had been learned before or during the crash course at Princeton. The rest of us clustered around both ends of the table and competed in a week-long fly-catching derby.

Ernie Zupancic from Boston College agreed to room with me, so we set out together in Guatemala City to find a cheap place to rent. At one address, a woman built like an oil drum sucked on her Camel cigarette so hard it sparked and crackled in front of us before she chased us off. A more agreeable landlady named Judith Braun took us in, and

Ernie quickly settled into his favorite cultural peculiarity—the siesta.

"Inertia is the biggest thing in my life," he would mumble whenever I tried to rouse him from his afternoon naps, after which he turned over and slept some more.

While we were at the resort in Antigua, I practiced in a gazebo near the swimming pool, where my classmates thought the solo from *Swan Lake* fit in nicely with the exotic bird songs and parrot squawks resounding all around them. My oboe playing pleased a British choir director of Guatemala City's Union Church even more.

"We are performing Mozart's *Exultate Jubilate* next week, and you must join us!" he exclaimed, when I met him after church one Sunday morning. He introduced me to a group of ex-pats and wealthy local amateurs who gathered every Thursday evening for wine, food and chamber music behind walls that bristled with protective barbed wire and broken shards of glass. During a rehearsal for one of their soirées in the fabulous home of the group's Guatemalan pianist, her young nephew in his parochial school uniform cracked the door open and peeked in. My hostess ran over to him and returned gushing, "Oh Miguel is so enchanted by the oboe! I have promised to go to Paris to buy him one."

Meanwhile, at the National Conservatory near the center of town, where I regularly encountered oboe students and their teacher, the first oboist of the Guatemala National Orchestra, Manuel Gomez, told me that he made only $200 a month and played on a thirty-year-old instrument. He also said he cut the best oboe cane of his life in the highlands above Guatemala City—information that would have great significance for me later on. More significant at that moment was my confrontation with the obscene disparity between rich and poor Guatemalans. Millions of natives lived on the land in that country much as they had for hundreds of years—barefoot, illiterate, parasite-ridden, and listless. A tiny minority of others—people mainly of Spanish descent who owned and controlled most of the wealth, lived pan-European lives, scarcely identifying (except for the money and privileges their country provided them) with Guatemala at all.

An accomplished baritone in our chamber music group was the American Director of AID (the Agency for International Development) in Guatemala. He had sung with the Washington Choral Society and was married to a soprano who had studied at Juilliard. He told me his warehouses were full of hybrid seeds that could dramatically increase corn production for native Guatemalans if they would only use them. Natives resisted, he said, because their ancient methods of agriculture had so depleted yields that many indigenous families lived too near the brink of extinction to experiment or invest in a better way. My friend said hybrid seeds were rotting in their containers while Guatemalan farmers' families starved to death!

"Pepe" Monsanto asked me one day how my labor union project was doing. I told him that I had infiltrated so many musical organizations by now I believed more strongly than ever that the arts could enhance a sense of Central American identity—through commissioned works; touring art exhibits; regional competitions; and things like that. His immediate response was, "Well, go ahead with that!" Assuming he had the authority to change my project and report it to Princeton, I jettisoned my notes on labor unions and headed straight for the Ministerios de las Bellas Artes. During the seven weeks that ensued, I investigated the direction and performance of music at student, professional, and amateur levels in Guatemala, El Salvador, and Costa Rica. I tested my hypothesis that tours, exchanges, and joint programs in the arts could contribute to an enhanced sense of Central American identity by sending and receiving lengthy questionnaires from one hundred professional orchestra musicians and twenty-two prominent business executives in Guatemala. I also interviewed fifty arts leaders and cultural affairs officers in the region and asked them to support regional arts programs that signified Central American unification in both form and substance.

A few days after returning from Guatemala, I made a brief first visit to the storied Marlboro Music Festival in

Marlboro, Vermont, where John Mack was recording Mozart and Schubert symphonies with Pablo Casals. The affectionate, exalted search for musical truth in that beautiful Vermont setting made an impression I would never forget.

John Mack began his thirty-five-year reign as Principal Oboe of the Cleveland Orchestra in September 1965, performing for George Szell one of the most difficult pieces, *Le Tombeau de Couperin*, by Ravel in his first concert in Severance Hall. Adrian Gnam was not on stage. His performance of Prokofiev's Fifth Symphony at Carnegie Hall had made me pretty sure that he would not survive as Marc Lifschey's replacement. Complying with the terms of their contract with him, the Cleveland Orchestra nevertheless retained Adrain for an additional season, during which he fulfilled his duties as fifth man in the oboe section mainly by drinking scotch and playing golf with John Mack. A few years later, Adrian took a job at the National Endowment for the Arts, before exchanging his reeds for a baton and becoming a conductor.

New Neo-Gothic dorm rooms opened in Princeton my second year, and I lived in one of them without a roommate. A history PhD candidate on the floor above me undertook my instruction in opera, guiding me on expeditions to the "new" MET at Lincoln Center only if I satisfied rigorous pre-performance homework assigned to me. (There were no "Met Titles" in those days.) He was such a brusque and dogmatic teacher that to call him "undiplomatic" would be an understatement! After Princeton, he went into the Foreign Service.

My courses at the Woodrow Wilson School now looked like this:

Fall 1965:
   Political Systems (Eckstein/Strange)
   Administrative Behavior (Egger)
   State & Local Government (Lockard)
   Research Seminar–Education & Manpower Policies
                              (Harbison & Mooney)

Spring 1966:
Interpretations of American Historical Development
(Lively)
Processes & Practices of Management (Corson)
Law & Social Control (Beaney)
Policy Research Conference—Urban Development
& the Community Action Program (Ylvisaker)

Harry Eckstein's course involved memorizing and applying his particular analytical template to old and modern societies, providing him with "grist for the mill" for his next publication. Meanwhile, Robert Lively assigned so many books on American history each week that it was all we could do to discern and remember each author's thesis and name—a practice antithetical to an English major accustomed to the music and subtlety of poetry. Paul Ylvisaker's course was the best offering of my second year at the Woodrow Wilson School. He himself was a very appealing human being—still Vice President for Public Affairs of the Ford Foundation, though he knew and told us that he was going blind. His course could have been called Great Men in Public Life in America, because our class meetings almost always involved encountering inspirational leaders such as Senator Robert F. Kennedy at his UN Plaza apartment (where he stirred the water in his piranha's fish bowl with his finger) and the great civil rights activist, Rev. Leon Sullivan from Philadelphia. Despite mutual respect and even affection, Paul Ylvisaker and I did not see eye to eye on my term paper at the end of the semester. He found my assessment of the potential for remedial therapy using the arts in prisons to be insubstantial and disappointing.

With a dance weekend coming up and having no prospects for a date, in a moment of desperation, I succumbed to the risky idea of inviting Jean Thomas. Her quick reply was bubbling with joy. She wrote that she had just agreed to marry Michael Russ, the boy she left me in Lenoir to visit.

In response, confessing that the Princeton invitation was a bribe, I wrote stoically, "A few years ago, I could have wished nothing more for you than the kind of maturity you have attained, the academic excellence that you have won for yourself, your continued musical involvement, and a happy marriage to a man worthy of your devotion. You were like an unblossomed flower that I flattered myself (as your mentor) with trying to help grow tall and straight in the sunshine. How regrettable that I tried to cut you for my own!"

It would be fifty years before a note passed between us again.

Inevitably, a policy conference was scheduled at which all of us involved with the Central American program were required to make oral presentations previewing the formal printed and bound documents that would follow. My proposals for using the arts to enhance regional identity among the five countries in the isthmus seem to have taken everyone but my roommate Ernie Zupancic by surprise! "Pepe" Monsanto had not told Professors Lopez and Bowen about my change of direction, and their predictable reaction was indignation. In my introduction to a nearly 24,000-word bound report, I would write the following:

"Finally, this is a policy report. It is not merely an exposition of data about the fine arts in Central America. Based upon convictions which I hope to have identified about the nature of the arts and their importance in society, and set in the context of the movement toward Central American integration, it calls for concrete programs of action and change; and it is in the success or failure of these programs that the report ultimately must be tested."

Professor Lopez declared that he was not competent to judge such work—that someone else would have to be brought in to do it; but in the end, he did grade my paper

"Pass-minus!"

Except for my undergraduate ROTC Honor Guard embarrassment at Davidson College, being out of step with authority was an unfamiliar role for me. But the liberal political consensus prevailing at Princeton in the mid-sixties bothered me for being orthodox rather than truly "liberal," in the sense of being tentative and open-minded;

and I resented the way virtuoso professors defended dogma behind conceptual fortress walls from which they sniped at their critics. I knew that righteous indignation is unattractive and usually counterproductive; but I also learned that it can be a powerful motivator. In an angry letter to Dean Marver Bernstein, I asserted that there was more Truth in a kind word than in most social science treatises! The sense of unfair treatment from my advisors and teachers at the Woodrow Wilson School burned within me throughout 1965-66, fueling my determination to demonstrate that my unappreciated report would have significance beyond its dusty place on the library shelves of Princeton University.

Fred Starr was my ally in the campaign that followed.

Central American Summer Music Scholarship Program

My portable Smith-Corona came in for a lot of use in 1965-66. I typed hundreds of letters on it during the winter and spring. Carbon paper had to be slipped between the letter page and an onion skin sheet to produce copies, and mistakes were corrected using a plastic liquid called "White Out." The stuff dried quickly and could be typed over a second time, but the corrected places were almost always illegible on the copies. Translating my earlier proposal for German students to attend the Brevard Music Center and return as soloists with the Transylvania Symphony I asked Henry Janiec if students from Central America could do something similar in the summer of 1966. They would be the first international students ever to attend the Music Center. If he said "yes," I promised to arrange competitive selection of the participants; fund their scholarships and travel; and oversee their activities in the United States. Henry gave me the green light to set things up and pursue funding, and he freed me to do the work by retaining from the previous summer a Converse College publicist named Frank Little as Director of Publicity. I was named Assistant Public Relations Director for the Central American program and assigned first oboe in a new ensemble called the Repertory Training Orchestra. My former Tanglewood roommate, Peter Hedrick, and his wife Libby were returning to Brevard that summer as the faculty oboists. (After Peter completed his studies with Robert Bloom at Yale and married his Oberlin sweetheart, he took Don Welles' job as Professor of Oboe at Ithaca College. Tanglewood's long tentacles continued to intertwine!)

Contacts I had made when I was on site in Guatemala, El Salvador, and Costa Rica gave me a starting point. I wrote to everyone I had met explaining my proposals that this would be the first-ever Central American arts program expressing regional identity, and requesting their help in selecting one winning participant from each of the five countries. Despite agencies such as ROCAP (the Regional Organization for Central America and Panama), there was no State Department Cultural Affairs overseer for Central America per se; consequently, I was forced to appeal to each Cultural Affairs officer in the five US embassies one by one. It was a bit like herding cats; because, in the end, only three of them cooperated. The effort persuaded me that "Cultural Affairs Officer" was a euphemism disguising a more honest job title: "US Anti-Communist Head-hunter!" In 1954 the Central Intelligence Agency participated in the overthrow of democratically-elected President Arbenz because he legalized the Communist Party in Guatemala and enacted land reforms that benefited peasants—an intervention that was assuredly not the **only** distortion of American democratic ideals inspired by the Cold War.

In the beginning, finding money was just as frustrating as establishing a fair method of selecting participants. I met with foundation directors in New York City and the heads of every agency in Washington I could identify who expressed interest in Central American development. And I wrote letters to many others, all without success. But late one afternoon, stepping off the train at 30th Street Station in Philadelphia and acting on a hunch, I called John Ronald Ott at the Presser Foundation. I told him that I was a graduate of Davidson College and that was enough! He responded enthusiastically, "President Grier Martin is one of the finest men I know in higher education. Come on over here and let's discuss your project." An hour later I had my scholarships.

Travel grants and *per diems* for the participants were also difficult to formalize. Local embassy officials had resisted all of my attempts to persuade them to pay for these expenses, and above them in the diplomatic hierarchy, no one yet had been helpful. Assistant Secretary of State for Latin American Affairs Howard Howland was my last hope. He had not replied to any of my letters, but at least had not yet turned me down. I poured out my dead-end frustrations to Fred Starr one evening while he checked the train schedule. Within minutes Fred had me standing on the platform at Princeton Junction with a sandwich in my hand, awaiting a train to take me to Washington, D.C. I walked in unannounced the next morning to see Sec. Howland and received his promise of travel grants from the Department of State. The pieces were now in place for the first Central American Summer Music Scholarship Program to become a reality.

Another Princeton campaign occurred in the spring semester in 1966. After requesting copies of the first winning grant applications funded under Title III of the 1965 Education Act, about thirty of them arrived from the Office of Education. Taken together they were a clinic in grantsmanship, as well as a demonstration of the weakness of money-first social engineering. Most of them were formulated quickly *a priori* and lacked substance in response to real needs. Title III eventually became known as the "woodwind quintet full employment bill"—an example of supply creating its own contrived demand. Eventually, thousands of "show-and-tell" concerts and performances funded under Title III would frustrate children whose enthusiasm for the arts was still-born in schools where full-time art and music teachers no longer had jobs. Almost unnoticed throughout the 1960s, in response to the Soviet challenge of Sputnik, arts programs in public schools everywhere were dismantled in favor of more math and science.

Someone told me that a brilliant but controversial cleric

was coming to Princeton University Chapel to preach. He was Episcopal Bishop James Pike. Watching him swagger up the aisle in a procession, I thought him too small for all of his elaborate ecclesiastical regalia. But in the pulpit he stood very tall; he was a charismatic and compelling speaker. Elucidating with convincing authority the thesis that Jesus was not born but **grew** into perfection as the Son of God, he cited two examples of Jesus' encounters with Samaritan women to prove his point. Called "Adoptionism," Bishop Pike's convictions eventually led to his excommunication from the Episcopal Church. I have nevertheless found his little volume entitled *Doing the Truth* to be the most instructive book on Christian ethics I ever read.

After returning from Nice, I continued to stay in touch with Hans Moennig, who took pride in my unexpected association with Marcel Tabuteau and often boasted of it. John DeLancie knew about it also, but when I met him twice again—once in Moennig's shop and once backstage after a Philadelphia Orchestra concert at the Academy of Music—both times he was surly and feigned non-recognition.

"You study around here, boy?" was his query in response to one of those encounters. An entirely different person welcomed me following a woodwind quintet concert at the Art Museum in Philadelphia, however. He was so pleased with his own performance that evening he was actually avuncular and embracing. Ironically, it was his good humor that prompted a long accusatory letter I wrote to him when I returned to Princeton that night. In my letter, I revisited and dramatized the life-changing first encounter we had had at Duke University and reminded him of his responsibility to young musicians like David Weber (just then applying to Curtis), who might be more talented than I was.

John Mack learned about it from his Curtis roommate, Lou Rosenblatt, backstage at the Kennedy Center following a Philadelphia Orchestra concert a few days later. Rosenblatt asked Mack if he knew a guy named Joe Robinson and told him DeLancie was furious about a letter I had sent to him!

Mack's reaction was to congratulate me and exclaim, "Way to go, Laddie! You just put another notch on your gun!" (It was that "notch" that almost cost me the most important audition of my life a few years later.)

Two major examinations were scheduled mid-semester—the Foreign Service Exam, which I flunked, and the Civil Service Exam, on which I performed poorly—but well enough to elicit one job offer from the federal government bureaucracy. It was a position in the Bureau of Labor Statistics at the Department of Labor paying $6,000 a year. Meanwhile, the Selective Service System instructed me to report for a physical exam in Newark. Conventional wisdom had it that the written part of that examination could be failed only by knowing the right answers and intentionally answering them incorrectly, in which case the respondent would be recognized as a cheat and pass anyway! I stood in lines in my skivvies most of the day, before being graded "One-A"—a status that would increase my draft-ability the closer I came to my 26th birthday.

Because of that, when an oboe opening was announced for the Air Force Band where my Tanglewood buddy Donald Hilts was serving, I rushed to apply. Positions in the West Point Band and the major service bands in Washington, D.C., were all coveted in the mid-sixties. Many of the finest instrumentalists of my generation played in them rather than be drafted and sent to Vietnam. My experiences at Davidson in the ROTC Honor Guard convinced me that I would make a better bandsman than infantryman. I auditioned for Colonel Gabriel in Arlington, Virginia, on my way home for spring break and was accepted. He gave me forty-eight hours to discuss the opportunity with my parents before accepting or rejecting a four-year Air Force commitment.

Dad was delighted when he learned that basic training would be required.

"Take it son," he urged. "It will make a man of you!"

Just then the telephone rang, and my mother left the den to answer it. When she returned, she announced that a man with an unpronounceable name wanted to speak to me. "He said it is urgent." The caller was James Yestadt, John Mack's golfing buddy from the New Orleans Philharmonic and Music Director of the Mobile Symphony Orchestra, with whom I had performed a concert at Brevard the previous summer.

"How would you like to be principal oboe of the newest professional orchestra in America!?" he asked. "We have the same salary and season length as Atlanta—thirty weeks at $160 a week plus $1,600 for teaching oboe at the University of South Alabama. No audition necessary. I'll send you a contract."

FANTASTIC! My dream job just fell from the sky! First oboe in a professional orchestra on the Gulf Coast was perfect! But I told him that between graduation from Princeton on June 14 and my 26th birthday on June 20 I was probably the most eligible man in the entire Selective Service System and I might be drafted. "But, of course, I would LOVE to take the job!"

"Joe, don't worry about it. Senator Sparkman, Chairman of the Armed Services Committee, is on our board!" was Yestadt's reply.

I understood then why there were so many protests all over America concerning the draft and the Vietnam War! It was in the sole discretion of local draft board clerks how to interpret draft status in a case like mine—whether I would be eligible because I was younger than twenty-six when I received my letter of induction, or ineligible because I would be older than twenty-six when I reported for active duty ten days later. As it turned out, my draft board clerk in Caldwell County chose the latter ruling, and Senator Sparkman had nothing to do with it.

"I accept your invitation!" I told James Yestadt enthusiastically when I learned of her ruling. After almost eight years of non-musical training, my career as an oboist was finally about to begin!

When John Mack heard the news, he was thrilled. But he warned, "You're a professional oboist now, Laddie. Don't expect any more reeds of mine to come your way!" An old

Wally Bhosys gouging machine with a guillotine on it and an arrowhead tube splitter were my graduation consolation prizes; but "Sink or swim!" was John Mack's last comment on the subject of reeds. I **never** got another one from him again.

The Southern Education Foundation announced an internship for which I applied that spring, and sometime mid-summer I learned that I was chosen to assist the Superintendent of Mobile County Schools on federally-supported grants in support of integration. At first, I thought that kind of public service would be compatible with my new orchestra job; but I quickly realized that making my own reeds would preempt every other activity in 1966-67.

Forgoing what felt like hypocritical graduation ceremonies at Princeton, I requested that my Master of Public Affairs diploma be mailed to me in Lenoir.

"Bringing the Americas Closer Together"

Early that summer Dad suggested buying me a car. Because he did the paying, he also did the shopping—for a Rambler American, the cheapest production car made in the US. It was a pale green sedan "loaded" with a heater, and I was thrilled to have it.

The Brevard Music Center was dramatically different in 1965. A resplendent new performance pavilion called (for Dr. Pfohl's parents) the "Whittington-Pfohl Auditorium" had been inaugurated with fanfare and fireworks while I was in Central America. If Transylvania Music Camp served youth through music as a Southern Interlochen, the Converse-led Brevard Music Center was more a Southern Tanglewood, serving the public through performances of fully-staged grand opera and musical theater. The migration to the Blue Ridge Mountains by music lovers from Atlanta and Charlotte mirrored that of New Yorkers and Bostonians each summer to the Berkshires; and the institutional symbiosis between the Brevard Music Center and Converse College was a brilliant idea. Director John McCrae and his Spartanburg

Opera Company found a perfect venue and much larger audience for their young singers, as well as a rich recruiting ground; and Henry Janiec brought stability and competence both to the administrative offices and to the podium of the Music Center. Singing filled the air at Brevard in 1966!

And so did Spanish.

Five musicians from Central America who won the Presser Foundation scholarships and State Department travel grants to attend Brevard came from only three of the five isthmus countries—Guatemala, Nicaragua, and Costa Rica; but they were nevertheless representatives of the first regional arts program espousing Central American unification and the first international students in the thirty-three year history of the Brevard Music Center. J. Humberto Ayestas, Assistant Conductor of the Guatemala National Orchestra, escorted them. Maestro Ayestas, who had played viola in the Baltimore Symphony for three years, helped me immeasurably "shepherding the flock" and acting when necessary as translator. He also conducted the Repertory Training Orchestra and performed as a violist in the Center's large ensembles.

Soprano Maria Blanco and pianist Julian Weston came from Costa Rica, violinist Gloria Alvarez and cellist Maria Juarez from Guatemala, and clarinetist Eduardo Perez from Nicaragua. A special concert honoring all of them was scheduled in the Whittington-Pfohl Auditorium on August 6. Maria sang arias from *Samson and Delilah* and *Carmen*, and Humberto conducted the concert which also included the premiere of a ballet score written by a Guatemalan composer. Joining the celebration, North Carolina Governor Dan Moore gave each Central American student a certificate bearing the state seal that appointed them to the "Order of the Long Leaf Pine," and he praised Henry Janiec and the Brevard Music Center lavishly for their international initiative.

But the best was still to come! One of Wyche Fowler's dearest Davidson College friends, Ervin Duggan, was a speech writer working in the White House. As a favor, he arranged for the Central American students to meet and be greeted personally by President Lyndon Johnson in the White House Rose Garden during their five-day post-camp visit to Washington, D.C.—funds for which had been donated by the Brevard Lions Club, the Hendersonville Rotary Club, and the BMC students themselves. Friends of the United States of Latin America and embassy officials in the Capital provided lavish accommodations for everyone. On August 26, the Washington International House presented us (I performed the Mozart Oboe Quartet) in a recital that was taped in its entirety for broadcast throughout Latin American by the Voice of America. Representatives from the Department of State, Congress, the White House staff, and the diplomatic community were in attendance.

A *Transylvania Times* headline for the story describing the Central American Summer Music Scholarship Program at the Brevard Music Center in 1966 unfortunately went unnoticed by my grave examiners at the Woodrow Wilson School.

"Joe Robinson Brings Americas Closer Together!"

With so many distractions, pressure built throughout the summer for me to get into performance shape and improve my reed-making. My future employer was on the BMC conducting staff, after all; and I could have lost my new job before it even started if James Yestadt changed his mind about my playing. While the Repertory Training Orchestra was an inspired way to attract young professionals to the Music Center and may have been helped them engage the notes of some of the greatest symphonic music ever written, it was no way to develop or demonstrate musical artistry. The "hit-and-run" reading sessions scheduled every afternoon disregarded intonation, ensemble and musical subtleties, and were mostly exercises in orchestral bad habits. Furthermore, many of the RTO's conductors were just "test driving" new batons at Beethoven's and Tchaikovsky's expense when they stood in front of us.

That summer I was able at last to replace Jean Thomas in my affections. My new love was another brown-eyed Southern beauty, from Aiken, South Carolina. She was "Miss

Aiken" in the same "Miss South Carolina" pageant Janet McGee won the year before, and she was one of the many Converse College singers appearing on stage at Brevard on stage that summer. Watching her in the musical *The Fantastiks* during the nostalgic hit song, "Try to remember a day in September . . ." etc., made my heart melt anew. Jeannie Martin was my romantic obsession throughout the year that followed.

John Mack surprised me with the news that Robert Shaw, the famous choral conductor and George Szell assistant, was about to become Music Director of the Atlanta Symphony Orchestra, replacing conductor Henry Sopkin in September 1967. He suggested I check out Atlanta as a second job before I even arrived at my first! I telephoned Wyche Fowler at once to ask if I could stay overnight with him on my way to Mobile. Wyche took me to see the brand-new Atlanta Falcons play (and win) their first NFL game while I was there.

Back in high school watching the New York Philharmonic on television one day, I told a friend that I would **never** want to join that orchestra! Washington's National Symphony was the height of my professional ambition—my career "consummation devoutly to be wished."

Dad and I agreed that a proper litmus test for my risky career choice would be either 1) to win principal oboe in the National Symphony Orchestra in Washington, D.C. (where I thought I could bring to bear all my years of academic extra-musical training in support of legislated arts programs) **within five years**, or 2) consider the oboe experiment a failure and go in another direction.

One might think it a fool's bargain on my side, since principal oboists can stay entrenched in their chairs for decades; but the $80 million Ford Foundation grants in 1966 made orchestras in America such a growth industry the demand for players actually exceeded the supply. As an example, when the second oboe position in the Baltimore Symphony opened up in 1967, principal oboist Joe Turner called John Mack to ask if he knew **anyone** who might be interested in the job. (Fifty years later, there would probably be 200 applicants!) Retirements announced at the top of the orchestral food chain always created "trickle-down musical chairs;" but the pace now quickened so much that Jimmy Caldwell came and went as principal oboe of the National Symphony within two years. (He left Washington, D.C. to join Anshel Brusilow and the ill-fated Philadelphia Chamber Orchestra.) Consequently, there was at least some chance, if things broke my way, that I **could** win the National Symphony job in Washington within five years.

rondo sinfonico

Mobile, Alabama

The resident full-time professional chamber orchestra in Mobile was a direct (if misguided) consequence of Ford Foundation initiatives—misguided because some fine print in the grant application guidelines that disqualified the Mobile Symphony from funding was overlooked. The orchestra's annual budget was not large enough to qualify it for funding. Despite the mistake, Music Director James Yestadt imported thirty players for performance of chamber orchestra and children's concerts in addition to reinforcing the mostly-amateur Mobile Symphony Orchestra whenever larger works were scheduled throughout the season. Assembling a resident ensemble late in the spring of 1966 was difficult; Yestadt had to cull most of us from the human and musical "recycling bin." Our group included retired instrumentalists, recovering addicts, down-

and-outers, etc. and a few beginners like me. Together with a new auditorium, our chamber orchestra represented a huge financial commitment by Mobile's civic leaders. Former All-American football player and Rhodes Scholar C.M.A. "Max" Rogers, III courageously took the reins as President of the Mobile Symphony and Civic Music Association Board of Directors. Several announcements from Max in the months ahead either canceled concerts or instructed us to wait a few days before depositing our paychecks.

Mobile itself, a beloved jewel of the Gulf Coast with proud claims to the best Southern hospitality and heritage, instituted the first Mardi Gras in America and was indeed a city of beautiful, semi-tropical gardens. Dripping Spanish moss, live oak trees hundreds of years old canopied Mobile's gleaming white shell-encrusted boulevards. Azaleas and bougainvillea bloomed lavishly as early as February, and residents were still sweltering in summer heat when I arrived mid-September.

Board member Anne Evans and her husband graciously hosted me until permanent housing could be found. Knowing that typical apartment neighbors would never tolerate oboe practice and late-night reed-making, after searching for a guest house or over-the-garage apartment among the dowagers of the town, Anne and I eventually spotted something behind an iconic white-columned mansion. It was a honeymoon cottage that had been used seventy or so years earlier by the ancient lady who offered it. Two huge camellia bushes crushed the roof and blocked windows on both sides of the front door; but inside were a living room, a tiny kitchen, bedroom and bath. I took it.

Even before unpacking, I bought a can of Raid with which to attack the giant roaches (called "water bugs") that crawled down from nearby live oak trees to live in the cottage. I tied a handkerchief over my face, sprayed under and behind everything, and in the morning, swept up my "winnings." The ugly creatures that lived in darkness died in sunlight. In the middle of the third night, loud gnawing noises that sounded as if a creature with big teeth were chewing its way through the baseboard into my bedroom woke me. Before rehearsal next morning, I went again to the hardware store—this time to buy four packages of D-Con rat poison. The salesman told me to put the containers—each of which had two compartments filled with stuff that looked like oatmeal—outside around the cottage, and to open one side first. Instructions on the box said, "If within 24 hours all of the contents of one side have been devoured, you may be sure you have a heavy infestation and should open the other side." Three hours later, all the contents of both the opened and unopened sides had been completely devoured.

That night one of my poisoned rats lost its grip on the rafters overhead and fell inside the wall next to me with a plop. I listened to it convulse and whine in mortal agony until dawn. The smell which I knew would soon arise in that tropical climate sent me packing early the next morning.

My second landlady, Mrs. L. G. Adams, was older than the first. Her husband, long deceased, had owned the first automobile agency in town. In fact, Mr. and Mrs. Adams were the first couple from Mobile to motor successfully to California and back. A young trumpet player from San Francisco agreed to share the over-the-garage apartment with me, reducing my rent to $90 a month. He brought with him a pet turtle that lived in the kitchen in a foul-looking dish into which he occasionally tossed flies, of which there was never a shortage of supply. The highlight of his life, my roommate explained, was to have been invited occasionally into fashionable Bay Area homes by wealthy socialites.

"Come in, Chicken Delight delivery boy!" they sometimes said, making him feel especially proud and welcome. "Go right on into the kitchen!" Sometimes they even offered him a glass of wine.

In the orchestra, he played second trumpet next to Mike Farrow, a rising star of the orchestra world who soon left Mobile for greener pastures in Indianapolis. My roommate left quickly also, unable to win tenure in the Mobile Symphony.

Sitting on my right in the center of the orchestra was a flutist from Curtis who had performed with John Mack in the New Orleans Philharmonic. She was a recovering alcoholic married to a much younger member of the cello section; and on my left, playing second oboe and English horn, was a local musician who st..st..st..st..stuttered badly. An acting principal clarinetist named Stanley, hired at the last minute fresh out of Curtis, replaced Al Genovese's big brother John (whose leg had to be amputated because of cancer), and he sat behind me.

Stanley wasted no time organizing a players' committee and getting himself elected chairman. It was probably not a good idea. On the afternoon he and the second clarinetist got into an argument, their shouting brought our Haydn symphony rehearsal completely to a halt.

"He's got a gun! He's got a gun!" Stanley cried as he dashed through the orchestra and threw himself at the feet of the personnel manager in the cello section.

That altercation prompted Stanley's move to the bass clarinet job in the New Orleans Philharmonic and effectively ended the professional career of his partner. Perhaps the most dramatic portent of things to come in the Mobile Symphony, however, happened at the beginning of the season, when the assistant concertmaster and his wife chased each other drunk and near-naked through the lobby of the best hotel in town. They had to be tackled and wrapped in blankets by house detectives, then bailed out of jail as a first exercise of duty by C.M.A. "Max" Rogers, III.

Dad had warned me about "going off the deep end" and I guess this was it! As a 32nd-degree Mason, he was concerned that being a musician would make me valuable only for what I could do and not for who I was. It was the old cliché of degraded character and social irresponsibility among artists that prompted his characterization of them as "Bohemian" when I was a teenager. By now I was learning that orchestra success had nothing to do with exemplary personal behavior or good citizenship—only with one's ability to play correct notes and meld quickly with others into an effective musical ensemble. Loss of social status from Princeton graduate student to Mobile Symphony musician was already obvious in Judge Johnstone's less-than-cordial welcome when I arrived to take his daughter Virginia out on a date. Virginia was Jean Thomas's "big sister" at Converse College and she was a Mobile debutante already at the top of the societal food chain. The judge made sure I brought his daughter home on time!

A particular scene made this change of status painfully obvious to my parents. They had driven to Mobile in March 1967 to visit me and attend the first in a series of "rush hour" concerts presented at 4:00 p.m. in a fancy downtown hotel. It was part of the orchestra's desperate search for new audiences. Taking their seats in a corner of the mostly-deserted ballroom, they found themselves separated by a sea of red satin-backed chairs from the few tipsy ladies who called out requests for their favorite Strauss waltzes. Their disappointment was palpable—Davidson phi beta kappa, a Fulbright to Germany, and a Princeton advanced degree all for this?

The first subscription concert back in September had been more promising. It included "killer" repertory for the principal oboist, and my few remaining John Mack reeds were dying by the hour. I was in a panic trying to make something of my own that I could play on. John Mack had often told me, "A reed a day keeps the psychiatrist away!" but he never said I would have to make ten just to get one!

Fortunately, something usable emerged at the last

moment, and several canceled weeks of concerts during the season gave me just enough time to survive as an oboist. My reed-making also began to improve when I realized that the tubes of cane do not grow round (often they are oval or even triangular) and discarded the arrow-head tube splitter John Mack had given me. Using a razor blade and a radius gauge instead, I selected precise pieces of the tube's circumference that yielded consistent, symmetrical reed openings. I believed that I could master reed-making once I gave it my full attention; but I was just beginning to understand that oboists and baseball sluggers rarely bat over .300!

THE MOBILE SYMPHONY AND CIVIC MUSIC ASSOCIATION

JAMES YESTADT, *Music Director and Conductor*

First Performance   Twentieth Season   October 10, 1966

Mobile Municipal Theater

Program

BERLIOZ————BENVENUTO CELLINI OVERTURE, Op. 23

BRAHMS————————————————SYMPHONY No. 3, Op. 90

    Allegro con brio
    Andante
    Poco Allegretto
    Allegro

INTERMISSION

DE FALLA————————————————EL AMOR BRUJO
                      (LOVE, THE MAGICIAN)

    Introduction and Scene
    With the Gypsies - Night
    The Ghost - Dance of Terror
    The Magic Circle - The Fisherman's Tale
    Midnight - Sorceries - Ritual Fire Dance
    Pantomime
    Dance of the Game of Love
    The Bells of Dawn

TCHAIKOWSKY————————————CAPRICCIO ITALIEN, Op. 45

The music world is similar to professional sports, insofar as instrumentalists are paid athletes of small muscle groups. All of us dream of advancing to the big leagues someday, and I was no exception; but just as few aspiring ballplayers ever make it to the pros, only about 15% of conservatory graduates actually go on to earn their living as performers. In Mobile I was already ahead of the curve. But my first opportunity to "move up" came when in March, thanks to John Mack's encouragement and a persuasive letter of recommendation, I was invited by Music Director Werner Torkanowsky to compete for Mack's former position in the New Orleans Philharmonic. Consequently, I drove over to New Orleans and auditioned in a junior high school auditorium following a children's concert.

Members of the New Orleans audition committee were already sitting out front with the maestro when I walked onto the auditorium stage with my oboe in my hands.

"Start with a D-flat major scale, two octaves!" sang out Torkanowsky. It was a command one might rather have expected at an all-State band audition, but I executed it perfectly. More appropriate orchestral excerpts followed— Brahms 1st, Beethoven 3rd, Rossini's *La Scala di Seta*, etc., and then *Le Tombeau de Couperin* by Maurice Ravel. Peter Hedrick had told me about *Le Tombeau de Couperin* when we roomed together at Tanglewood; but I still had never heard it or seen the oboe part. And the only notes I brought with me were published in Southern Music's *Vade Mecum*, a compilation of standard orchestral excerpts that included newer ones (those not yet in the public domain) altered by an editor in order to get around copyright laws. Taking a chance, I played the *Vade Mecum etude* as if it were authentic Ravel and confounded everyone on the committee longer than I should have before an oboist came forward to explain what was going on! Despite that fiasco, the audition ended successfully when New Orleans' personnel manager came over to ask, "Tell me, what are they paying you in Mobile next year?"

"$165 a week," I replied.

"Fine, we'll match that!" he said.

Wow! It was great to be offered John Mack's former chair! But I turned it down.

"The job is more prestigious than Mobile's," I said. "If you think I'm good enough for it, you should pay me what it is worth. I will come for $175 a week."

His answer was, "Sorry . . . we can't go that high."

Meanwhile, Ernestine Whitman, a friend of mine from Brevard who played second flute in the Atlanta Symphony, invited me to stay at her parents' home and attend a performance of *The Nutcracker*. She wanted me to judge for myself whether young Patrick McFarland, a student of Ray Still who was playing first oboe in Atlanta, would pass muster with Atlanta's new Music Director, Robert Shaw. I knew Shaw's conception of fine oboe playing had hatched in John Mack's nest in Cleveland, so I doubted if he would. And sure enough, as soon as the opening for Principal Oboe in the Atlanta Symphony was announced, I flew at once to Cleveland.

John Mack met me at the airport and took me to his home to spend the night. He did not touch my reed, but listened carefully to the oboe solo from Bach's *St. Matthew Passion* ("*Ich will bei Meinem Jesu Wachen*").

"Excellent opening selection for a choral conductor," he said approvingly! Only three other oboists auditioned in Severance Hall when I did, one of whom was known to me from the Princeton Chamber Orchestra. It probably helped that John Mack sat beside Robert Shaw throughout. When all of us finished playing, Shaw congratulated me backstage in his distinctive, slightly breathless, stammering tenor voice, saying, "Mr. Robinson, you are a promising musician with a lot to . . . to . . . to learn . . . but, but, but . . . then, **so am I!**"

"Thank you. That is a perfect basis for our relationship, Mr. Shaw," I answered happily. "I promise to do my best."

He told me the job would pay $200 a week for thirty weeks and promised a contract mailed soon to me in Mobile. On the way back to the Cleveland Airport, John Mack leaned over in the car and said intently, "Listen, Joe. I am only going to tell you this one time: **stay away from Robert Shaw**. People who get too close to him live to regret it!"

A notorious figure in the Southern resistance against school integration and the Civil Rights movement was George Wallace, two-time Governor of Alabama prohibited by the state constitution from running for a third term in office. In 1966 his wife Lurleen ran instead. Many Alabamians still acted as if the Civil War had never been lost, and some of them in Mobile even claimed that the noxious odors drifting down from paper mills north of town were the stench of continuing federal government interference in their state. During my nine months in Mobile, I did not see at a concert, meet in a restaurant, sit in a church pew, or at any other place and time encounter and interact with any black people at all. The demographic majority were as invisible to me in Mobile as they had been in Lenoir when I was a boy. It was not a city I wanted to live in for long.

Two important pieces of administrative business remained before I left Mobile. The first was to help choose (with pleasure) my successor, John DeLancie's graduating Curtis student that year. And the second was to serve briefly on a committee selecting William C. Denton to be the new administrative director for the orchestra. Bill Denton would soon play a role in my professional development more important than either of us knew! Meanwhile, too late, the personnel manager of the New Orleans Philharmonic called to tell me he could indeed meet my price of $175 a week.

At home in Lenoir, Dad, now enervated by worsening emphysema, retired from the insurance business, and Mother threw herself more intensely into palette-knife landscape oil painting—which she could do without leaving Dad at home alone. My brother Ed got married. Taking stock of my first season as a full-time professional oboist, despite some social dislocation in Mobile and another failed romance, I was proud to have sustained myself as a reed-maker and survived a season with the Mobile Symphony Orchestra. It had been a wonderful opportunity to play great orchestral music that was new to me. Meanwhile, I had won two auditions in more prestigious ensembles and increased my annual compensation per week by 25%—altogether a promising start to my musical career.

The Reston Music Center

If you can "watch the things you gave your life to, broken, and stoop and build 'em up with worn out tools . . ."

James Christian Pfohl validated this element of Rudyard Kipling's prescription for successful manhood by reinventing Transylvania Music Camp in Reston, Virginia, in the summer of 1967. Using the same "tools" as always, he networked his way into the company of real estate mogul and Utopian builder Robert E. Simon (R. E. S. Town— "Reston"), a man whose holdings included Carnegie Hall, and won support from him for housing and training the best high school instrumentalists in America every summer in Northern Virginia. After that, he gave full expression to his ideas in a brochure—"anything that can be printed . . . " and, using a list obtained from a friend at the Music Educators National Conference headquarters in Washington, D.C., announced two full scholarships for string players from the 100 best high school orchestras in the country. The brochure, on which my name and photograph appeared, described the entire curriculum, schedule, and instrumental faculty for the Reston Music Center. It was real!

Reston itself was a courageous experiment in multi-use holistic community planning. Laid out on a bucolic tract in the Northern Virginia countryside, Simon's grand design included a high-rise residential tower lakeside twenty miles from Washington, D.C., as well as other high-density homes, shops, and restaurants. Pathways throughout Reston enabled children to walk to school without crossing a street. Fifty years later, Simon's concept would be almost commonplace; but in 1967, it was too futuristic to succeed. Gulf Oil and John Hancock Insurance Company rescued Reston in exchange for watering it down, adopting a more-typical suburban configuration. Besides compromising Simon's vision, his new partners took a dim view of summer music-making in the steeplechase field across from the entrance.

Pfohl charged ahead anyway, trusting that other sources of support would materialize. His new summer camp opened on the date announced and welcomed dozens of young musicians from all over America at a registration station manned by volunteers in the town's new Elementary School. Driving into Reston, most of the parents and students noticed the construction underway in a patch of pine woods down the hill from a huge blue and white circus tent. At registration they learned the tent would be their concert hall and the tent village eventually their housing. In the meantime, they would live with hospitable Reston families. This news disenchanted and offended one family so much, they turned around on the spot and drove all the way back to Albuquerque!

It is a tribute to the power of music that so many others stayed. Skunks nesting beneath their tents and showers that ran cold when the students moved in did not dissuade them. Sleepy teenagers with instruments in their hands emerged from the woods every morning and slogged through rising morning mist up the sunlit steeplechase field to the blue and white circus tent. A joyful cacophony soon filled the air, and "Service to Youth Through Music" worked its magic once again!

Presser Foundation scholarships and State Department travel grants continued in force for a second year, giving five other Central American students the opportunity to live and work at Reston. Humberto Ayestas was once again their translator, guide and mentor. A scrawny young student from Masaya, Nicaragua, who arrived at Dulles Airport carrying only his trumpet and an almost-empty suitcase, became a hero of the camp when he performed brilliantly at the season-ending student recital.

Danny Werts, who along with David Weber had been my first oboe student in Charlotte, was now a full scholarship student of composer Milton Babbitt at Princeton University. He and I were roommates who shared an apartment in the high-rise building overlooking Lake Reston. We often accompanied Dr. Pfohl to a nearby grocery store for steak and watercress.

"Boys, I need muh 'cress!" he would exclaim happily as he sorted through each leafy bundle. One-night Danny and I watched him at the entrance of the building far below, imploring his secretary for a goodnight kiss.

Among the outstanding musicians who attended the Reston Music Center that summer were the son of an army general, oboist James Ryon, who went on to an outstanding career as performer and teacher, and Cynthia Siebert, a pianist who founded and ran The Friends of Chamber Music in Kansas City. Cynthia's sister, flutist Renée, would one day welcome me to the front row of woodwinds in the New York Philharmonic.

Pianist Byron Janis was soloist at the Reston Music Center's final concert of the summer. Priscilla Rappolt, the newly-hired second oboist of the Baltimore Symphony, was tuning the Steinway grand piano when a ferocious late-afternoon storm blew the concert tent down upon her. She escaped serious injury by crawling underneath the piano. Despite the calamity, in the best show business tradition, the concert took place as scheduled that night in the local high school auditorium.

A personal triumph for me that summer was "closing the deal" on a request for $50,000 from Jack Bowman, owner and CEO of Virginia Gentleman and other fine bourbons in Fairfax. His generous contribution extended the Reston Music Center several years beyond its inaugural season and confirmed my potential as a fund-raiser!

Atlanta: Getting Started

As in Mobile, the first order of business was to find housing in Atlanta that would allow me to work on reeds and practice at any hour of the day or night. Once again wealthy symphony volunteers put their heads together and recommended the guest house of one of their members.

They said it would be a perfect place if renovations were finished in time.

Margaret Sims, despite being elderly and wheelchair-bound, was a Southern lady too lovely and rich not to remarry. Her much younger husband, Ben—long a bachelor born in Birmingham, Alabama a century too late—had been Personnel Director for the Lockheed Corporation in Marietta until Attorney General Robert Kennedy's threats of lawsuits for his racist employment practices forced him to retire. In Atlanta, he found and married Margaret and her three-acre spread at the corner of Northside Drive and Mt. Paran Road. Dressed daily in one-piece bib overalls and wearing heavy mud-caked brogans, Ben trudged around their little plantation pushing a wheelbarrow like an ordinary laborer, digging footings for a lap pool and working in the gardens below their house. His fleshy, effeminate face was adorned with myopic rimless round glasses and a military buzz cut—both incongruous atop his tall muscular body. The Sims' guest cottage itself was a cute one-bedroom version of the main house—board-and batten wood-framed painted loden green shutters with a fireplace. Ben had just finished restoring it when I arrived.

In the early months of our association, Ben invited me occasionally to the big house for breakfast, where Margaret welcomed me warmly and Ben did all the work. He arranged fresh flowers; set the table beautifully; cooked and served the most lavish assortment of Southern specialties—cheese grits, biscuits with pepper jelly and homemade preserves, scrambled eggs with crunchy little sausage patties, broiled pink grapefruit (the menu was always the same); and he cleaned up afterwards. Conversation on those occasions was politely constrained—usually about the Atlanta Symphony or the weather. Ben always spoke in muted tones in Margaret's company. When he and I were alone, however, his honeyed Southern accent roiled with suppressed political fury and an unremitting hatred of the Kennedys. The morning after Bobby was shot in California in 1968, Ben came giggling to knock on my cottage door and report "good" news!

The cover story in *TIME* magazine that week posited that wicked thoughts inevitably engender wicked deeds. Unrestrained hatred sooner or later breeds tragedy.

Atlanta was a city of about one million residents in 1967, energetic and "rarin' to go—"a city too busy to hate!" Although Lester Maddox, Georgia's segregationist "Anti-Governor," would soon inhabit the new Governor's Mansion, Mayor Ivan Allen and Editor Ralph McGill were Atlanta progressives much admired throughout America. Major corporations were rushing to establish regional offices in a city that touted itself as **the** business, banking, and distribution center of the Southeast. John Portman's rakish open-atrium design for the Regency Hyatt Hotel, with its "space-capsule" elevators and rotating rooftop restaurant, epitomized the promise of a resurgent downtown. The arrival of professional sports teams and the prospect of a huge new international airport fueled a surge of civic pride in Atlanta. Atlanta was on the move and the arts rode the wave.

A plane crash at Orly Airport in Paris on June 3, 1962 killed 106 of Atlanta's cultural leaders, a tragedy that motivated creation of a major arts center in their memory.

It included a new 2,200-seat concert hall for the Atlanta Symphony scheduled to open in October 1968. Until then Robert Shaw would have to conduct Opening Night in the Atlanta Arena, a smelly barn of a place that hosted the circus and rodeo every year, and other subscription concerts of the 1967-68 season in the Atlanta Civic Auditorium. Both venues had terrible acoustics.

My first rehearsal with the Atlanta Symphony took place in Clark Howell Junior High School on a September afternoon late enough for orchestra members with "day jobs" (which was most of them) to finish their work. Even Concertmaster Martin Sauser closed his insurance office in Decatur before grabbing his violin and heading for the school. Robert Shaw, determined to put his "best foot forward," wisely programmed Beethoven's *Ninth Symphony* with its triumphant choral section for Opening Night. Sputtering a few self-conscious words of welcome to everyone, he announced, "Ladies and Gentlemen, let's begin with the third movement."—the easiest one for him to conduct. He was dressed in what we soon recognized as his rehearsal "uniform"—a metallic blue shirt open at the collar with a towel tossed over his left shoulder; and by the time of the rehearsal break, he was dripping so much perspiration we believed the rumor that his nickname at the Cleveland Orchestra was "Sweaty-Pie!"

I was in my chair scraping on a reed during the break when the flutist next to me drew from his pants pocket a large switchblade knife, which (ZING!) he opened in a flash! Looking slyly at me and chuckling, he began to clean his nails with it. Warren Little, a denizen among local musicians of the Atlanta Symphony, was a full-blooded native American who had studied at Eastman and returned to rejoin his hometown orchestra. People told me Warren played baritone saxophone in local strip joints and was licensed as a union enforcer to carry a gun in his car. His wife was the beautiful principal bassist of the orchestra, whom he was reputed to have defended in brutal ways from time to time.

"Crunch, crunch, crunch" went the switchblade.

I made my first mistake as Warren's colleague when I looked over at his grimy fingers and exclaimed, "Say, Warren, I'm glad to see you've got something there that can do the job!" Warren Little was truly the Godfather of the Atlanta Symphony; and, during our six years together in the orchestra, he was never without that knife.

Back at my audition for Robert Shaw in Cleveland, no one told me that my new job in the Atlanta Symphony would be entitled "Co-Principal Oboe." Consequently, when I arrived at my first rehearsal, I assumed that the first oboe chair was mine. Pat McFarland was already warming up on the other side of second oboist Jean Cavanaugh where my assistant should be, apparently reconciled to his change of status. An incident three days later, however, called that into question. Shaw's first hire as Music Director was Alan Balter, a brilliant young clarinetist from Oberlin whom Shaw looked for as soon as he stepped on the podium at the dress rehearsal of Beethoven's *Ninth*.

"Where is Mr. Balter?" he asked, surveying the orchestra.

From behind the first violin section, Alan waved sheepishly at him.

"Wait a minute! I am Principal Clarinet of this orchestra, Mr. Shaw," Leroy Johnston interrupted, jumping to his feet behind me and shouting, "This is **my** chair!"

We held our breath in anticipation of would happen next.

"Well, Mr. Johnston, I am M-M-Music Director of this orchestra," stammered Shaw, "and I demand that you to move aside im . . . im . . .**immediately**!!"

"Sir, I will not do that," said Leroy shaking with emotion—whereupon he crashed to the floor, overcome by stress of the confrontation. Stage hands rushed from the wings and pulled him off stage, and I never saw clarinetist Leroy Johnston again. Meanwhile, Pat McFarland, cooperating with the new regime, stayed the course as my assistant and was rewarded the next season with a promotion to Solo English horn, where he distinguished himself for more than forty years.

"Get out of bed and get dressed!" exclaimed a voice in my telephone early one Sunday morning. "I am coming to pick you up!" It was Wyche Fowler. "We are going to go hear 'the next Peter Marshall!'" he said. John Randolph Taylor's preaching at Church of the Pilgrim in Washington, D.C. had caused eager parishioners to line up around the block to attend his services. And this was to be Randy Taylor's first Sunday as new Senior Pastor of Atlanta's Central Presbyterian Church. We **had** to be there!

Central Presbyterian was one of those downtown churches proud to remain in the city—as solid in its sense of urban mission as the limestone blocks it was made of. Operating a daycare center and homeless shelter and soup kitchen directly across from the Georgia State Capitol, it served as the rallying point for thousands of mourners who came to Atlanta for the funeral of Martin Luther King, Jr. in April 1968. By that time, I was fully engaged in the musical life of the church. Annette Sparks, wife of a Davidson College fraternity brother, was the superb organist, and a charismatic fellow named Don Robinson conducted the choir, which I joined as a mediocre second tenor. I also played oboe obligato parts and preludes and offertories when needed. "Randy" Taylor hooked me with his first brilliant sermon, for which he chose the perfect scriptural verse: "In the beginning was the **Word**." (John 1:1).

In my second year as a professional oboist, the Atlanta Symphony Orchestra season was blessedly short (just thirty weeks), with subscription concerts performed only once a week. At that pace, I could just about keep up with reed-making. In the much busier years that ensued, I would have to fly to Cleveland many times for rescue. John Mack was always welcoming and unstinting with his assistance; but he never again gave me a reed of his own to play on.

A different kind of trip occurred in the spring of 1968, when Warren Little invited me to go with him to Nashville for a country music recording date and an audition with the Nashville Symphony's new Music Director, Thor Johnson. Principal flute and principal oboe positions were both open;

and Warren told me that even though he was not interested in the job, winning it would provide "horizontal leverage" that might improve his contract in Atlanta. I should do the same. Warren said he would do the negotiating for both of us if our auditions were successful. Things went as he predicted, and we were both invited to join the Nashville Symphony. Thor's offer to me was $250 a week plus three weeks of summer employment in his Peninsula Music Festival in Door County, Wisconsin. When Warren explained to Robert Shaw what had happened, Shaw immediately matched Nashville's weekly salary rate for both of us. Additionally, he covered the summer part of my Nashville offer by sending $500 to the Marlboro Music Festival in Vermont for the privilege of my auditing there. We agreed to call it a "professional development grant" paid for by the Atlanta Symphony's Board of Directors, but I feel certain Shaw wrote the check himself.

Georgia is a "right to work" state. Despite that, ancient Personnel Manager Harry Robkin told me I would have to join the local musicians' union or risk being black-balled by my colleagues. He said guest artists would refuse to perform with the Atlanta Symphony if I did not. In 1967 there were around 1,100 members of the Atlanta Federation of Musicians, only 300 or so called themselves full-time, and only about ninety of whom were in the classical field. Twenty-five members constituted a legal quorum. Because union meetings were scheduled when Atlanta Symphony players could not participate, our work dues rose unchallenged year after year.

In the fall of 1970, I was finally able to attend a meeting in the ballroom of the old Biltmore Hotel. On stage in front of me a few beefy men who looked like gangsters were running the show. When dispensing with a reading of the Treasurer's Report was moved and seconded, I rose in protest to complain that I had been a member of the union for years and had never seen a financial statement.

"I would like to **hear** the Treasurer's Report!" I said.

Annoyed discussion ensued on stage before a man in a dark suit approached the lectern and read a few incomprehensible numbers, after which he stepped back and glowered at me. I hadn't learned anything from his report; but as I left the ballroom following the meeting, I found the doorway blocked by a beefy guy whose breath was hot in my face as he growled,

"Dawn y'lack the way we do bidness down he-uh, baweh?"

That is when I realized that union reform and oboe playing were not going to be compatible!

An impatient community mandate supported Robert Shaw's intention to upgrade the Atlanta Symphony, and complicity with the local union was needed to facilitate replacing weaker players with stronger ones. Prior to arriving in town as the Atlanta Symphony's Music Director, Shaw had secretly observed orchestra rehearsals and concerts and assessed each player, targeting the ones he decided had to go. By moving rehearsals to 10:00 a.m. in the 1968-69 season, he forced players to choose between their day jobs and the orchestra, which took care of some of the weaker musicians. Others were shoved aside by newcomers like me, and several others were recruited and hired without audition by Concertmaster Martin Sauser acting as Shaw's agent.

Two Michaels

In form as well as substance, Music Director Robert Shaw emulated his Cleveland mentor, George Szell. He made Atlanta's harried and over-worked librarians copy into every player's music the precise marks that were in Szell's own scores—even to the extent of spelling out every note of a trill. Sometimes it seemed there was a special instruction above every single note of the music! Szell's timings were the touchstones of Shaw's interpretive success, and Shaw's secretary, Eddie Burrus, or his favorite contralto, Florence Kopleff after she moved to Atlanta, often sat at a table just off stage with a stopwatch, checking to see if the orchestra's tempos precisely conformed to Szell's. When they did not, Shaw would growl "Da capo!" and we would play the piece or movement again from the beginning. If Szell wore a metallic blue shirt with a towel over one shoulder for rehearsal, Shaw did the same. If Szell had several assistants listed on the masthead of his Cleveland Orchestra programs, Shaw would need them also.

He found the first one in Rome in the class of Franco Ferrara—the famous "fainting maestro" forced to exchange lecterns for concert podia because of his embarrassing disability. Michael Zearott was accompanist for Jasha Heifetz's master classes at UCLA and the university's first Ph.D. in Music before traveling to Italy. After finishing his studies with Ferrara, Zearott came to Atlanta affecting the continental manner of a great maestro, with stringy black hair flowing and a jacket carried casually over one shoulder. In addition to flambouyance, Zearott possessed perfect pitch, a photographic memory, and prodigious keyboard skills—none of which were Shaw's! In order to bring him into line and "teach him who was boss," Shaw forced Zearott to accompany the Robert Shaw Chorale on a tour in the summer of 1967, during which time he bullied and harassed him continually at the keyboard.

For all of his musical gifts, conductor Zearott had a fatal flaw—he lived in a musical dream world. For example, following a particularly unfortunate concert in Milledgeville, Georgia when Zearott begged me to tell him if I thought he had conducted well, I said that his own performance itself was brilliant but bore no relationship at all to what was going on in the orchestra. He might as well have been conducting a recording! Zearott was out of touch in other ways also, too self-absorbed to be socially graceful. Despite this, I liked him. I liked his theatricality and zest for music, his extravagant language, and his deep-throated laughter. We double-dated a few times (his girlfriend was a hefty blond named "Blue" Calhoun); and we played tennis and even cooked peach pancakes together at my guest house. In the spring of 1968, Michael Zearott became the last winner of the Mitropoulos Conducting Competition in New York City. His prize was assignment to the Monte Carlo Opera, where seasoned European pit musicians quickly ate him alive!

Robert Shaw needed a more compliant assistant as a buffer between himself and the brilliant but prickly Zearott; so he turned to another of his mentors, Julius Herford of Indiana University, to find twenty-one-year-old Michael Palmer—a keyboard artist and conducting phenom from Indianapolis. This second Michael joined Shaw before the beginning of the 1967-68 season and stayed with him for ten years. He was as unassuming as Zearott was pretentious; as eager as Zearott was surly; as relentlessly cheerful as Zearott was brooding. He was a Midwestern **innocent** in love with music and a perfect Shaw factotum.

If Robert Shaw feared the orchestra, Michael Palmer disarmed us by revealing no fear at all. When he was called upon on short notice to replace Shaw, as he often was (the excuse for Shaw's absences being "hemorrhoids" rather than "drunkenness"), Palmer's equanimity of the podium amazed us. On these occasions, he conducted important works with little or no preparation blithely unaware of the music's difficulty or the orchestra's disrespect—demonstrating once again the truth of Thomas Gray's old adage: "Where ignorance is bliss, 'tis folly to be wise!" Michael Palmer was a very gifted musician who became one of the important American conductors of his generation.

Robert Shaw

Robert Shaw's biographer, Keith Burris, refers continually in Deep River to Shaw's insecurities in front of an orchestra. He says that Shaw came from Cleveland to the cultural backwater of Atlanta not only to liberate himself from slavish subordination to George Szell, but to escape national scrutiny while he exorcised his demons—demons which every member of the Atlanta Symphony recognized as soon as our rehearsals began with him. At the same time, everyone in the orchestra marveled at the "other" Robert Shaw—the one who conducted the chorus in the last movement of Beethoven's Ninth later that week with absolute confidence and supreme mastery. Our collective perception of two very different conductors in the same man never changed or abated during my six years with Robert Shaw in Atlanta.

While it is true that Shaw urged instrumentalists to play more like singers—i.e., with "longer vocal lines," and exhorted choristers to sing more like instrumentalists— with greater precision and clarity, in the case of singers, he knew (and knew that he knew) precisely how to achieve unsurpassed choral results, and in the case of orchestra musicians, he was totally unsure of himself. He could never forget that he was not an instrumentalist or even a well-trained musician. In the one case, he possessed power **and** authority, and in the other, power without authority. He often protested that it was not his idea to seek the music directorship of the Atlanta Symphony; it was the orchestra's Board Chairman who sought him and begged him to take the job. As an oboist with nearly eight years of "non-musical insurance," I recognized Shaw's psychological "cop-out" perfectly!

Perhaps that is why Robert Shaw and I got along. Both of us strove to prove something—he to his minister/ father that music was as redemptive as religion, I to my conservative parents that artistic excellence was compatible with the middle-class values they cherished. In Nice Marcel Tabuteau had convinced me that Absolute Truth inhabits "good notes"—something Shaw affirmed in word and deed every day; and this shared conviction both motivated and discouraged us. Motivated because it impelled us to "scorn delights and live laborious days;" and discouraged because we knew the musical perfection we sought was unattainable. Our best efforts were never—**could never be**—good enough! Deep down both of us felt inadequately prepared for our jobs.

Growing up, neither of us learned to play the piano or completed conservatory training. Shaw studied English, Philosophy, and Comparative religions at Pomona College, perhaps explaining his pretentious preference for convoluted rather than ordinary patterns of speech—e.g., "Your execution was substantially more handsome in the reprise, Mr. Robinson," as well as his ferocious social conscience. I studied English and economics at Davidson College, and my liberal political bent mirrored Shaw's enough to please him. He was never certain of my skills as an oboist, however, until they were confirmed by the New York Philharmonic audition many years later.

Robert Shaw was a powerful, kinetic, and handsome man. But he was ungraceful both on and off the podium; and his boyish looks ("Ah shucks!") in middle age were deceiving—a deliberate repudiation of the long-haired, courtly conductor stereotype. As Shaw's biographer Keith Burris has pointed out, Shaw could smile and chill a person at the same time with an intense blue-eyed gaze; and he tended to punctuate even casual conversations with nervous, breathy cackles. He lumbered hunch-shouldered when he walked, despite sometimes taking a cute little skip on his way to the podium. Returning for a final solo bow after performances, he would hang his head as if embarrassed. (Keith Burris is convinced that Robert Shaw was a sincerely humble man; but I agree instead with Shaw's old friend Thornton Wilder, that "mock-humble" would be a better characterization.) Shaw desperately craved adulation but hated himself for craving it.

On the podium without a chorus, Shaw clung to the beat the way frightened riders cling to the lock-bar of a roller coaster. In many of those early ASO concerts, dripping profusely, he would stare down at the score, tracing the progress of the music with one finger and throwing blind cues to solo players (when he remembered them) with another. Even the rhythmic pulse sometimes betrayed him. Performing Tchaikovsky's *Romeo and Juliet* on a tour in Florida one night, Shaw lost his place and stabbed into empty air a few times after the orchestra had finished the piece. Mortified, he fled in his tails and white tie out the stage door and disappeared into the night. Michael Palmer told me Shaw talked about purchasing one-way airline tickets to remote parts of the world that evening. When he returned in time for our next concert in Tampa, he announced that he had reserved the city's best restaurant, "Las Novedades," for the entire orchestra following our performance—dinner that included an open bar, the restaurant's famous signature dish, "Pompano papillote" and unlimited amounts of delicious Spanish wine. Buses were scheduled to transport us. Altogether, it was the most extravagant act of atonement I have ever witnessed. (And I was not the only member of the orchestra who drank too much that night!)

It is my opinion that Robert Shaw's championing of new music, which he professed to be a moral duty, was really a subterfuge—a way of avoiding comparison with other great conductors' mastery of the symphonic classics. Conducting the complex music by Charles Ives, for example, insured him the upper hand, because all of us in the orchestra struggled just to play Ives' notes and stay together.

"Try harder" was the mantra for every Shaw concert. The tension we experienced in his performances was relentless and unremitting. What a difference young James Levine made when he came to guest conduct! His music-making was so effortless, natural and joyful, it was as if windows had been flung open and fragrant spring air filled the rehearsal room! Both Robert Shaw and James Levine issued from Szell's Cleveland Orchestra, but they were the antithesis of each other in terms of musical technique and temperament.

Shaw was lionized in Atlanta. He was to the Symphony what Norm Van Brocklin was to the Falcons—a national figure whose presence itself validated his organization. America's "Culture Boom" was happening everywhere in 1967, and Atlanta rushed to participate. Matching funds quickly released $1,750,000 for the Symphony from the Ford Foundation, making impressive growth possible in the orchestra's size and season length for many years to come.

My contract for the 1968-69 season read "Principal Oboe for 36 weeks at $250 a week." My salary as an oboist had almost doubled in two years. I felt that I was on my way!

Summer 1968

In June, I revisited Central America and stayed for a week in Guatemala City with Davidson College exchange student Fernando Rodas and his family. A surprising thing happened while I was there. Walking along a downtown street one morning, I noticed what looked like arundo donax (oboe cane) growing in a vacant city lot; and on a hunch, using my pen knife, I cut down a couple of stalks and, chopping them into 4-to-5-inch lengths, put them in my suitcase to bring back to the States. Later that month at my parents' home in Lenoir, I scattered the little tubes all around the back yard to cure in the sun. Then I deposited them in a plastic bag and forgot about them for five years. It was one of those pieces of Guatemalan cane that yielded the reed that won me the New York Philharmonic Principal Oboe audition in December 1977!

After Guatemala, despite suffering serious stomach distress, I flew on to San Salvador to perform the Bach Double Concerto for Oboe and Violin with a local virtuoso, Miguel Serrano, and then to San Jose, Costa Rica, for a reunion and recital with soprano Maria Blanco.

John Mack had told me to wait until he gave the word before applying to the Marlboro Music Festival, but I was serving food in the dining room when he arrived for dinner in July 1968. Tony Checchia, the Philadelphia bassoonist whose compliments so encouraged me when I was in the Princeton University Symphony, was personnel manager for Rudolph Serkin at Marlboro; and he had arranged a room for me in a wonderful eighteenth century guest house nearby. He invited me to audit rehearsals and concerts for a month and even to play a woodwind quintet with the great clarinetist, Harold Wright, as an audition for the following year. Shaw's subsidy made that possible.

Marlboro was musical heaven! In 1951 Rudolf Serkin, Adolphe Busch and Marcel, Blanche and Louis Moyse envisioned a retreat for themselves in the wooded hills of Southern Vermont, and a cluster of white-washed frame buildings at tiny Marlboro College became their summer home. Inspired by the beauty of Nature away from pressures of commercial performance, they searched with other of the greatest musicians in the world for musical truth on their own terms.

For me Marlboro was a place where I could play golf with John Mack at Mt. Snow and schedule REAL oboe lessons with him on campus. In one of those, tooting through a Barret articulation study on a reed constructed from one of the 100 pieces of cane Marcel Tabuteau mailed to me shortly before he died, I was interrupted by John Mack when he asked intently, "Where did you get that gouge?"

(Tabuteau had told me in Nice, "The gouge is EVERYTHING!" but how John Mack recognized **by sound alone** the gouge's subtle contribution to my finished reed was something he never adequately explained.)

In a later lesson, Mack showed me how to replace a defective octave key pad with a piece of bottle-stopper cork and ferrule cement obtained at a hardware store in Brattleboro, initiating a process that inspired replacement of a thousand other pads over the years and fostered self-reliance in the maintenance of my instrument. Eventually I learned to do just about everything except pin a crack.

Most importantly, Marlboro was a place where I could listen to John Mack play chamber music; attend the orchestra's recording sessions for Schubert and Mozart Symphonies; and hear Pablo Casals confirm Marcel Tabuteau's precepts about the Interpretive Art of Music. If the venerable old cellist—ninety-one years old and still heralded as "the greatest living classical musician"—used different terminology, his obsession with "playing music between the notes;" extending the curved musical line; inflecting every note and phrase "up" or "down"; articulating incisively; and respecting rhythmic pulse was the same as Tabuteau's. Casals described **"nuances"** as "ups" and "downs" formed "within their dynamic." That is, every dynamic level (which Tabuteau described with numbers instead of the familiar letters, pp, p, mp, mf, f, etc.) was a zone within which nuances could be sculpted. Formed in this way, "ups" and "downs" could be strung together like pearls on a thread or roll like waves, imparting forward motion and coherence to music by revealing the time signature in the melody. Both Marcel Tabuteau and Pablo Casals regarded "up-down distributions" in the same way, conceiving of musical phrasing in binary form fifty years before computers!

Conducting the Marlboro Festival Orchestra, Casals was less concerned with (or took for granted with such a great ensemble) the mundane matters of precise ensemble and accurate intonation than with "straight notes." Those were what really upset him.

"Ugly! Ugly!" he bellowed when cellists persisted in holding unchanging tones. "You call that music?" A straight note was to Casals like a dead limb on a tree—better cut off and thrown away! He knew that music, like every other organic thing in Nature, must change shape, color, texture and pulse to be alive.

"Never play the same music twice the same way!" was something he also preached continually. Mutability is indeed the *sine qua non* of life.

Casals was obsessed with revealing the architecture of the music. Notes on the page, he said, were just a blueprint. It was up to performers to build the composer's "house!" And Casals constantly reminded everyone what a privilege it was to do this: "Dear friends," he would say. "Believe me . . . **we musicians** are the **most fortunate** human beings."

John Mack warned me that if I didn't sit on the front row at orchestra rehearsals and hang onto every word that fell from Casals' lips, he would never play golf with me. It was an unnecessary ultimatum. I absorbed Casals like a sponge! At one of his afternoon master classes, for instance, when Casals used cellist Ron Leonard (future Principal Cello of the Los Angeles Philharmonic) as his guinea pig, he spent three hours explaining the tension inherent in dotted rhythms.

"Lahee-ya-DAH!" he sang over and over again, exploding the last syllable to demonstrate the propulsive force of the dot between the dotted eighth and sixteenth notes. Dotted figures, he insisted, are not just inert arithmetical subdivisions; they are **little rhythmic engines that motivate the melody!**

Since that afternoon, I have never played them any other way.

In August, I traversed the Upper Peninsula of Michigan and boarded a car ferry in Grand Haven that took me across Lake Michigan. From there I drove north to Fish Creek, Wisconsin, to participate in the Peninsula Music Festival. Thor Johnson had invited me to play second oboe, despite my rejection of the full-time position with him in Nashville. In beautiful Door County, I once again encountered Walter Jouval, the remarkable Israeli oboist who had followed John Mack as principal in New Orleans, whom I had met at my own audition for his job the previous year. When Jouval left New Orleans to join the National Symphony, he did not know that Jimmy Caldwell had already agreed to return to Washington, D.C. as soon as the last year of his contract with the Philadelphia Chamber Orchestra was completed. That deal made Jouval a sacrificial lamb unfairly dismissed after one season. He was fortunate to have landed in the oboe chair I rejected in Nashville.

Despite training in Paris, Jouval was avidly reforming his reeds to comply with requirements of the Tabuteau School, eager to learn whatever I could teach him. In exchange for a few John Mack reed secrets, he taught me how to use slip knots to finish tying cane on the staple; how to double-tongue (saying "kitty-kitty" to express two articulations with one stroke of the tongue); and how to "circular breathe" (to inhale while playing). These tricks of the trade were enormously helpful to me throughout my career.

Jouval was a powerful, barrel-chested man, broadly-educated and multilingual. I admired his exuberance and his devotion to his wife Dvora and their two young children. Before the last concert of the Festival in Fish Creek, he asked Thor Johnson if I could play first oboe on the program's opening overture. He said he would take the second part himself. It was an extraordinarily gracious gesture that set the stage for my replacing him in Fish Creek the following summer. We remained friends for many years.

Second ASO season: 1968-69

The grand opening of the Memorial Arts Center in the fall of 1968 created great excitement in Atlanta. For the occasion Shaw chose the Gloria by his friend Francis Poulenc. Our season was now thirty-six weeks long, with subscription concerts performed three times instead of once. As the only principal oboe player, my work load had jumped in one year by a factor of more than six. Consequently, when I wasn't practicing, rehearsing or concertizing, I was changing the curve of my gouging machine blade (John Mack congratulated me for "falling through the ice") or chopping and scraping oboe cane. There was little time for anything else.

Despite this, I continued my determination to foster arts programs in support of Central American unification, by developing and discussing with Robert Shaw in February an elaborate proposal to send the Atlanta Symphony Woodwind Quintet on tour to the five countries of the isthmus from May 20 to June 22 during the summer of 1969. In terms of diplomacy, the proposal expressed my favorite diplomatic principle of "cultural sharing" rather than hit-and-run "cultural display." Atlanta wind players were to collaborate in shared performances and open rehearsals in every capital city (but most intensively during a week-long residency in San Salvador) with local musicians, teachers, and students. We would coach ensembles, teach private lessons, repair instruments, and share sources information about tools and supplies.

Defending my approach, I wrote in a ten-page proposal.

"This project is based on the premise that exemplary performance and the intensive sharing of musical techniques are not mutually exclusive goals. Excellence is inspirational where there is strong identification between those who have attained excellence and those who aspire to it. By sharing performances with local musicians, both in recitals and in concert with the National Orchestra of El Salvador, the Atlanta Symphony Woodwind Quintet will demonstrate that its own levels of performance are accessible. The gap between performers and listeners, between visitors and hosts, will be narrowed."

I estimated costs for the entire tour at slightly less than $5,000.

Copies were mailed to the Office of Cultural Presentations, the Council on Leaders and Specialists, the Office of Inter-American Programs within the Bureau of Educational and. Cultural Affairs within the U.S. Department of State, as well as to embassy cultural affairs officers in Central America; but only one component of the proposal (thanks to Robert Shaw who paid for it once again himself) came to fruition. Packages of woodwind quintet scores and parts were sent to the national orchestras of Guatemala, El Salvador, and Costa Rica as "gifts in friendship" from Robert Shaw and the Atlanta Symphony Orchestra. Quite a lot of regional press acknowledged the gifts.

(Pictured below are Robert Ebersole, Cultural Affairs Officer at the U. S. Embassy in Guatemala City, and Conductor Ricardo del Carmen, Music Director of the Guatemala National Orchestra, examining some of the music.)

Meanwhile, over at Emory Law School, my friend Wyche Fowler decided that by baby-sitting Mayor Ivan Allen's office after hours, he and other law students could respond effectively to citizen complaints and requests that came into City Hall overnight. Being Atlanta's first "Night Mayor" gave Wyche a launching pad for a political career that eventually propelled him from the Atlanta Board of Aldermen to the United States Senate. George Mason Miller III, meanwhile, still struggling to finish his PhD. with John Hope Franklin at the University of Chicago, arrived in Atlanta to begin teaching Black History at Morehouse College.

Robert Shaw's commitment to racial equality in Atlanta's musical life expressed itself early and often in his growing friendship with conductor Wendall Whalum, his inclusion of singers from Morehouse and Spelman College in the Atlanta Symphony Chorus, and his programming of music by black composers such as T. J. Anderson, John Lewis and William Grant Still. Chamber music groups dispatched from the ASO often performed in Atlanta's segregated schools. At the first of these in which I played, during a question and answer session that followed our woodwind quintet recital, a young lady in the back of the audience waved her arm, stood up, and asked loudly, "Hey, Oboe! Why does yo' eyes bug out when you play that thing?" At which Warren Little fell from his chair onto the stage and roared with laughter!

As time passed, Warren's teasing and taunting turned hard-edged and threatening, making life difficult especially for Alan Balter and me. One of us seemed always to be the target of Warren's practical jokes or scorn. In a rehearsal of Stravinsky's *Pulcinella,* for instance, in the "Tarantella" section, Warren began furiously tapping his foot out of time next to me during an oboe solo. Shaw looked up in surprise as I crashed and burned. When Warren's turn came a little later in the piece and I did the same thing to him, he stomped my ankle so hard it bled into my shoe.

"The trouble with you, Big Daddy," I said through my pain at the rehearsal break, "is that you can't take your own medicine!"

"Come out in the parking lot," he growled, "and I'll show you some medicine!" It was just the beginning . . .

At first Robert Shaw would call me offstage before concerts or have the Personnel Manager put little notes on my stand advising me how to improve the oboe part. Later he preferred post-concert critiques downstairs in his dressing room, where he sometimes stepped pink and steaming from his shower and conducted inquisitions in his birthday suit.

"I cued you three times tonight in the Hindemith, g-g-g-goddammit Robinson, and you didn't come in on time! What's the matter?" he growled, scratching himself immodestly.

"Yes, yes, I know, Mr. Shaw," I explained, looking around the room. "I have been in a reed slump this week and had to sacrifice response for the sake of a decent tone. I'm sorry."

"Listen!" vigorously stroking his back two-handed with a towel, "I can't tell one tone from another; but if you don't c-c-c-come in when I cue you, I'll have to find an oboe player who will!"

That is when the lead horse pulling my three-horse reed chariot became "Response" instead of "Tone" or "Pitch/Pitch Stability!" Marcel Tabuteau had underlined the importance of response when he insisted, "A big tone comes from a little tone, and not the other way around!" or "The most beautiful tone is the 'dolce tone,' and the 'dolce tone' is closest to **zero**!" But for years I resisted response in favor of a having bigger oboe voice. The confrontation with Robert Shaw reminded me of Tabuteau's maxims and moved me along the tonal continuum closer to Philadelphia (John DeLancie) and further away from Cleveland (John Mack). Because of that, Mack would tell me that, despite playing pretty well, I sounded as if I had "a concentration camp tone!"

Most young players in small American orchestras cannot obtain the best oboe cane. That is why I asked Walter Jouval to translate into French a direct appeal from me to some of the wholesalers on the list John Mack had given me when I was in Europe. As soon as I received his translated letter and sent it with a $25.00 personal check to six or eight of those cane growers, the results were amazing! Donati returned a box the size of a small chair full of uncured cane. Brignone and Rabbia sent assortments of tubes that looked like organ pipes—sized for English horn, clarinet, and baritone saxophone as well as oboe. Marcelle Ghys returned a note explaining that since all of her good tube cane was sold already, would I please accept a bundle of 300 gouged pieces instead? I still have some of it.

"Faithful obedience to the wishes of the composer" was a mantra much-recited by Shaw and many other conductors early in my career; but one particular experience called its validity into question. The Southeastern Composers Forum was a professional association celebrating members' creative talents and rewarding the best of them with performances by the Atlanta Symphony Orchestra. One of the winning compositions in the spring of 1969 was a woodwind quintet which we were invited to record. Listening to the playback of the first movement in the recording booth with the score in his hands, Warren Little noticed that the time signature was 4/4 instead of the cut time (2/2) we had been playing. When Warren pointed out the discrepancy and apologized to the composer for recording his music at a tempo that was twice as fast as indicated, his reaction was, "Really? I didn't notice. It sounded great to me just the way you played it!"

Interlochen's Arts Academy Orchestra came to perform in Atlanta that spring, conducted by Nicholas Harsanyi. I had not followed Harsanyi's career since leaving Princeton, but it had obviously spread out a bit. On the program was the Fifth Symphony of Dmitri Shostakovich, during which a stunning, raven-haired oboist knocked my socks off with her playing of the heavenly solo in the third movement. I ran backstage to meet seventeen-year-old Elaine Douvas and tell her that she was destined for greatness!

Emory University called to invite me to join their Music Department as an adjunct faculty member. Someone was needed to teach a young graduate student from Mt. Holyoke some oboe lessons for credit, so I readily agreed. Elizabeth Couture was a radiant young woman with delicate features, fine-spun brunette hair and sparkling blue eyes. During our third or fourth lesson, she acted so preoccupied and distracted I thought she must be ill. When the lesson was over, I walked with her into the hallway and asked if everything was alright. Her answer was a wild embrace and kiss full on the mouth! It was the impetuous beginning of a courtship that continued for nearly a year.

Summer 1969

Liz Couture's Roman Catholic family lived in Massachusetts. Her father and brothers were home builders—that is, they dug the foundations, poured the footings, plumbed, wired, and constructed houses themselves. They even built the house her parents lived in. Liz and I stopped to see them on my way north to Marlboro. The plan was for her to fly to meet me the last week of the Peninsula Music Festival, after which we would drive back from Fish Creek to Atlanta together. Despite her attractiveness, I was not as much in love as she was.

A familiar face beamed when I asked if I could join him for lunch my first day at Marlboro. It belonged to Seth McCoy, the magnificent black tenor who had soloed with us in *Messiah* the previous season. Seth introduced me to his neighbor at the table, someone named Oscar Pereira. Oscar was a violinist from Goa who said he was auditing at Marlboro thanks to Alexander Schneider, whom he knew because of an article in *TIME* magazine. Oscar told an amazing story. Schneider's string quartet was touring India, which Oscar said he followed from town to town until he and Schneider could meet. That's when Oscar poured out his heart, telling Schneider how desperately he wanted to be a classical violinist despite scant opportunity in India. He begged Schneider to help him find a way to come to the United States. Several discouraging months passed before a letter came from Schneider, inviting Oscar to come to Marlboro to audit chamber music sessions and even to play in the orchestra with Pablo Casals! Acting on blind faith, like the first emigrants to America, Oscar sold everything and smuggled his money and wife into Canada. She was to wait there until word came from him that he had found employment in an American orchestra.

Just that same morning, Martin Sauser, the Atlanta Symphony Concertmaster and Personnel Manager, telephoned to ask me to keep an eye out for Marlboro string players who might be interested in joining the Atlanta Symphony Orchestra. I had no idea how well Oscar Pereira played violin, but I told him about the Atlanta opportunity and called Sauser as soon as we finished lunch. Sauser said Oscar should come immediately to Atlanta for an audition.

"That's great, Joe! Thank you very much," sang out Oscar in his melodic Indian voice. "But I have no car and no money even to take a bus. How can I possibly get there?"

We had only minutes to ponder the problem before Sauser called again.

"Mr. Shaw says if your friend is good enough for Marlboro, he's good enough for us! Spell his name, and I'll send him a contract."

Robert Shaw (probably at his own expense) sent Oscar to Indiana University the next year for some catch-up work with the great violinist Josef Gingold, after which Oscar remained a grateful and productive member of the violin section of the Atlanta Symphony for many decades.

Seth's story was scarcely less dramatic. He had grown

up in the thirties with grandparents on a farm south of Greensboro, North Carolina. In order to hear classical music, he took the bus into town on Saturdays and listened to recordings in the public library. After enrolling in college at Greensboro A&T, he changed his mind about playing football when he saw how big the college players really were and joined the glee club instead. Seth served for two years in the U. S. Army in Korea, then moved to Cleveland, Ohio, where he worked as a mail clerk in the Post Office for thirteen years and earned spending money singing in black churches on Sunday. His big dream in that era of "Black Capitalism" was to own and operate his own barber shop someday. But people began attending church services just to hear him sing; and one day one of them put him in touch with a voice teacher at the Cleveland Music School Settlement named Pauline Thesmacher. Seth told me Ms. Thesmacher fell on her knees after their first lesson and begged God to protect her from harming his amazing voice! She arranged for Seth to sing for Robert Shaw, who is reported to have wept when he heard him. Shaw immediately invited Seth to join his Chorale on a tour of South America—the beginning of a spectacular career that led Seth to the Bach Aria Group, the Marlboro Music Festival, and the Metropolitan Opera House. Wherever he went in the world, on stage or not, Seth McCoy exhibited a transforming radiance that people never forgot.

By contrast, Leonard Arner came from New York City to Marlboro and was repulsed by the Casals cult. He stayed only for about a week. When he learned that I had a graduate degree from Princeton University, he confronted me to ask incredulously if it were true.

"You went to Princeton and you still want to be an oboe player? Are you crazy? You have been trained to drive a Cadillac, and you prefer a second-hand Jeep? Man! Get out of this business while you still can!" (He really meant it.)

The concert hall at Marlboro College was an open-sided converted gymnasium, not too different from the old one at the Brevard Music Center. Visitors, being careful not to disrupt rehearsals, tiptoed into it quietly through the birch trees and sat reverently watching Pablo Casals conduct the orchestra. I had never witnessed age so venerated. The old cellist's words and gestures were all being recorded for posterity. When his limousine arrived each day, his beautiful young wife Marta opened the door and assisted him to the concert hall. As soon as he appeared on stage, members of the orchestra jumped to their feet while concertmaster Jaime Laredo assisted him onto the podium. A bass stool on which he sat while conducting awaited him there. Sometimes, whenever the music stirred him sufficiently, Casals would rise from that stool and lift his right arm above his head, pointing heavenward. Just the sight of it made the audience gasp and hold their breath!

Pablo Casals was about to conduct Beethoven's Second Symphony one Sunday afternoon when he fumbled putting on his rimless glasses. He blinked through them for a few seconds, unable to see the music in front of him, and returned them to his coat pocket. He then closed the score and conducted the entire symphony with his eyes shut. Despite a few miscues, it was one of the most inspiring performances of my life!

At Marlboro, every participant's weekly schedule was posted on Monday morning. An artistic "Sanhedrin" headed by Rudolf Serkin and Frank Solomon decided who would rehearse what with whom, and at what point the music would have "ripened" sufficiently for public performance. My first great challenge was the Woodwind Quintet by Villa Lobos, in which I worked with the legendary horn player John Barrows and the great bassoonist, Sol Schoenbach. Paula Robison played flute and Larry Combs clarinet. Our performance went well enough for my stock to rise a bit—aided significantly by exhibitions of my Frisbee prowess with Rudolph Serkin's son John in front of the dining hall.

Joe Turner from the Baltimore Symphony and I were the busiest oboists at Marlboro in 1969, both participating in several recording sessions with Pablo Casals; but we still found time for an unusual tool-making adventure that summer. Joe said we should make our own shaper tips (the steel profilers that determine the shape of gouged cane before it is tied onto extensions of the bore called "staples"). Few shaper tips were mass-produced in those days (Angelo "A," Brannen "X," and Prestini "#1," to name a few) and they were notoriously inconsistent. A local tool-maker agreed to sell us some cold-rolled steel stock about 10 mm wide and 5 mm thick; and, with heavy bastard files, we set about forming shaper tips free-hand. It was very tedious . . . we were like a couple of kids playing with clay! But eventually we decided we had something usable and hardened the pieces of steel with a blowtorch and some heated motor oil. The process made us pretty good friends. I actually preferred my shaper tip and used it in Atlanta until I dropped it on the floor and broke one of its "ears" off.

John DeLancie's star Curtis graduate, nineteen-year-old Richard Woodhams, came to Marlboro for a visit. Dick had just won the Solo English horn audition at the New York Philharmonic, but turned that job down to take Principal Oboe in the St. Louis Symphony, replacing the great Alfred Genovese. When all of us learned that Genovese was playing. J.S. Bach's *Double Concerto for Oboe and Violin* at Dartmouth College that weekend, Joe Turner and Dick agreed to go with me to hear him perform. Before setting out in my pale green Rambler American, we were warned that wildfires burning in the White Mountains near our route might envelope parts of I-91 and we should be careful. They were right. A stringent, smoky haze worsened by the hour as we drove north along the Connecticut River.

Our nostrils and eyes were stinging when Dick suddenly shouted from the back seat, "Holy crap! Stop the car! Something is on fire in here!"

Dick's tossed cigarette had blown unseen back into the car and lodged itself behind my suit jacket. A smoldering hole about the size of a softball was widening in the seat cushion next to him and burning away the edge of my coat. Luckily, it had not yet burst into flames. As soon as possible, I pulled over on the interstate; and using my Championship Frisbee, carried water up from a little stream running alongside the highway to put out the fire.

At Dartmouth, Al Genovese was surprised to see us. He apologized for using a student's reed, explaining that he had been learning to fly all summer and had no time to make a reed for himself. We thought he sounded wonderful anyway!

I got a different kind of assignment (or perhaps opportunity) near the end of my stay at Marlboro. It was to perform with Blanche and Louis Moyse in a chamber music concert on July 24 at the library in Bennington, Vermont, for which there would be several rehearsals in the Moyse chalet near Brattleboro. Our time together there was enormous good fun! Their extrovert personalities and irresistible French accents reminded me of Marcel Tabuteau. In addition, Blanche was a fabulous cook! Omnipresent but not obtrusive in the Moyse home during the week was an attractive young secretary named Janet White whose job it was to coordinate the activities of the Moyse Trio and Brattleboro Bach Choral Society. She rode with us up the mountain to Bennington for the recital, which was a big success. Several glasses of wine preceded our return trip home, and Janet and I found ourselves in the back seat of Louis' car being tossed around on the curving road like a couple of teenagers. Quite spontaneously, also like teenagers, we began "making out!" While Louis glowered at us in the rear-view mirror, we careened faster and faster down the mountain toward Brattleboro. Blanche was alarmed and exhorted him repeatedly to slow down; but he ignored her and continued driving like a madman. Five years later Louis Moyse married Janet White!

Back at Fish Creek in August, I was principal oboist now and quite comfortable in the role, but in a rehearsal one morning, Thor Johnson turned on me with surprising fury. He accused me of being inattentive and insubordinate—of sabotaging the rehearsal and undermining his festival! I didn't know what I had done to provoke this reproof, and I felt unfairly stung and embarrassed by it. I decided later that the outburst was a preconceived tantrum dramatizing, as Toscanini often did, his authority and extraordinary concern for music. Shaw tried something like that in Atlanta one time, when he ripped off his wristwatch and smashed it onto the stage floor. Perhaps I just happened to be in the maestro's line of fire that day. Anyway, we got along splendidly after that.

Like Southern Vermont, Door County, Wisconsin, is a beautiful summer resort, famous for its white fish boils on the beaches of Green Bay and for its delicious fresh fruit in season. Thor and his chubby young assistant, cellist Harold Cruthirds (we called him Harold "Two-thirds") lived in a rakish vacation home around the bay from Fish Creek. Other famous musicians such as John Krell (piccolo player from the Philadelphia Orchestra) and Robert Marcellus (clarinetist of the Cleveland Orchestra) also summered in the area. Liz loved it when she came to visit.

Our trip home to Atlanta was less decisive than Liz hoped it would be. In spite of my great affection for her, I remained noncommittal. A newcomer to the Atlanta Symphony Orchestra's first violin section was about to change everything.

Atlanta: 1969-70 season

In the fall of 1969, Mary Kay McQuilkin arrived from Knoxville, where she had replaced her former violin teacher at the University of Tennessee for a year. Several attractive young women joined the orchestra that season, but she was the prettiest.

At the end of a rehearsal one day, she walked over and sat down next to me.

"Could I take a few oboe lessons from you sometime?"

She had tried playing the oboe and liked the way I sounded. She was petite and shapely—quite sexy-looking in the mini-skirts that were the fashion of the day; and she had driven into Atlanta in a brand-new gold Oldsmobile Cutlass convertible. When she told me she grew up in a Methodist family like my own on the other side of the Appalachians and after watching her organize and host a luncheon for the ladies of the orchestra, I became seriously interested. Her violin credentials were impeccable—Ivan Galamian and Dorothy Delay at the Juilliard School; and she also played piano well enough to assist with that instrument when needed in the orchestra. She was intelligent. Her vocabulary and use of the English language impressed me, and best of all, she was only twenty-two years old. At twenty-nine myself, I knew it was past time to get married. Maybe Mary Kay McQuilkin would turn out to be the girl of my dreams! (Michael Palmer and Wyche Fowler had both tied the knot during the previous summer.) By comparison with her, lovely Liz Couture faded as a prospect. While it hurt me to hurt Liz, we both knew the risks of courtship.

Despite the attraction, my relationship with Mary Kay did not develop too quickly. I was surprised to learn that she did not share my high opinion of herself—her beauty, talent, and intelligence. At Juilliard, she was so embarrassed by her Tennessee origins, she hid her Southern accent beneath an affected veneer that re-appeared like a rash in every stressful social situation. Competing with Itzhak Perlman and Pinchas Zuckerman at Juilliard was hardly reassuring, even though she held a full scholarship and made straight "As." Her father's premature death the year before also had left its scars, and her domineering mother was not ready to give her up. Nevertheless, I noted hopefully that despite her inferiority complex, Mary Kay possessed courage enough to live on her own in New York City. Maybe she would have the nerve to marry me!

Mary Kay's and my first date was a dinner party hosted by Wyche Fowler and his pretty bride Sue. Sue was an excellent cook and a regal hostess, proud of her social command and jealous of her recipes. Sue intimidated Mary Kay. Fernando Rodas, who was visiting from Guatemala, sat next to Mary Kay at our table that evening. She was dressed stunningly in a bright yellow miniskirt. I assumed that Mary Kay hardly spoke a word during dinner because of Sue. Instead, she twisted and squirmed incessantly.

After dessert Wyche announced, "Hey everybody! I have an idea! Let's go down to City Hall for the victory celebration of Atlanta's new mayor, Sam Massell!"—which is what we did. It was an exciting political event new to us, where people cheered and jostled each other, trying to get close to the winning candidate.

In order for Mary Kay to get a better view, I hoisted her up onto a chair next to Fernando; but she protested and tugged hard at her dress, whispering coarsely into my ear, "No, no! Take me down, Joe! Fernando was **groping me** under the table all through dinner!" I was astonished—but in retrospect more impressed than offended to learn that my mousy little Latin friend had it in him!

It was an unsettling start, but Mary Kay's and my relationship ripened throughout the winter. We visited my parents and her mother and began to talk seriously about getting married. Colleagues in the orchestra twittered when, instead of sounding the tuning "A" one morning, I played Dulcinea's love theme from Strauss' *Don Quixote*, and aimed my oboe straight at Mary Kay. I didn't have a ring, but February 23, Mary Kay's birthday, seemed like a propitious time to "pop the question." We had scheduled a celebratory birthday dinner in a chic new restaurant called "The Abbey"—a converted Episcopal church in midtown Atlanta, and we dressed up as well as we could for the occasion. Apparently, the extra sartorial effort did not compensate for our lack of sophistication, because the pompous maitre'd seated us in a noisy back corner of the restaurant next to the busing table, and an equally pompous wine steward protested loudly, "Just a **half** bottle, Sir?" when I ordered Lancers before dinner. All romance and sense of special occasion were dispelled by the time our mediocre dinner finally arrived. So much for proposing marriage!

Arthur Fiedler was an early guest conductor in Atlanta and a tough taskmaster with a great ear. He recognized immediately that our home-grown timpani player, who was as bald as one of his timpani sticks, did not play in tune— something Robert Shaw missed but which Warren Little had known for a long time. During run-out concerts around Georgia on a tourlet one time, whenever the timpani could be heard in Tchaikovsky's *Fifth Symphony*, Warren wheezed and shook in his chair next to me. I discovered the reason when I saw him during intermission loosening two of the most remote tuning screws on Gene Rehm's timpani. Every note Gene struck in the Tchaikovsky after that sounded like a hound dog howling!

Failure in Boston

Despite the vagaries of reed-making, by mid-season of my third year in Atlanta, I felt confident enough to audition for Assistant Principal in the Boston Symphony "just for the fun of it!" I wasn't about to give up first oboe in the Atlanta Symphony to be Ralph Gomberg's assistant in Boston, but Warren Little had shown me the value of "horizontal leverage" in contract negotiations. I doubted that Shaw would excuse me from two important rehearsals on the day of the audition, to my surprise, he said "Go ahead! Let's see how you hold up against national competition."

Until that time, I had won four auditions in a row—for the Air Force Band, the New Orleans Philharmonic, and the Atlanta and Nashville Symphonies, just by appearing and playing on the spot. I didn't think it necessary to prepare for Boston either, except to practice some of my opening selection, the *Symphonie Concertante* by Jacques Ibert. Consequently, when I arrived at Logan Airport in the spring of 1970, it was with the same smug attitude as always: "I will play; they will like me; and I will win!"

My plan was to take a cab from the airport to Symphony Hall and arrive early enough for plenty of time to warm up and adjust my reeds. Massive protests against the Vietnam War were going on in Boston that afternoon, however, and all taxi service from the airport was canceled. I had to take a train that made me late.

An attendant who was waiting for me at the Symphony Hall stage door rushed me downstairs into a large room where oboists who had already played were milling about, waiting for the audition committee's decision regarding their fate. One of them was David Weber, my former student, now at Curtis. Everyone stopped talking when I entered and watched as I fumbled to put my instrument together. My mouth suddenly went so dry, I could barely wet my reed. And the first quick notes I played unnerved me because my low C did not speak. Certain that it was an adjustment problem, I grabbed a screwdriver from my oboe case and loosened the screw on the C key's stem about half a turn. I was just checking the result when a proctor tapped me on the shoulder and said, "They're waiting for you, Mr. Robinson!" I followed him upstairs and tiptoed across a carpet into the center of the stage of Symphony Hall. A chair and stand were there behind a large white screen shielding me from the audition committee. Auditioning in that spot was quite literally blowing into a bed sheet.

"Start with the Ibert cadenza!" a loud voice commanded. (I recognized it as Ralph Gomberg's.) The second note of the Ibert cadenza is a dramatic high D-flat, which I pronounced with as much authority as possible. But OUCH!! It was a quarter-step **sharp**! The adjustment I had made downstairs loosened the connected E key too much, making every ensuing high D-flat (and there were many of them) grossly out of tune. And there was nothing I could say or do about it behind that screen. I wanted to shout, "Hey, everybody, I know I'm playing out of tune; can I please have a screwdriver?" but I was the twenty-fourth oboist to audition that afternoon and the committee was in no mood to grant an exception or extension. The wheels that wobbled early now fell off completely, and I fumbled one passage after another.

A kind of "out-of-body" perspective possessed me in Boston. The real "Joe" was up in the balcony, looking down upon a contemptible incompetent! My skin tingled, and I was filled with self-loathing—the significance of which was not so much that I was losing the audition, as that I was discovering the meaning of fear trying to win it. Until that afternoon, I never thought that I would lose anything but a particular job by not winning an audition! But I was wrong. That afternoon I lost my "audition innocence!"—my nerve and my confidence

On the flight back to Atlanta, I pondered what had happened beyond the excessive twist of a screwdriver and winced remembering David Weber's disenchantment as he peeked at me on stage through the stage curtain. He was not the only young oboist that afternoon checking out the "mongrel" they had heard about who won the Atlanta Symphony first oboe job! That guy (like most of them, it must be said) did not even advance to the semi-final round of the competition. Wayne Rapier, Oboe Professor at Oberlin and a New England Conservatory graduate who had studied two years with Marcel Tabuteau, won the job. When I told Shaw what happened in Boston, he was **not** impressed.

In mid-May, Michael Palmer conducted Handel's magnificent little *Concerto in G Minor for Oboe and Strings*. At intermission Janet McGee, looking as radiant as ever, called me to the edge of the stage to congratulate me and introduce her mother. Only a month before my wedding, I guessed correctly that I would never see the former "Miss South Carolina" again. *Atlanta CONSTITUTION* critic Bob Rohrer, in his review of the concert the next day, wrote, "The orchestra's principal oboist, Joseph Robinson, joined an ensemble of symphony performers in an excellent reading . . . that exhibited **the rich tonal qualities and mastery of nuance that consistently mark his performances.**" Following the concert, Dad found Robert Shaw backstage and asked him if he thought I had any talent . . .

More portentous at the end of my third year with the Atlanta Symphony was Bob Rorher's summation of Robert Shaw's programming for the season: "Music Director Robert Shaw is to be commended for the fact that of the 62 works he included in the series, 35 were composed in the twentieth century—some 15 of these since 1940."

Getting married

It is a fact of musical life that most performers suffer from symptoms of anxiety or "stage fright." Even Pablo Casals claimed to feel a "crushing weight" in his chest before playing in public. My own apprehensions, especially after becoming a professional oboist reliant on my own reed-making, had more to do with fear of my reed's inadequacy than anything else; but some anxiety, however vaguely felt and quickly dissipated, was always present before concerts.

A late-spring tour in 1970 that took the Atlanta Symphony to several smaller towns en route to Miami featured pianist Theodore Lettvin as soloist in the glorious *Second Concerto* of Johannes Brahms raised the stakes. I felt fine in the first movement of the Brahms; but midway through the second, a painful sensation of urgency took my breath away. It passed quickly and I was able to continue playing for a few more measures before the second wave hit me with such force that beads of perspiration popped out on my forehead. In a panic, I whispered to the oboist next to me, "Sandy, I **have got** to get out of here! Cover me!" She pushed her chair back to make room as I stumbled past her through the cello section with my oboe held high. Both Shaw and Lettvin looked up in astonishment. A huge oboe solo was just around the corner. "Quick, tell me!" I cried as I fled the stage, "**Where** is the bathroom?"

Fortunately, the spasm was quick and decisive; and after an embarrassing one of my own, I made it back on stage in time for Brahms's third movement! There had been no choice—either I fled the stage myself or everyone else would have to! My new-found vulnerability frightened me.

"This is humiliating and intolerable!" I thought. "It could totally ruin my career!"

During the next afternoon, I relaxed on a beach towel in the sun recovering from whatever food allergy or virus afflicted me. Fortunately, Shaw thought it was the oboe and not my gut. My gastrointestinal tract recovered, but the psychological damage it caused did not. Normal stage fright accompanying future concerts morphed into something sinister and more dangerous—an irresistible, provocative concern about the state of my colon! And any inquiry at all into that part of my autonomic nervous system triggered peristalsis which no mantra of reassurance could suppress. A phobia emerged full-blown on that tour to Florida that was to torment me throughout the rest of my career—so much that when I retired from the New York Philharmonic three decades later, the toilet off-stage in Avery Fisher Hall was dubbed by some of my colleagues "The Joe!"

The summer of 1970 was supposed to be **mine** at Marlboro. I was the only returning oboist, confident that my standing with Tony Checchia and Rudolf Serkin was secure. When their invitation for my return to Marlboro arrived, I responded that I was honored but could attend only five weeks because of promises made to Thor Johnson at the Peninsula Music Festival. Three other members of the Atlanta Symphony, including Concertmaster Martin Sauser, were accompanying Mary Kay and me to Fish Creek in August. I knew that many Marlboro "insiders" came and went every summer at their own convenience and we really needed some money to help pay for our wedding. To my astonishment, Tony reported that Serkin did not accept my proposal. "All or nothing!" was the verdict. Consequently, in what was one of the worst miscalculations of my career, I decided **not** to return to Marlboro in 1970.

Out of the blue Mary Kay received her own invitation to play with Pablo Casals in the Marlboro Festival Orchestra. It came from her former Juilliard chamber music coach Felix Galimir. Thrilled by this wonderful coincidence, she drove over immediately to discuss how to respond. Standing in the living room of my Mt. Paran cottage, she called Tony Checchia to tell him she would love to participate.

"Psst, Mary Kay!" I interrupted, "Ask him if you can bring your husband with you . . . er, that is . . . in the event you are married!" (That was not the marriage proposal either of us intended!)

"Sure, you can," said Tony cheerily. "You can occupy a perfect honeymoon cabin surrounded by birch trees down the hill from the concert hall. By the way, **who** is your fiancé . . . ?"

My black friend George Miller called frequently, asking to get together. In response to a particularly urgent request, I suggested meeting for dinner at my favorite downtown restaurant "The Midnight Sun." He was "Professor Miller" now, teaching Black History at Morehouse College, but I still related to him as my "black little brother" whom I encouraged and counseled as before. Halfway through dinner, George stopped eating and patted his dangling lower lip with his napkin. Looking up and, speaking nervously, he said, "There is something I have to confess." My mind raced through a list of possible peccadilloes, addictions, crimes, etc., wondering what advice he sought from me this time.

"My psychiatrist says that I **must** tell you . . . (he hesitated) . . . that **I am in love with you!**"

Taken completely off guard by this revelation, and as shaken and confounded as I had been back at Cincinnati Conservatory, I blurted impulsively, "George, whatever that means, don't . . . don't **feel** that way! "Isn't being black enough of a handicap? You want two of them? Just don't **do** it!" My reaction was well-meaning, but without any understanding of what it meant to George.

(A recent sermon by Randy Taylor suggesting that society holds together only if most people do not "prosecute their lust" was in my mind when I spoke that way.)

Many years later, as he lay dying of AIDS, George telephoned to tell me how grievously I had wounded him with my words that evening.

Despite George's confession at "The Midnight Sun,"

which I dismissed as smugly as if I had told someone to stop smoking, we maintained our close friendship. In May he came for dinner at my little guest cottage, where I cooked for him my only edible menu—barbecued chicken, Uncle Ben's white rice, salad, and a rum-soaked oatmeal cookie topped with coffee ice cream and whipped cream for dessert. We chatted amiably for a long time afterwards on the screened-in back porch at twilight.

Early the next morning, Ben Sims banged on my door. "I saw you out here last night eating dinner with a nigger!" he roared. "If that happens again, you will be evicted! Do you understand me?" His pink face burned and his eyes blazed.

"No problem, Ben," I said. "I will leave today!"

And so I did. And I never saw or heard from my bigoted landlords again.

Church friends named Grace and John Bansley invited me to stay with them in an Ansley Park basement apartment until Mary Kay and I married on June 20—my thirtieth birthday.

Because Mary Kay's mother was in no emotional or financial condition to stage a traditional wedding in Knoxville, we decided to marry in Atlanta at Central Presbyterian Church. Robert Shaw learned that John Mack would be coming from Cleveland to play for us, and he offered to conduct sections of J. S. Bach wedding cantatas and splice them together himself. Chorale soloists Seth McCoy, Peter Harrower, and Florence Kopleff, as well as string and keyboard players from the orchestra, performed a half-hour recital before the service. Mary Kay and I organized the entire ceremony and wrote our own vows, encouraged and guided by the Reverend John Randolph Taylor, who pronounced us "man and wife."

Dad was my Best Man, and my brother Ed, Dennis Rash, and Wyche Fowler were groomsmen. Uncle Bill McQuilkin escorted Mary Kay down the aisle and gave her away, and Mary Kay's sister Susan was her Maid of Honor. Our processional music was the Lutheran hymn, "A Mighty Fortress is our God," and our recessional was the exuberant finale of Widor's "Toccata." Randy Taylor told us afterwards that although he used our service repeatedly as a model for others, he never experienced any future wedding with music as spectacular as ours. Generous parishioners baked the wedding cake and hosted our reception in the church basement.

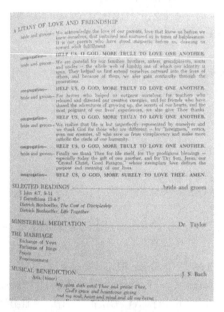

Back to Marlboro

Mary Kay's gold Oldsmobile Cutlass convertible—a symbol of her freedom and glamorous young adulthood lost before they were scarcely won—was sold to help pay for our wedding. Nevertheless, we were giddy that evening driving north up I-85 in my dull gray Volvo coupe, headed for an inexpensive honeymoon cottage in Myrtle Beach my mother had reserved for us. Because I forgot to bring any cash with me, we had to drive late into the night in order to find a "MasterCard" motel in South Carolina that could accommodate us. Next day after church, we found our cottage at Myrtle Beach to be a pretty seedy place which was, at least, right on the ocean. Both of us acquired fiery sunburns almost as soon as we arrived.

In contrast to the blistering beach, we drove north in splendid summer weather toward Vermont, anticipating a more successful honeymoon in the cool birch trees of Marlboro. Michael and Jean Palmer arrived almost immediately! I forgot that when Michael asked me if he could observe Casals at work with the Marlboro Festival Orchestra, I had said "Sure," never imagining that he and Jean would come so soon and stay so long.

While Mary Kay entered easily into the mainstream of orchestral life at Marlboro, I remained stranded on a sandbar of musical uselessness for the entire month. I ate and served in the dining hall with everyone else and attended rehearsals and concerts, but was never invited to participate musically in anything. The expectation that I had "finessed" Serkin's residency requirements by arriving as Mary Kay's husband was mistaken. Oboists Georges Haas and Rudy Verbsky (who would marry Serkin's daughter Judy) were firmly established in the center of the orchestra. Listening to them one morning and feeling sorry for myself, I went to Tony Checchia to complain about the way they sounded. He was sympathetic but told me Casals didn't care about that. Only on our last Sunday afternoon at Marlboro, when Serkin himself stopped to give us a ride up the hill to the auditorium, did he ever acknowledge my presence on campus.

"Why haven't you been playing this summer?" he asked ironically!

The Peninsula Music Festival was more welcoming. But handing off Mary Kay's 300-year-old Grancino violin to her (I was trying to be gallant by carrying it), it dropped and cracked. Thank goodness Martin Sauser saved our marriage from cracking by recommending a luthier in Chicago and scheduling an appointment for repairs. While we were in Chicago, I visited William Brannen, a well-known young woodwind repairman whose shaper tip ("Brannen X") was very popular at the time. Bill urged me to start a business like his in Atlanta.

"You'll be a wealthy man . . . a wealthy man in no time!" he exclaimed repeatedly.

As soon as Mary Kay and I returned to Atlanta, I told Pat McFarland what Brannon had said. Chicago was Pat's home and place of musical training, and he wasted no time arranging an apprenticeship with Brannon during the ensuing summer. Soon after that, Pat established the McFarland Double Reed Shop in Atlanta, quickly becoming "an (almost) wealthy man!"

An excellent young musician arrived in Fish Creek to play second oboe that summer. He was Michael Hennoch, a student of Ray Still's at Northwestern who later joined his teacher in the Chicago Symphony. As soon as the festival in Wisconsin ended, Mary Kay and I stopped in Chicago to exchange a loaner violin for her repaired Grancino, and drove sweltering through oceans of Midwest corn fields back home to Atlanta. We immediately traded my gray 1969 Volvo in for a blue 4-door model that had air conditioning.

Atlanta: 1970-71

Mary Kay and I made our nuptial nest in a duplex on Huntington Road, east of Peachtree not far from the Memorial Arts Center, and filled the place with hand-me-down furniture. Living on my salary, we saved Mary Kay's for a mortgage down payment whenever we could afford a house of our own. Another young couple with two little girls and a Basset hound lived in the unit behind us. Every morning at dawn their Basset hound, chained on a landing right outside our bedroom window, wailed mournfully, begging to get in. The effect was the same, but I much preferred our rooster's wake-up call back on the Wilkesboro Road! Sitting at my reed desk one spring morning, I watched the window sill in front of me erupt in a swarm of termites.

Robert Shaw's elegant home was situated in a much finer part of the same neighborhood, within walking distance of our duplex. Instructed to meet him there for a musical consultation one afternoon, I rang the doorbell and mistook a handsome middle-aged lady for Shaw "in drag!" Maxine Shaw, whom I had never seen or met before, looked surprisingly like her husband! She greeted me unceremoniously and pointed to a room at the end of a long hallway, where Shaw sat at his piano, surrounded by colored pencils, pens, and piles of music and manuscript paper, plunking out notes of a score in front of him two fingers at a time.

The score Shaw was studying was "To Thee Old Cause," written by his Juilliard friend William Schuman for solo oboe, strings, brass, and percussion. Harold Gomberg and Leonard Bernstein had premiered it in celebration of the New York Philharmonic's 125th anniversary in 1968. Set between Brahms' *Tragic Overture* and Beethoven's *Ninth Symphony* on the Atlanta Symphony's September 24, 1970 Opening Night program. "To Thee Old Cause" presented enormous musical challenges for me as an oboist and enormous emotional challenges for Shaw as a conductor. The assassinations of Martin Luther King, Jr. and Robert Kennedy and the death of his towering mentor George Szell the previous year had shaken Shaw; and he identified passionately with the Walt Whitman text which inspired the piece's composition.

Regarding our first performance, *Atlanta CONSTITUTION* critic William Weaver raved that "To Thee Old Cause" on Opening Night was some of the best work of the evening: "Joseph Robinson . . . played the demanding solo part with tremendous beauty and control; the phrases were extremely long; and dynamic demands, as well as musical requirement, were played flawlessly."

The *Atlanta JOURNAL* critic John Schneider wrote: "Schuman's music conveys the helplessness of despair through the lament of the solo oboe, rising occasionally to an unearthly keening above the numbness of granite blocks that sound in the brass and piano. The extraordinary control oboist Joseph Robinson achieved in his mournful melodic line added greatly to the moving power of the performance." Probably no collaboration bound Robert Shaw and me as closely together as this one did. He and I performed "To Thee Old Cause" twelve more times.

1970-71 was the third year of my multi-year Atlanta Symphony Orchestra contract, negotiated on behalf of the board by its then-new manager, William C. Denton. It stipulated a base salary of $200 a week for thirty-nine weeks. The orchestra was growing so rapidly, it may have been Robert Shaw's vision of "The Cleveland Orchestra of the South" that motivated his decision to add additional players to the flute and oboe sections. I doubted that he consulted Warren Little about the idea. In a discussion with Shaw six months earlier, I suggested the "perfect "candidate for the new Assistant Principal Oboe position—my former student David Weber, soon to graduate from Curtis. On my recommendation Shaw invited David to audition—the only oboist I know of who did so. After meeting David at the Atlanta Airport, I drove him to Symphony Hall, and guided him on stage through several predictable excerpts. Shaw sat listening alone out front. After David sight-read the oboe part for Stravinsky's *Violin Concerto,* Shaw offered him the job. Meanwhile, his fiancé Vendla auditioned for the flute position and was also accepted. So, David and Vendla Weber joined the Atlanta Symphony in September as newlyweds, both employed in the same orchestra right out of conservatory. It was a wonderful wedding present!

Psychological warfare with Warren Little continued

sporadically. Whenever Alan Balter was the object of Warren's scorn, I hunkered down, grateful not to be in the line of fire. Principal trumpeter John Head was the other "strong man" in the orchestra, with whom Warren seemed to have made—like Hitler with Stalin—an accommodation. Their spheres of influence overlapped chiefly in matters of union governance, which they skillfully divided between themselves. "Paying tribute" to Warren one Saturday morning in his Buckhead teaching studio, I surprised him with a very large bottle of bourbon. His delight at the gesture bought relative peace between us for the next month or so.

Leopold Stokowski came to guest conduct. Was I really going to play for the maestro of *Fantasia*—the architect and music director of the great Philadelphia Orchestra whose *Nutcracker* was the first classical recording I ever heard? Stokowski's program included Beethoven's *Fifth*, Stravinsky's *Petrouchka*, and *Mysterious Mountain* by Alan Hovhaness. The first rehearsal of the Beethoven began with an unanticipated slash of Stokowski's long right hand—a sudden "karate chop" thrown from in front of his face toward the orchestra—"Wham!" Surprised, we fell all over ourselves trying to respond with the familiar "Ta, Ta, Ta, Tee!" Several slashes later, we finally were finally able to play those opening four notes satisfactorily. Stokowski was not about to dictate every subdivision of the beat the way Shaw did. Like good chamber musicians, we were expected to listen more carefully to each other and create our own ensemble.

At the rehearsal break, I rushed to the podium.

"Mr. Stokowski, what a thrill it must have been to hear Marcel Tabuteau play that first movement cadenza!" I exclaimed.

The ancient maestro looked at me suspiciously for a moment, trying to divine my motives. His expression finally relaxed and he said to me, "Oh . . . **no** . . . **no** . . . the other one . . . what's his name? . . . played it better!"

(He meant John DeLancie.) I wondered if Stokowski knew that Toscanni's and his own portrait were the only ones adorning Tabuteau's studio wall in Philadelphia.

Throughout the week Stokowski repeatedly called out timpanist Gene Rehm and a substitute trumpet player for their bad intonation, and he continually berated the violin sections for their laziness and inattention.

"What are you doing here?" he harped. "Isn't this music good enough for you? This is your life! Wake up! Try harder! Play better! What is wrong with you?"

As Music Director of the Houston Symphony, Stokowski commissioned "Mysterious Mountain" by Hovhaness, and he must have thought he owned the piece. In our third performance of it, instead of impelling us toward the concluding fortissimo climax indicated in the score, he inverted the composer's intentions without warning and signaled a long, incredible diminuendo down to nothing! Stokowski was not the only conductor I would encounter who thought his genius surpassed that of the composer.

Opportunity in Washington.

A major Atlanta Symphony tour was scheduled in the middle of the 1970-1971 season. It began on February 8 in Baton Rouge and proceeded up the Mississippi Valley into Iowa, where one of our three buses over-heated. The driver used his ignition battery to inch us forward far enough to limp onto a snowbound pig farm in the middle of nowhere. He filled up his radiator there, while members of the orchestra threw snowballs at each other. A few days later, I was driven from a Sandusky, Ohio motel to the campus of Oberlin College. Ken Moore, the former Davidson College Wind Ensemble conductor and Wilfred Robert's bassoon professor at Oberlin Conservatory, asked me to apply for the oboe vacancy created when Wayne Rapier won Assistant Principal in Boston. Consequently, I spent much of one afternoon at Oberlin, being interviewed, performing and looking around, after which Dean Emil Dannenburg congratulated me and said he would offer me the job if Oberlin's "mystery candidate" did not take the job. (The conservatory that rejected me as a transfer student eleven years earlier was about to invite me to join its faculty!) As I was leaving, the dean whispered the name of their "mystery candidate" . . . Jimmy Caldwell!

My heart leapt within me! If Jimmy took the Oberlin job, the National Symphony principal oboe position in Washington, D.C. would open up precisely in my fifth season as a professional. And if I succeeded in that audition, I would win both the job of my dreams **and** the bet with my father! I was also one of the only people in America to know about the opening! Moreover, William Denton, the orchestra manager whom I helped employ in Mobile, was about to leave Atlanta and become Managing Director of the National Symphony, giving me an important friend and advocate in Washington, D.C.

("If God be for us, who can be against us!" In the best Presbyterian sense, success seemed foreordained.)

Regrettably, it was not foreordained for David and Vendla Weber—at least not in the Atlanta Symphony. Throughout the season, neither of them was assigned any meaningful parts. Instead Shaw followed George Szell's example of "putting the orchestra's best foot forward"— using assistants only to double or play when they could not be heard. In February, David and Vendla were told their positions were a luxury the Atlanta Symphony could no longer afford. Remarkably, however, they were able to land on their feet in Alabama, playing principal oboe and flute respectively in the Birmingham Symphony until it folded.

On March 4 a major snowstorm delayed our arrival in New York City and erased our afternoon rehearsal, threatening the Atlanta Symphony's first-ever performance in legendary Carnegie Hall. Somehow the concert took place anyway, winning me favorable mention in *Musical America's* review of *Mathis der Mahler* by Hindemith. The final concert of the tour was in Washington, D.C. where I performed on the Kennedy Center Concert Hall stage imagining it to be my future home!

The oboe world was stunned when Jimmy Caldwell so abruptly changed direction—resigning in Washington and going to Oberlin to teach. Everybody expected him to inherit his teacher's positions in the Philadelphia Orchestra and at the Curtis Institute. But Jimmy was a true intellectual who felt that orchestra playing was "blue collar" work—too repetitive and stultifying. Studying at Curtis with John DeLancie had put him on the "high road" to extraordinary early success as an oboist, but he now yearned for the free inquiry and creative diversity promised by my kind of liberal education. At Oberlin Jimmy Caldwell would become a national leader in Baroque performance practice; a rare instrument and glass collector; President of the American Banzai Association; and a computer whiz. It is ironic that my development proceeded precisely in the opposite direction—from liberal arts to the oboe, from the general to the particular. When an audition to replace Jimmy Caldwell was scheduled for the second week of April, 1971—despite its following three performances of Bach's magnificent *St. Matthew Passion* with Shaw in which I played five major arias for English horn as well as the first oboe part, I applied immediately. Tape protected my badly bruised lower lip (caused by the English horn reeds) and covered my bottom front teeth the morning I flew to Washington. There was no time to prepare.

In the warm-up room backstage at the Kennedy Center, an affable competitor named David Weiss introduced himself as Assistant Principal of the Pittsburgh Symphony. He was practicing "Pan," from the "Six Metamorphoses for Solo Oboe" by Benjamin Britten, the solo piece he had chosen to begin his audition; and his virtuosity impressed me. Eventually three of us were left standing for the final round—Georges Haas, David Weiss, and myself. I didn't worry about Haas, whose strident tone offended me so much at Marlboro; but I wasn't sure about Weiss. My reed certainly sounded good enough to win. But fate intervened again—this time not anti-war protesters or instrument maladjustment, but condensation in my upper octave key. Attempting to play the notoriously tricky passage in the first movement of *Le Tombeau de Couperin,* all of my high notes gurgled and sputtered so much, Maestro Dorati himself came to the edge of the stage to ask if anything could be done about the problem. National Symphony English hornist Richard White quickly volunteered to go downstairs to help me solve it. Dick and I tried everything we knew to dry out my recalcitrant octave key; but, when I returned to the stage and tried the passage again, my octave key did not open at all. That's when Dorati dismissed me with a wave of his hand and awarded the job to David Weiss.

Knowing how much I wanted to join the National Symphony, David told me to keep my bags packed! He said he was determined to return home to California as soon as Barbara Winters left her Co-Principal position in the Los Angeles Philharmonic. (He had been circling above her seat like a vulture for years.) At that point I did not hesitate to grant myself a career extension. Reed-making was way too hard for a five-year apprenticeship. Dad and the insurance business would just have to wait!

John Mack was disappointed but looked forward to some remedial work he planned for me next summer at the Blossom Festival School in Kent, Ohio. Mary Kay and I were both participating.

Kent/Blossom Festival: 1971

The Kent/Blossom Festival School was established in 1968 by George Szell and Louis Lane as an educational component of the Cleveland Orchestra's new Blossom Festival summer home—their "Tanglewood" in Ohio. As soon as we arrived, Mary Kay and I moved into a dormitory room on the campus of Kent State University and pushed two double bunks next to each other in order to sleep together without falling on the floor. We then picked up schedules for the week and drove out into the bucolic Ohio countryside in search of Blossom itself—the beautiful new pavilion where Cleveland Orchestra concerts took place. Unfortunately, we lost our way coming back to Kent. Because my first assignment was to play second oboe to my former student and colleague, David

Weber, in a rehearsal of a Mozart wind serenade—and I had just missed half of it, our coach Robert Marcellus (the great principal clarinet of the Cleveland Orchestra) interpreted my late arrival as a deliberate, unprofessional protest against my placement in the ensemble and was furious. As a result, I found myself unscheduled and at liberty during whole blocks of time each week for the rest of the summer.

One afternoon Mary Kay and I returned to our dorm room in a romantic mood to find an overweight French horn player named Philip Myers sleeping in one of our top bunks. For some reason, he chose to nap in our room instead of his own down the hall. Phil was ten years younger than me, in his second year at Blossom, and already principal horn of the Atlantic Symphony Orchestra in Halifax, Nova Scotia. He too had run afoul of a Cleveland Orchestra mentor and was as out of favor with administrators as I was. We were like two schoolmates on perpetual recess, playing games to fill each week's unscheduled time. Phil had been undefeated as the number one player on his Carnegie-Mellon tennis team and could tear the racket out of my hand with his serves, so one set of tennis was enough of that. Ping pong did not last much longer. Phil gave me nineteen points and won every game, despite the fact that I had grown up with a ping pong table! (He had the fastest reflexes and best eye-hand coordination I had ever seen.) I surpassed him only in Frisbee, which was reason enough not to do much of that. Golf was the one game in which we competed evenly and it quickly became our pastime of choice. We often played several rounds a week, followed by a trip to the Red Barn—a.k.a. the "Dead Barn"—for Phil's heroic conquest of the menu. Boy, it was wondrous to watch him eat!

The musical highlight for both of us arrived with Pierre Boulez, who came for two weeks to coach Schoenberg's monumental Woodwind Quintet. Arguably the most serious piece ever written for woodwind quintet, the Schoenberg is an early twelve-tone composition difficult both to play and to hear—which makes every performance of it a special event! John Mack attended ours and proclaimed it a triumph. The work with Boulez that summer was the best musical training I ever received in a modern musical idiom.

The Cleveland Orchestra's first concert included the Brahms' *Second Piano Concerto* and Beethoven's *Seventh Symphony*. John Mack's fat tone drooped enough during the Brahms to worry me, but in the Beethoven, he sounded magnificent. At my oboe lesson the next morning, I raved to Mack about his tone in the Beethoven.

"Would you like to try the reed?" he asked quickly.

"Of course," I said, panting like a dog awaiting a treat

"You can play it," he said, "but **don't look** at it. No peeking allowed!"

Gingerly I placed the reed into my mouth and sped off as if in a Ferrari, tingling with amazement, wondering, "How in the world does he do that—a tone like mahogany, eager and supple, a huge dynamic range and such stable pitch?"

"Wow!" I exclaimed, "This is fantastic!" (To me his reeds always were.)

Now examining it, I saw shiny unscraped bark almost from the heart behind the tip all the way back to the thread. It was a short-scrape reed unlike anything I had ever seen John Mack play.

"One of my students at the Institute (the Cleveland Institute of Music) came into his lesson last spring with a short-scrape reed that worked beautifully," he explained. "It reminded me where our reeds come from. More stable high notes; easier response; a more colorful tone, etc. Scraped 'short' that way, his finished reed was 2 millimeters longer than mine."

"Go and do likewise!" he commanded.

Back in Atlanta the next season, I faithfully drew a pencil mark across my reeds halfway between the tip and the thread and scraped only in front of the line. Within weeks, my reeds also were more responsive, more stable, and sharper in the high register despite being two millimeters longer.

Hungarian conductor Istvan Kertesz conducted the Cleveland Orchestra in Dvorak's *New World Symphony* early in the summer, transforming that familiar music into something monumental, incandescent and unforgettable! Members of the orchestra petitioned to have Kertesz named George Szell's successor (Szell had died of cancer in 1970); but the Cleveland Board of Directors, in one of the catastrophic decisions in the history of American orchestras, chose Lorin Maazel instead. No conductor could have been more **unlike** his predecessor. Szell was a perfectionist maestro who said he required twenty-six painstaking years to build an ensemble that expressed his absolute musical will. Maazel, by contrast, was a musical relativist—whimsical, arbitrary and unpredictable. When his appointment was announced, several principal players of the Cleveland Orchestra resigned on the spot.

Despite the turmoil and declining morale of the ensemble in 1971, the Cleveland Orchestra was **still** the Cleveland Orchestra, precise and in many other ways without peer in the world—except for one performance we attended when Louis Lane conducted Tchaikovsky's *Little Russian Symphony*. Lane missed a time signature change and went on beating in 4/4 time while the orchestra played in two. Whole groups of players fell away from the pulse like tender meat from a bone! Only two stalwart members, the timpanist and principal trumpet, sustained a barely-recognizable sinew of melody long enough for the rest of the orchestra to reconstitute itself and finish the symphony together! Except for that one near-calamity, each concert we heard at the Blossom Festival in 1971 was a revelation and an inspiration.

Atlanta: 1971-72 season

"Governor Jimmy Carter's on-stage endorsement at an Atlanta Symphony concert earlier in the spring prompted a letter from me to him on June 3, 1971. In it I thanked him generally for his enlightened, gracious leadership of state government and particularly for his support of Georgia's best orchestra. I also requested a meeting as soon as one could be scheduled. Three months later I paced nervously in an anteroom of the State Capitol rehearsing my pitch for increased state funding to the Atlanta Symphony when a door opened behind me and Jimmy Carter's trademark toothy smile welcomed me into his office. Unfortunately, that famous smile faded almost as soon as I sat down and began to speak. The Governor had done his homework and was not about to sit for long listening to my vacuous preamble! He interrupted me and quoted "chapter and verse" from several relevant pieces of state legislation unknown to me— ones dealing with nonprofit subsidies and abatements, etc.; and he was still citing specific dates and numbers when he stood up, walked around his large desk, and escorted me out of the office. Shocked by the brevity of our encounter, I stood for a few moments in the anteroom, properly chastened for my ignorance of the law and ashamed for wasting Governor Jimmy Carter's time. I was also really impressed by the mental acuity and executive efficiency of a man who would soon become President of the United States!

Oboist Eric Barr joined the Atlanta Symphony as second oboe in September 1971. He won the job in a spring shoot-out with Michael Hennoch when Shaw decided Eric and I made a better team.

Eric and his young wife Cathy and Mary Kay and I became best friends in Atlanta. On stage, Eric's and my partnership was generally exemplary until one of us fumbled a passage and caused the other to snort, sputter or giggle. The pressure required to play the oboe makes it impossible to hold the reed in one's lips and laugh at the same time; and Eric had an especially short fuse. In one unforgettable children's concert performance of the "Cygnets" from Tchaikovsky's *Swan Lake*, no dancing oboe chicks could be heard at all! A tiny miscue had sent Eric diving beneath his stand, where he gasped open-mouthed and stared bug-eyed at his oboe in his lap as if it had broken. At the same time, whining with tears running down my cheeks, I spat the reed from my mouth and pretended it had cracked! Shaw looked up, astonished to see his oboe section in hysterical disarray!

Offstage Eric's and my partnership was also both

productive and hilarious. Late into the night we explored the arcane frontiers of gouging machines, shapers and reed-making, mitigating our inevitable frustration with six packs of beer and riotous laughter. One evening a "Eureka!" moment of discovery confirmed Tabuteau's adage: "The gouge is everything!" A particular blade curve, like alchemy, had changed bad cane into good and loser reeds into winners! Eric kept that gouging set-up unchanged for eight years, saving it for special occasions. It helped him win Principal Oboe in the Dallas Symphony in 1973.

Robert Shaw chose programs in the Atlanta Symphony's 1971-72 season that paired symphonies of Johannes Brahms with major orchestral works by Charles Ives—an intriguing idea that backfired badly! Shaw, always drawn to the singing melodies of Brahms whose *German Requiem* was a concert staple throughout his career, also had an affinity for the music of Ives—the Yale-educated Hartford insurance man whose celebrity was achieved by means almost as unpredictable as Shaw's and whose quirky creations quoted patriotic Americana and Protestant hymn tunes well-known to Shaw. While Brahms symphonies were exactly what conservative listeners in Atlanta loved and would pay for, the thorny, incomprehensible sounds of Charles Ives chased them away in droves. Early in February 1972 the Executive Committee of the board, foreseeing a massive deficit because of a drop in subscribers from 5,500 to 3,300, asked for—and received— Robert Shaw's resignation as Music Director of the Atlanta Symphony. The city was stunned!

On tour the morning after learning the news, I sat at the breakfast counter of a cafe in Florence, South Carolina with Assistant Conductor Michael Palmer, who looked red-eyed and sleepy.

"Listen, Joe," he whispered conspiratorially between mouthfuls of hot cheese grits, "I am going to need your support. The board has just invited me to take over for the rest of the season—planning, programming, personnel, conducting . . . everything!"

He was practically jumping out of his skin, despite

exhaustion from the previous late-night phone calls. He was like a U-boat commander who surfaced prematurely and began firing his little deck canon in every direction all at once. My advice to him that morning was, "Michael, watch out. Be careful. Go slow!"

The "Save Shaw" campaign which *TIME* magazine later characterized as "The Battle of Atlanta" sprang up immediately and enlisted foot soldier/church choir members from every part of the city. Its command center was the home of an elegant young socialite named Mrs. Caroline Hitz (whom Shaw would later marry), around whose dining room table Mary Kay and I sat with "young Turks" Bobby and Betty Edge and Neil and Sue Williams—all of us stuffing envelopes with appeals for $20 down payments on subscriptions for the Atlanta Symphony's next season. Checks made payable to "Robert Shaw and the Atlanta Symphony" were returned to us by the thousands—more than half from people who had never subscribed to the orchestra before. Confronted with this overwhelming public affirmation and a sold-out season next year, the symphony board quickly rescinded Shaw's dismissal and reinstated him as Music Director—action that confirmed his affiliation with the orchestra for another twenty-two years. ("Captain" Palmer, meanwhile, slipped quietly back beneath the waves of command!)

Shortly after Shaw's reinstatement, Wyche Fowler decided to run for President of the Atlanta City Council. Mary Kay and I attended his "kick-off breakfast," at which symphony colleagues performed some chamber music. Conducted by clarinetist Alan Balter and calling themselves the Atlanta Little Symphony Orchestra, they wore little blue-and-white campaign buttons imprinted "ALSO for Wyche" and performed Mozart's delightful *Divertimento* in D Major, K. 251. Columbus native Eric Barr played the important oboe part. As far as anyone knows, Wyche was the first politician to run for office in the State of Georgia with Mozart, and it earned him a lot of favorable press. America's infatuation with culture was sufficiently "booming" in 1971 to inspire bipartisan passage of a bill in the U.S. Senate on May 2 that authorized by a vote of 76 to 14 a five-fold increase in funding for the National Endowments for the Arts and Humanities. (Twenty years later the arts band wagon Wyche jumped onto so enthusiastically as a young public official—by then laden with sacrilegious Mapplethorpe photographs he was accused of voting to fund, rolled backwards over him and unexpectedly killed his reelection to the United States Senate!)

When I lived in Cologne in 1962-63, even though the city had been almost totally destroyed by Allied bombing seventeen years earlier (the Cathedral miraculously survived), it once again supported two major orchestras, an opera company, and a conservatory. Professional musicians lived on their salaries without supplemental income and ordinary people attended performances regularly. I saw "Tosca" for the first time in Cologne for $.85. Residence there so convinced me that arts organizations need NOT be the purview and responsibility of just a few wealthy citizens, that in a letter to Clyde Burnett, Entertainment Editor of the *Atlanta JOURNAL* written on February 20, 1972, I argued that, in contrast to Germany, it is wealthy Americans who carry the burden of arts patronage almost entirely upon their own shoulders as a kind of cultural *noblesse oblige*—until they tire of the responsibility or are financially threatened by it. This tradition of predominantly private "ownership" makes the survival of arts groups uncertain and raises the socioeconomic costs of participation too high.

"Arts organizations are public institutions that deserve public support!" I argued—a notion that still resonated positively in 1972.

Politicking Oboe Player

My involvement in politics had begun with volunteer support for Congressman Charles Weltner and continued, of course, for Wyche himself. But beyond typical campaigning, I sought to express in public policy my conviction that symphony orchestras, like libraries and museums, are repositories of precious achievements of Western civilization deserving greater support from public funds than, for instance, the 5% of our orchestra's annual budget authorized by the Atlanta Board of Aldermen. In this aspiration, Wyche was my ally. He agreed with me that Robert Shaw's surprising reinstatement revealed a broader arts constituency in Atlanta than was previously suspected and he knew that every one of those new subscribers could vote!

We met for lunch early in March to discuss the phenomenon. Wyche understood that, in the same way people who never use public libraries still believe in their necessity, Atlantans who never previously attended classical concerts had demonstrated in the "Save Shaw" campaign their willingness to support the orchestra. He said if I wrote it for him, he would introduce a bill to the Board of Aldermen increasing local funding to the Atlanta Symphony. Here was my chance to use Woodrow Wilson School training in translating personal priorities into public policy! I went home that afternoon and penned the following:

"Whereas, thousands of Atlantans rushed recently to the aid of Conductor Robert Shaw and the Atlanta Symphony Orchestra . . . ;"

"Whereas, many Atlantans who have never attended concerts consider the orchestra their own cultural resource . . . ;"

"Whereas the Atlanta Symphony Orchestra . . . should belong to and serve ALL the people instead of just a privileged few;"

"Whereas, the City of Atlanta presently contributes less. than five percent of the Atlanta Symphony's annual budget . . . ;"

and "Whereas, the City of Atlanta should . . . establish a clear policy of greater responsibility for the Atlanta Symphony Orchestra;"

"BE IT THEREFORE ORDAINED that [the Board of Aldermen] authorize the Mayor of the City of Atlanta to enter into an agreement with the Atlanta Symphony Orchestra whereby the Atlanta Symphony Orchestra will hold four afternoon concerts for families in the Civic Center Auditorium of the City of Atlanta and will receive from the city the sum of $100,000." Stipulating that the orchestra would be exempt from paying any regular charges and fees for use of the Civic Center Auditorium, the bill was introduced by Wyche on March 6, 1972.

Now the battle for passage began in earnest. Despite administrative resistance to the idea of giving away what the Symphony was trying to sell and skepticism that there would really be sufficient public interest in free concerts, supporters of the orchestra undertook an exhaustive telephone campaign urging four members of the powerful Finance Committee to recommend the bill to the full Board of Aldermen. Impassioned appeals from Robert Shaw, black composer T. J. Anderson, and Wyche failed to persuade the Finance Committee, however, which by a vote of 4-0 on March 17 rejected our proposed ordinance. Wyche was quoted in the *Atlanta JOURNAL* as saying, "I am utterly flabbergasted!"

Just as surprisingly, four days later on March 21 the *JOURNAL* announced a compromise approved by the entire Board of Aldermen which authorized an increase in Atlanta Symphony funding by $25,000 from the city, **if** Fulton and DeKalb County Commissioners together matched that amount. Our truncated proposal was still alive, but the compromise stipulated that approval of $15,000 from Fulton County and $10,000 from DeKalb had to be approved within six weeks, or else Atlanta's conditional authorization would lapse.

Wyche warned me that a tripartite agreement involving the city and two other county governments was virtually unprecedented and would be very tricky. And he was right. Dozens of letters, calls and meetings were required to persuade Fulton County's Commissioners to approve their $15,000 on time. Meanwhile, DeKalb County Commission Chairman Clark Harrison dragged his feet. Just two days following an optimistic April 4 meeting with Wyche and me, he told the *Atlanta JOURNAL* that our motion had been tabled and could not come up for reconsideration unless at least $5,000 were found from some other source in the county.

Fortunately, a powerful editorial by the *JOURNAL's* chief Arts and Music Editor, Chappell White, published on Sunday, May 7, changed his mind. A few days after it appeared, the DeKalb component of $10,000 was finally approved . . . but TOO LATE! By refusing to extend the deadline for positive consortium action in a vote two weeks earlier, the Atlanta Board of Alderman apparently had doomed the project they proposed in the first place!

It took Wyche's heroic intercession once again, with a second motion-to-extend that passed on May 16 by a vote of 11-3, to assure that the Atlanta Symphony would in fact receive $50,000 of new public funding. Victorious at last, Wyche and I succeeded in doubling local funding to the orchestra, more than reimbursing it for all the salary it had paid me as Principal Oboe up until that time!

6-A The Atlanta Journal   Tuesday, May 16, 1972

SYMPHONY SUBSIDY OK'D BY LAST AGENCY

The Atlanta Symphony will get that extra $50,000 subsidy from three metro Atlanta governments, it now appears.

The Board of Aldermen, which approved its $25,000 donation Monday, was the last of the three agencies to act.

But Alderman Cecil Turner served notice that he will ask for reconsideration, leaving the final action in doubt for two weeks.

The city's money would be matched with previously approved donations of $15,000 from Fulton County and $10,000 from DeKalb County.

Officials have said that a $50,000 federal grant also may be available.

THE SYMPHONY has promised to give four concerts, free to the public, in return for the donation.

Alderman Marvin Arrington said he was withdrawing his support from the proposal, since it made no provision for black artists such as James Brown and Aretha Franklin.

The donation was approved by an 11-3 vote. Two weeks ago the aldermen had apparently killed the plan when they voted not to extend the time they would wait for the money from DeKalb.

I was ecstatic. At last my schizophrenic training had found a meaningful, unifying focus! Furthermore, the clouds of jealousy and paranoia that formed around future successful forays into the arena of public policy produced only distant rumbles this time.

"He should stay out of management's business."

"He's not on the Board."

"Don't we pay him to play the oboe?"

"What's he getting out of this?"

Comments and questions like these would grow louder throughout my career, as I attempted to combine effective advocacy with exemplary musicianship.

Summer 1972

A more threatening thunderhead now took the form of vengeful Warren Little. In his roles as both chairman of the orchestra's contract negotiating committee and president of the Atlanta Federation of Musicians, Warren had for weeks promoted the idea of establishing a pension plan for the orchestra. Two attorneys were selling non-participatory pensions to orchestras around the country and installing themselves as trustees. There was an obvious need to protect retired musicians, but I believed that these attorneys, with Warren as their surrogate, were selling plans in self-serving, disingenuous ways.

Warren called a meeting of Atlanta Symphony musicians to discuss the progress of contract negotiations, at which he introduced his new friends. The attorneys spoke with persuasive fervor, arguing that a "non-participatory" pension plan would cost players nothing at all—an opinion Warren eagerly endorsed. With my own recent politicking out of the way, I was able to devote two weeks to critiquing their plan. The result was a ten-page document written on June 2, 1972 displaying demographic information about the orchestra and contrasting tax-exempt annuities with non-participatory pension plans. In it I argued that financial obligations incurred by symphony boards of directors on behalf of their musicians are "fixed sum" amounts, regardless whether they pay for salaries or fringe benefits. Because salary and pension fund contributions are interchangeable obligations, "a pension plan that costs nothing" is impossible! The report disclosed that average seniority was only 6.5 years, with two-thirds of the members of the orchestra under the age of thirty. Between the two of them, Warren and Jane Little held ten percent of the total seniority of the eighty-seven member Atlanta Symphony, for which they demanded full pension credit—including years when the orchestra was volunteer and paid no salary at all. Since fixed-benefit plans reward those closest to retirement at the expense of newcomers, my analysis made Warren and Jane Little look like crooks. And Warren was furious. Fortunately, Mary Kay and I were due to leave town soon for our second summer at the Kent/Blossom Festival School!

Before packing up and prompted by my antipathy to Warren and his hostility, I wrote a letter to Shaw requesting a raise in my salary equal to Warren's, arguing that while Warren was teaching dozens of flute students each week and playing club dates at night, I sat working on reeds. Referring to an upcoming audition for Principal Oboe in the Montreal Symphony (just announced), I said it was one I would disregard if Shaw agreed to my terms of $400 a week for the 1972-73 season. He surprised me once again by responding, "Take the Montreal audition. If you win, we will talk!"

Back at the Kent/Blossom School, Mary Kay and I were old-timers well-known to many musicians of the Cleveland Orchestra and comfortable among them. I felt almost like a junior member of the orchestra, playing golf so often with John Mack and his friends and performing with them at Blossom in Handel's *Royal Fireworks Music*. Mary Kay's affable new violin teacher Jaime Laredo inspired and encouraged her. New student oboists that summer included two extraordinarily beautiful and accomplished young women—Elaine Douvas and Pamela Pecha, both of whom would go on to major-league orchestral careers. Elaine's performance of Charles Loeffler's *Two Rhapsodies for Oboe, Viola and Piano* was a revelation, both inspiring and unforgettable. Oboist James Ryon, whom I had met at Reston, was also there.

"Wow! Sounds like chocolate mousse!"

At my first lesson with John Mack, his rich dark oboe tone stunned me anew. Just as in the previous summer, he offered me his reed to play on and examine. Good grief! Cane was dug out everywhere and even the thread had been nicked with the knife where he scraped all the way back.

"What happened to the short-scrape reed?" I asked incredulously, feeling betrayed as well as confused.

"How many times do I have to tell you, Joe? **Scrape the reed for the way it works and not the way it looks!**"

Insight comes in unpredictable and surprising ways. During the ten years I played on John Mack's reeds, I often tore them apart to measure multiple points on each blade with a micrometer. Like a myopic Michelangelo, I meticulously carved cane to tolerances of hundredth of a millimeter. My little sculptures looked like reeds, but they rarely played. Even the short scrape pattern I had adhered to for the previous year produced uneven results. But fourteen spoken words changed everything:

"Scrape the reed for the way it works and not the way it looks!"

I had heard those words before without fully comprehending them. Tabuteau himself had told me, "Do not impose a scrape upon the cane." Now, instead of being a sculptor carving cane, I became a mechanical engineer diagnosing and directing **the flow of the cane's vibrations**.

In a previous encounter, when Mack adjusted my reed with a magical touch of his knife, I shouted, "Stop! Why did you scrape there? How did you know to do that?"

"Make a thousand reeds and ask me that question, Joe!" was his imperious reply. After a puff on his big cigar, he added, "The cane was vibrating more in the northeast corner; I felt it on my lip."

He could feel it!

A whole new perspective of reed-making was born at that moment—kinetic instead of static: scraping to induce action here and obstruct it there, rather than sculpting inert material. Balancing eager vibration with a clear in-tune tone was the goal. Except for the reed's total length, I never measured anything again! I conceived of "negative" scraping as that which inhibits hyper-vibration of the sides (the chief source of "rattle" and spreadness), and "positive" scraping as that which encourages the reed's vibration in the center. The value of positive scraping was reinforced when I brought a reed to Mack that had eluded proper balance for hours.

"I know this is a good piece of cane," I told him, "but the reed says 'a' as in 'quack' instead of 'ah' as in father. It is a 'so-near-and-yet-so-far' reed!"

Mack adjusted it with three or four tiny concentric "Cee's" just left and right of the center near the back of the tip, and by shattering a shibboleth never to scrape the center of the reed, he made it perfect! I used it in a performance of Gounod's *Petite Symphony* that night, after which conductor Robert Marcellus whispered to me, "I haven't heard oboe playing that fine since Marc Lifschey was in the Cleveland Orchestra!"

(Marcellus was such a lord of the clarinet in Cleveland, he charged more for lessons than anyone else in town. They were so expensive in fact, Mack once told me. "Joe, the two biggest threats to public safety in Cleveland: are junkies and clarinet players!")

One morning an attractive lady hurried toward me on campus and introduced herself as Margaret Baxtresser, Professor of Piano at Kent State University. She said her beautiful daughter Jeannie was Principal Flute of the Montreal Symphony. Jeannie had called to ask her mother to contact me as soon as possible. First-round auditions for Principal Oboe had not yielded anyone good enough, she said, and Jeannie hoped I would be willing to fly to Montreal immediately to compete for the job. The audition finals were happening day after tomorrow!

Shaw's gauntlet, thrown down in response to my request for a raise—namely, that I win in Montreal before we could even talk about a raise, had discouraged rather than challenged me. I rationalized that flying from Cleveland to Montreal for the audition would be inconvenient and expensive—and I probably wouldn't want to live in that frigid city anyway. Now, complimented by Jeannie's interest in me and encouraged by the presence of my Marlboro friend Larry Combs' position on the committee as Principal Clarinet—even without time to prepare, I changed my mind and decided to go.

Franz-Paul Decker was Music Director of the Montreal Symphony, born and educated in Cologne—something he revealed fraternally before the audition. (He had read about my Cologne/Fulbright year in my bio.) Facing me at the center of a wide table, he sat with members of the audition committee spread out on both sides of him like open arms. Jeannie Baxtresser, Larry Combs, and bassoonist David Carroll had all welcomed me warmly and encouraged me as I played; and, after seeing a bit of Montreal itself, I was enchanted enough by its quasi-European charm to wish I had taken this opportunity more seriously. Placed on the stand in front of me was Richard Strauss's tone poem "Don Juan," in the middle of which is a beautiful, extended oboe solo so seductive it is a staple at every audition. I was ready and eager to play it.

"Play from the beginning, Mr. Robinson!" was the surprising command from Maestro Decker.

I had not looked at the difficult tutti passages of the opening, most of which are doubled by violins, so it felt like sight-reading to play the angular kinetic music in cut time (2/2) that starts the piece. Unfortunately, buried in the middle of it is a tiny little measure in three/four time.

"Stop!" shouted Decker as soon as I misread it. "Play that passage again from the beginning!"

Still misunderstanding the rhythm of the three/four bar, which I expressed as a triplet, I was stopped and told to try again. When I made the same rhythmic mistake a third time, Decker slapped his hand on the table and waved me out. I had broken the most important law of auditions, which is: **Give no reason for complaint!** Twenty-two-year-old Peter Bowman from Boston University beat me and got the job.

Back at Kent State Robert Shaw approached me down a classroom hallway. (He had come to conduct "Elijah" at Blossom with the student chorus.) As soon as he saw me, he asked, "How did it go in Montreal?"

"I came in second," was my sheepish reply.

"Then I guess we d-d-don't have anything to discuss!" he said, and walked on by.

Atlanta: 1972-73 season

The first "free concert for families" sponsored by the City of Atlanta was scheduled for Sunday afternoon, October 1, 1972 in the Civic Center Auditorium. It would prove or disprove the premise that inspired it—namely, that off-putting social conventions and high-ticket prices discouraged wider audience participation in Atlanta Symphony concerts. In the same way the gift of a tree that requires planting might inspire ambivalent feelings in its recipient, the new city and county money obligating the Atlanta Symphony to produce extraordinary concerts was received with mixed feelings by the orchestra's administrative staff and directors. $50,000 from a private donor supporting business as usual would have been more welcome! Still doubting that there would be much public interest in a free event, the orchestra gave away whole blocks of tickets to various government agencies ahead of time—to Department of Children's and Families Services, to the Fire Department, etc.; and only one nine-square-inch announcement instructing interested readers to return self-addressed envelopes for receipt of their tickets was purchased by the orchestra and placed in the Sunday edition of the *Atlanta JOURNAL-CONSTITUTION* on September 24. A photograph in the *JOURNAL* three days later revealed that a mountain of mail (estimated at 12,000 pieces) had already been received by the orchestra staff.

CONCERT MAIL

Secretary Brenda Vaughn and Richard Thompson, assistant manager of the Atlanta Symphony Orchestra, are swamped with mail from persons who sent self-addressed envelopes requesting tickets for the free concert by the orchestra to be sponsored by the City of Atlanta at 3 p.m. Sunday at the Civic Center. The city provided $25,000 to sponsor a series of four free concerts by the orchestra in the 1972-73 season.

Robert Shaw hosted and conducted the concert with gusto. His program began with the *Egmont Overture* by Beethoven, followed by William Grant Still's *Afro-American Symphony*, the Saint-Saens Second Piano Concerto, *Romeo and Juliet* by Tchaikovsky and a symphonic arrangement of music from Bernstein's *West Side Story*.

Reviewing the event in the *JOURNAL* on October 2, Music Critic John Schneider wrote, "Any doubt that many more people are interested in the Atlanta Symphony Orchestra than attend the regular concerts was dispelled when the symphony office was deluged with mail requesting tickets . . . " Characterizing the audience as "unhabitual" and acknowledging particularly the large number of young members in attendance, he wrote in summary: "The city's initiative in making such concerts possible puts a valuable seal of official recognition on the artistic growth of this community and the overwhelming response of the public is proof that the decision was the right one." The event precipitated thereafter an Atlanta Symphony tradition of free summer concerts in Chastain Park.

Mary Kay and I routinely mailed our annual union dues to the office of the Atlanta Federation of Musicians in September at the beginning of each season. Unaware that the union office had changed locations during the summer of 1972, we posted our check to the old address. Three concert versions of *The Marriage of Figaro* conducted by James Levine were scheduled to begin on Thursday, October 12; and since all the rehearsals for them had gone so well (as usual with Levine's confident, breezy conducting), everyone anticipated especially joyful Mozart that evening. But at eight o'clock Warren Little, although reported to be in the building, was still not sitting in the principal flute chair. I supposed there must a problem backstage with a singer's costume, or something. Fifteen minutes past time for the performance to begin, Concertmaster and Personnel Manager Martin Sauser, greatly agitated, rushed to me from the wings and whispered in my ear:

"Joe, give me $170 immediately, or this concert cannot take place!" he exclaimed.

Flabbergasted, I replied, "Good grief, Marty! I don't have that kind of money out here on stage with me, and we left our checkbook at home. What are you talking about?"

"Warren is head of the union, and he says the orchestra cannot play tonight unless the Robinsons pay their union dues!"

"But I mailed the check last week," I said. "Was it to the wrong address? Tell Warren we paid our dues already!"

Jimmy Levine watched standing just off stage, his arms folded across his chest and his baton twitching impatiently when Warren sauntered through the orchestra and took his seat next to me. He was chuckling with self-satisfied malevolence.

"Thank Marty," he snarled. "He wrote the check for you!"

Throughout the performance I felt as if I was playing in a war zone. But as soon as the concert ended, an enraptured member of the audience approached me and exclaimed, "Oh, Mr. Robinson, this Mozart was so, **so** wonderful . . . **Don't you wish the whole world were like a symphony orchestra?"**

In the middle of all of the political activity going on back in April, Mary Kay and I bought a house. It was a four-bedroom colonial at 928 Beaverbrook Drive in a pleasant neighborhood northwest of Atlanta, and it cost $41,500. A friendly banker loaned us $9,000 for the down payment and a $30,000-mortgage from Nationwide just about covered the rest. Although we moved into it on May 24, we had to wait until fall to throw ourselves into a whole spate of home improvements—covering gutters; stripping and replacing wallpaper; painting every room; installing drapes; even sanding and refinishing the den floor ourselves. We moved the back door to enlarge and modernize our kitchen and fenced the back yard for our Cocker spaniel puppies, "Treble" and "Bass." During all of this activity, we were assisted by two childless Scots friends from our church choir named Neil and Doreen Mathieson, who had practically adopted us. Neil sorted things in an industrial warehouse, and Doreen was a seamstress who made beautiful hand-crafted drapes and curtains. They knew very well that we played in the Atlanta Symphony, but it was a joke how often they asked, "Aren't you two ever going to get **a proper job**?"

In the third year of our marriage, our lives were full, in sync and generally satisfying. As Southerners, Mary Kay and I were at home in Atlanta, exhilarated by its growth and youthful energy. On Sunday afternoons, we could walk from Central Presbyterian Church with friends Dave and Carol Conklin across a pedestrian bridge to Atlanta-Fulton County Stadium to watch Tommy Nobis and the Falcons play football. We saw "Sweet Lou" Hudson shoot lights out for the Hawks and Hank Aaron dog it in the outfield, take two strikes, and then hit the ball out of the park for the Braves. We hiked and slept in Georgia's mountain state parks and ate sweet corn muffins, liver and onions, and coconut cream pie at our favorite restaurant, The Colonnade, on Cheshire Bridge Road. Even though orchestra life distorted normal social patterns by requiring us to work when our friends did not, concert seasons perpetuated the delightful school-year pattern known to us from childhood—summer vacation from June to September!

The hundreds of concerts I performed with Robert Shaw sharpened my rhythmic sensibility and expanded my tone. Especially sitting in front of the soprano section of a chorus and imitating their singing improved the range and quality of my musical expression. Mary Kay and I were amazed to see Shaw transform ordinary church-choir singers into the finest symphonic chorus in America and fortunate to share the many thrilling performances of choral masterpieces he loved so much and conducted so well. Whatever demons stoked Robert Shaw's fire—and I thought his performances of Bach's *Passions* were often anguished acts of public atonement, the fire itself was born of Shaw's fierce, inextinguishable faith in the redemptive power of music.

In his Philosophy course back at Davidson College, Professor George Abernethy first introduced and explained to me the Aristotelian concept of "entelechy"—i.e., the necessity inherent within things to fulfill their organic potential. Today we call it DNA. Ministers in my tradition call it "vocation." The Atlanta Symphony Orchestra could have been our professional home throughout our entire careers. But I was exhilarated by the success of Wyche's and my campaign and still believed in the rising priority of the arts in America. Consequently, I believed it was my "calling" to join the National Symphony and work in Washington, D.C. on behalf of the arts. Even if "Camelot" no longer existed there, the memory of it still seduced me.

Meanwhile, my partnership with Warren Little cried out for divorce! Like two strong magnets, we had alternately attracted and repelled each other for six years. Warren was unquestionably a great player, with a huge singing tone that inspired me in unforgettable performances of Brahms First Symphony, *Petrouchka*, the second movement of Beethoven's Third Piano Concerto, *Daphnis and Chloe* and many other famous flute soloes. We collaborated on stage successfully most of the time, and off-stage Warren could be as charming as he was charismatic. But he was always a compulsive Alpha Male—the unchallengeable switchblade-toting chief of the village; and he was a bully. He once told me if I didn't keep my nose out of his union business, "it would wind up at the bottom of the Chattahoochee!"—a threat that prompted me to discuss with my lawyer a "peace bond" requiring Warren to post a significant amount of money with the court against his doing me bodily harm. Sitting next to such a person was no longer conducive to good music-making or to my psychological well-being. And Shaw acted powerless to do anything about it. Mary Kay agreed that it was time to go!

True to his stated intention and right on schedule, David Weiss played for Zubin Mehta and won Co-Principal Oboe of the Los Angeles Philharmonic; and the announcement of an audition to replace him in the National Symphony arrived just at the time of Mary Kay's and my reflections about our future. Being runner-up to Weiss two years earlier convinced me that I would be the front-runner this time. Like a dramatic *deus ex machina*, winning in Washington would extricate me from my Atlanta predicament and make my sacred dream come true! In anticipation of that happy outcome, I fantasized about what our new life could be like—perhaps residing in the Watergate and walking over on spring days under cherry blossoms to rehearsals and concerts at the Kennedy Center! Dad would understand why it took me seven years instead of five to win our bet. Unfortunately, like an addict too obsessed with ends to care about means, I was too fixated on the fruits of victory in Washington to prepare for the challenge of winning them.

Final auditions for Principal Oboe in the National Symphony happened on Friday, March 30, 1973. The Atlanta Symphony was performing a concert that night at Berry College in Rome, Georgia, seventy miles to the northwest, making my window of opportunity very small; but there was no way I could not participate in Washington. Personnel Manager Armand Sarro agreed to schedule me first in all the rounds of competition, and Delta posted flights to and from National Airport that would just about work. Fortunately, the weather on Friday, March 30, also was perfect.

On site at the Kennedy Center, I found proper focus by disregarding what others around me were doing. I chose a good reed, warmed up carefully, and dealt on stage successfully with all of the prescribed first-round excerpts. Movements of woodwind quintets played after lunch with principal players of the orchestra, most of whom knew me already, went so well other candidates had to wait while Maestro Dorati and the audition committee discussed my candidacy on the spot—after which Sarro rushed to me, shook my hand, and exclaimed enthusiastically, **"Congratulations, Joe! You've got it!** You have won the job! Please wait here because Dorati needs to talk to you as soon as he has finished with the others."

"But Armand," I protested, "you know I can't do that!" (My heart was about to burst with joy.) "I have to catch a cab to the airport immediately! My plane leaves at 4:00."

"Oh, that's right," he said. "Listen, I will call you Monday morning about terms!"

"Shazam!"

Suddenly I was Captain Marvel, soaring above everything even before my plane took off! The flight to Atlanta was a euphoric dream. I kept thinking that the musical seed planted in the Lenoir High School Band nearly twenty years earlier was about to bloom as "Principal Oboe of America's National Symphony Orchestra!" I couldn't wait to tell Dad, John Mack, and Mary Kay! She would be waiting at Berry College for me with my concert clothes in her arms.

Two hours usually suffice for the drive from the Atlanta

Airport up the I-75 corridor to Rome, Georgia, but not on Friday afternoon in rush hour traffic—not even close! I arrived at Berry College at intermission of the concert, just as Mary Kay and other worried colleagues ran toward me off the stage to ask why I was so late. Their anxious questions bounced off me like hailstones on a windshield. In response to all of them, I said, "I just won in Washington everybody! I won! I won!" No matter that Shaw was furious or that he had to jerry-rig the orchestra to perform the first half of the program without me. To him and Personnel Manager Marty Sauser, I gave the same explanation: "Traffic out of Atlanta was impossible tonight and it made me late; but I am going to be principal oboe in Washington, D.C. next year! Sayonara! Auf Wiedersehen! Goodbye!"

Regret for disrupting the Rome concert or upsetting my colleagues did not disturb my sleep over the weekend. Rather, like a child on Christmas Eve I anticipated Santa's Monday morning gift of a telephone call from Armand Sarro spelling out the terms of my new contract in Washington, D.C.! Saturday and Sunday dragged on interminably.

On Monday morning, rising with the sun, I puttered around the house, checking my watch every fifteen minutes or so until I reckoned the National Symphony's executive offices would open. I knew Armand Sarro would need some time to settle in, perhaps drink a cup of coffee, and check his schedule before calling me. Sitting beside the telephone in our bedroom, I waited in tortured uncertainty as 9:00 came and went, then 10:00 and 11:00 a.m. Finally, at 1:00 p.m., in a mood shredded by frustration and dismay, I rang the administrative offices of the National Symphony and asked to speak to the Personnel Manager. Armand Sarro himself picked up the receiver.

"Mr. Sarro," I cried, "I have been waiting at the edge of my bed since early this morning to receive your call!" (He must have sensed the desperation in my voice!) "Is anything wrong? What's happening?"

After a moment, he said drably, "Hey, man. What can I tell you?" His tone was completely matter-of-fact. **"Some**

girl played after you left (Sara Watkins from the Honolulu Symphony) **and changed everybody's mind!** Sorry **about** that . . . "

What? **Crash! Boom!** Wait a minute! . . . In that instant, my dream was dead!

Atlanta in April is a débutante dressed for her cotillion. Azaleas, dogwoods, and wisteria bloom everywhere in gaudy, lacy, prolonged profusion. Spring lingers in Atlanta coquettishly, languorously—in no hurry to yield to the white heat of summer. It is the best time of year.

But for me in 1973 spring was a season of dreary despondency. I avoided contact with friends and colleagues and withdrew within myself to a place where shame and humiliation live. Despite being happily married and well-employed, I was emotionally bankrupt and at a professional dead end. The goal that had guided me (my lodestar) was gone . . . burned out. What direction would I take now? And should I even stay in music? Like a raft stuck in an eddy, for two weeks I bobbed around uncertainly, as life cascaded by me on all sides.

"It's Bill Montgomery," said the flute teacher's cheerful voice on the other end of the line. "We are upgrading our oboe position in the Music Department at the University of Maryland and wonder if you would be interested in returning to College Park?"

Interested? Interested? I jumped at this miraculous, face-saving consolation prize and arranged an interview immediately. If I could not get to the District of Columbia one way, I would go another!

Negotiations with Chairman Eugene Troth took a few weeks following my successful interview at the University of Maryland; and Mary Kay required some time to apply and be accepted on fellowship into the Graduate School, where part of her work would involve performing in the University's resident string quartet. Obtaining tenure as Assistant Professor of Oboe was easy. Troth and I agreed upon a salary of $13,000 a year.

When everything was in order, on May 26, 1973, I wrote

Atlanta Symphony Orchestra League President Joseph Haas to inform him that it was "our intention **not** to remain with the Atlanta Symphony beyond the end of this current season"— we had decided instead to join the Music Department of the University of Maryland. "We are committed . . . to the principle that the arts are a potentially enriching dimension of life for everyone, not just the privileged few," I continued. "We welcome the opportunity, as members of the musical community of a great public university and of the Nation's Capital, to try to influence formulation of cultural policies consistent with that principle. Congratulations are due Robert Shaw and you on the Board of Sponsors for increasing your orchestra's professionalism. Certain growing pains have been inevitable, but I am sure that the Atlanta Symphony will continue to flourish along with its city. We shall watch its development with a mixture of pride and nostalgia."

When John Mack heard about my letter, he was beside himself.

"Joe" he cried, "What the hell are you doing? Don't give up 90% of what is possible in our field—principal oboe of a major symphony orchestra! Don't do it! Don't do it! I am heart-broken!"

intermezzo

A Second Coming

Ten years earlier, I had been the one heart-broken, and love-sick and disillusioned—a refugee from the Music Department of the University of Maryland. Now I was returning as its new Professor of Oboe! Quonset hut offices were gone, replaced by a spacious brick music building which was already a bit too small for the burgeoning department; but my old friend Emerson Head was still there to welcome me. He and I would share a significant trumpet/oboe recital later in the spring semester. Despite many ironies, returning to the University of Maryland seemed the right thing to do.

In retrospect, it surprised me that leaving the Atlanta Symphony did not inspire protests by Robert Shaw or anyone on the board or in the orchestra's management. Perhaps Mary Kay and I had given everyone the impression that we regarded the Atlanta Symphony a stepping stone rather than a career destination. Or perhaps it was because Shaw had already engaged two of John Mack's best students, Elaine Douvas and Betty Camus, to replace Eric Barr and me for the next season. Church friends who elected me a Ruling Elder of Central Presbyterian in June were more distressed to see us go; and our beautiful black Cocker spaniel "Bassie" looked quite sad when we returned him to his breeder, Mary Barnes, for the promised show dog career that would lead him to "Grand Champion" of the breed as "Liz-Bar's Magic of Music" a few years later. "Treble" accompanied us happily to College Park.

After an exploratory trip to Maryland in early June, Mary Kay and I devoted the entire summer of 1973 to prepping 928 Beaverbrook for sale. We invested more than 12% of its purchase price in improvements by the time we sold it for $52,240 on September 17. Net capital gains for sixteen months of ownership exceeded $5,000—more than a 13% return on our 16-month investment. Just four days after selling in Atlanta, we bought 9220 St. Andrews Place for $53,000 near the campus of the University of Maryland. A contingency permitting the sellers to remain an additional two months forced us to rent elsewhere until December 1. During that time, we settled in Laurel, Maryland in the home of Bob Windsor, a starting tight end for the New England Patriots. What furnishings we had brought with us from Atlanta were stored in his spacious living room. On Halloween evening, slipping unnoticed out the front door with some trick-or-treaters, Treble ran into the street and was killed by a passing car.

Mary Kay's immersion in the academic courses and musical organizations of the Graduate School proceeded smoothly and successfully. She enjoyed performing with her teacher, Joel Berman, in the University of Maryland String Quartet and playing concertmaster of the University of Maryland Orchestra; but my position on the faculty was less clear-cut. Six oboe students, only one of whom could really play, enrolled for lessons. I filled some contract hours by initiating a course for wind octet, coaching the students from the first oboe chair Marlboro-style. The Departmental faculty woodwind quintet almost never met because of the illness and disability of one of its members. Consequently, I was assigned to faculty committees that engaged me in meaningless busy-work six hours or more each week. The best thing about my schedule was the freedom between lessons and meetings to reconsider Marcel Tabuteau's precepts and to undertake repairs (something John Mack called "draining swamps") for which playing three concerts a week in the Atlanta Symphony had left no time. I had protested to John Mack for years, for instance, that I could not trill—a complaint which always elicited the same reaction from him: "Well, Joe, how much are you practicing trills?" At Maryland I finally confronted the problem head-on by repeating a difficult trill study as an inviolate discipline for one hour every morning for a month. To my surprise, at the end of that regimen, my fingers were practically flying off the keys!

Meanwhile, our proximity to Washington, D.C. was musically meaningless—Mary Kay and I might as well have lived in Nebraska! Whatever freelance work there was in the District of Columbia was consumed by a cadre of the same resident musicians year after year, with a player named Gene Montooth gobbling up all of the important oboe parts. (I substituted for him only once.) People involved with the National Endowment for the Arts or supporting it in Congress were unknown or inaccessible to me; and, except for bringing my oboe students to hear Sara Watkins play the Brahms Violin Concerto solo part and Beethoven's *Pastorale Symphony* with the National Symphony one night, I had no contact at all with the Kennedy Center. In terms of oboe playing, my musical life at the University of Maryland was as impoverished as it had been when I was a graduate student ten years earlier—this time restricted throughout the entire school year to only a couple of recitals on campus in College Park.

The first of those recitals included the Mozart Oboe Quartet. The evening before the recital, after I had practiced all of the difficult passages in the Mozart and checked my reeds, I decided not to go to bed too early. Instead, absentmindedly rearranging things on my desk, I found a little plastic bag with some forgotten tubes of cane in it. They were the ones I had chopped down in a Guatemala City vacant lot five years earlier. With a "nothing-to-lose" attitude, I tossed several pieces of that Guatemalan cane into a glass of hot water, barely soaking them before gouging one. It snagged on the blade and tore a little at one end, but I shaped it and tied it onto a staple anyway. Fifteen minutes later, I ran into the kitchen with the finished reed in my oboe and exclaimed, "Mary Kay, listen to this! You are **not** going to believe your ears!"

It was one of the best reeds of my life! And Mozart never sounded better!

In the second recital, the one in the spring semester, I played English horn in Aaron Copland's *Quiet City* with Emerson Head on trumpet. The Guatemalan tubes were too small for English horn, but they once again produced an amazing oboe reed. My performance of the *Six Metamorphoses after Ovid for Solo Oboe* by Benjamin Britten sounded so good I mailed a recording of it to Dick Woodhams c/o the St. Louis Symphony. His extravagant compliments in response made me wonder if I had made a mistake once again by moving into musical obscurity at the University of Maryland! Was history repeating itself?

The motivation impelling our flight from Atlanta had been more negative than positive. Warren Little was an intolerable colleague, and my pride was severely wounded by the two failed National Symphony auditions. On the other hand, the invitation to join the faculty of a major university was no small achievement. Academia provided an alternative career track almost as prestigious and desirable for oboists as a first chair position in a major orchestra; and a Doctor of Musical Arts degree was not even required for me to obtain mine!

Mary Kay and I were optimistic when we arrived in College Park. But we quickly began to realize that many of our expectations were misguided or naive. Incompetent students, insufficient performance opportunity, virtual exile from Washington, D.C., all of these things were disillusioning; and worst of all was the poisonous faculty culture within the Music Department that made every teacher not huddled in a gathering of two or more colleagues the object of scorn and slander by those conversing. It was a snake pit!

Distracting family concerns also dominated our year in College Park. In November Mary Kay surprised me with the good news that she was pregnant, and midyear my mother surprised us with the bad news that surgery was necessary to remove the cancerous upper lobe of her left lung. Dad had never fully regained his strength from the stroke four years earlier and his emphysema was worsening. It was time to think about moving closer to my family in North Carolina.

Just then Nicholas Harsanyi, Dean of Music at the North Carolina School of the Arts, called to invite me to join his faculty in Winston-Salem as Instructor of Oboe and member of the resident Clarion Wind Quintet. In a letter written on

April 9, 1974 he offered, in exchange for fifteen hours of oboe and chamber music instruction, a base salary of $12,500 plus $1,500 more for work with the International Summer Program from June 16 to July 18 in Italy. I would also be compensated "as the oboist of the Piedmont Chamber Orchestra and whatever you earn as a member of the Clarion Wind Quintet;" **and** he threw in $1,000 for moving expenses. As daunting as it was to relocate so near the expected birth date of our first child, Winston-Salem promised a better homecoming and more challenging and varied musical opportunities than the University of Maryland. Even though Eugene Troth begged me to reconsider and offered to appoint me his fundraising assistant if we stayed at Maryland, we sold our St. Andrews home for $59,000 and prepared to leave. Soon after Kathryn Grace Robinson was born in Silver Spring on May 31, we loaded a U-Haul truck with our things and headed for North Carolina.

Finally, I understood that the career I dreamed of when Dad and I made our bet in 1966 was founded on a false premise—namely that a particular **status** rather than inherent musical excellence justified my life as an oboe player. Not winning the coveted prize in Washington, D.C.— which I preconceived to be the **only** acceptable validation of my career, made me feel that I had failed completely. In fact it was skulking away from Atlanta to the obscurity of campus life in College Park, Maryland, that gave me the chance to rebuild my career from the inside out, rather than the other way around. My new orientation continued in Winston-Salem, where "good notes" rather than "prestigious professional achievement" became my goal.

North Carolina School of the Arts

America's first state-supported school of the performing arts was nine years old in 1974.

The brainchild of James Christian Pfohl, Governor Terry Sanford, and author John Ehle, its authorization as the "Tippy-toe School" by a mostly rural legislature in 1963 is one of the classic case studies of American state politics. The school's stated mission was to provide "professional training, as distinguished from the liberal arts instruction, of talented students in the fields of music, drama, the dance and allied performing arts, at both the high school and college levels of instruction, with emphasis placed upon performance of the arts, and not upon academic studies of the arts."

Winston-Salem won a statewide bidding war for location of the school by raising nearly $1 million in two days to use in renovating a large public high school near Old Salem as its campus centerpiece; to add appropriate new facilities for dance, drama, and the visual arts; and to construct dormitories for both high school and college students—50% of whom were mandated to come from North Carolina. Composer Vittorio Giannini arrived from Juilliard to be the school's first president. It was his good idea to invite members of established chamber groups, such as the Clarion Wind Quintet and the Claremont String Quartet, to be the resident faculty of the school. Noted choreographer Agnes DeMille and Atlanta dancer Robert Lindgren quickly established an admired School of Ballet; and the School of Design and Production, which soon separated from the School of Drama, was already supplying technicians to theaters everywhere in the United States when I arrived in 1974. Giannini, with the help of founding trustees Jim and Mary Semans, also instituted for music students an International Summer Program in his native Italy.

Following Giannini's death in 1966, another Juilliard composer, Pulitzer Prize-winning Robert Ward, succeeded him briefly as president. (Giannini argued that **only** composers had an overview broad enough to encompass all of the performing arts.) Soon after signing my contract in the spring of 1974, Robert Ward stepped down as president to become a member of the Music School's faculty. He was succeeded by a third composer named Robert Suderburg, at whose pompous academic ceremony in September 1974, he was installed as the institution's first "chancellor," a title more appropriate now that the School of the Arts was incorporated into the seventeen-campus University of North Carolina system.

Long and lanky Robert Suderburg looked younger than his thirty-nine years, with a shock of yellowish hair that fell across his forehead like Robert Shaw's. He acted younger, too. He came from a Contemporary Music project funded by the Rockefeller Foundation at the University of Washington to Winston-Salem convinced that audiences unfamiliar with Schubert might just as well fall in love with Suderburg! Programming his own music and that of his trombonist/ friend Stewart Dempster, Suderburg wasted no time shaking up things in the School of Music. Assuming that he and I were "newbie" kindred spirits, he whispered in my ear in the stairwell one day, "Joe, we must get rid of the people around here who think this place should be another Curtis or Juilliard!" And on another occasion, again completely misjudging my own musical priorities, he said, "It's time to slam the museum door shut on Beethoven and Brahms! All of their music has been recorded already." (I wondered what Marcel Tabuteau and Pablo Casals would have thought of that!) Later in the year, conducting *Ancient Voices of Children* by George Crumb, Suderburg choreographed it (I had to hop around on stage like a cricket, dressed entirely in white) and engaged both his young son and wife as soloists. The production made Harsanyi's skin crawl!

Conflicts between the dean and the chancellor developed on many fronts, perhaps most of all between their soprano wives. Janice Harsanyi was a classically-trained singer and favorite of Eugene Ormandy who performed frequently with the Philadelphia Orchestra. Elizabeth Suderburg was a contemporary music specialist whose angular, acerbic voice perfectly reflected her angry, frustrated personality. She resented being a chancellor's wife presiding at fund-raisers in the cultural backwater of Piedmont, North Carolina. Nicky, on the other hand, embodied Old World musical values and Old World social charm. On the podium, he looked like Eugene Ormandy and conducted with similar enthusiasm, authority, and grace. Just as Harsanyi had rescued my professional musical potential in Princeton ten years earlier, he now revived it as my employer in Winston-Salem. The School of Music under his leadership was a true conservatory, aimed at preparing young instrumentalists for careers in performance—not a factory turning marching bandsmen into music educators or a laboratory fomenting new music. Describing their aesthetic and stylistic differences, one might say that Suderburg was the musical hare and Harsanyi the tortoise! I tried to disregard their feuding, but my bias was obvious. Fortunately the two men were in agreement when Suderburg wrote to me on May 12, 1975, "On strong recommendation of Nicholas Harsanyi, Dean, School of Music, your salary has been raised from $12,500 to $13,500 for 1975-76." Back home in Lenoir, Dad boasted to his friends, "Joe is a professor at the University of North Carolina!"

An excellent student oboist transferred from the University of Minnesota into the college division when I arrived at the North Carolina School of the Arts. She was Marian Buswell, a young woman who looked and behaved like a combination of Marilyn Monroe and Goldie Hawn but played first oboe with impressive skills and melodic flair. As a professional, she became principal oboe of the Kansas City Philharmonic and later of the Phoenix Symphony; and in a remarkable coincidence, her NCSA pal Mike Schindleman, who mostly played English horn at the School, invited Marian into his section (he was second oboe in Phoenix) and spent most of his career with her. Terry Bell was an eager but mediocre student in my studio early on. She came to her lessons so often wearing the same cotton dress, she reminded me of Little Orphan Annie. She told me she lived with her mother in a trailer in Granite Falls, and that her little half-brother in Bloomington, Indiana was a violin-playing genius. (I thought, "I bet he is!") His name was Joshua Bell! Mark Biggam stayed on in Winston-Salem as an accomplished composer and oboist; and Debbie Giesler, the daughter of a Moravian minister, continued playing oboe in community groups in and around Durham long after she graduated. Another of my most important students at the School of the Arts was Robin Driscoll who studied with

Betty Camus and John Mack after me, then went on to play first oboe in the Pittsburgh Opera and substitute frequently in the Cleveland Orchestra. His fastidious work developing better gouging machines and measuring devices has been admired for decades.

My written final exam for oboists in December 1974 included the following questions:

1) Tabuteau spoke often of himself as founder of the "American School" of oboe playing. What did he mean by this? What are the primary characteristics which distinguish the "American School?"

2) As a teacher, Tabuteau is probably most famous for his "number system." To what did this refer?

3) What is meant by "inflection"—what Tabuteau called the "up-down distribution?"

4) John Mack claims that Tabuteau's most helpful rule was to "put the notes on the wind." What did Tabuteau mean by that rule?

5) Explain the "inner work" of a singing slurred interval—the means by which the oboe . . . may approximate the glissando of a stringed instrument.

6) What is tone color? Explain what adjustments are necessary to change color and maintain constant pitch.

7) What are the three basic ways of altering the pitch of a single note on the oboe? Discuss their interrelationship and explain why one adjustment may be better than another.

8) Who are these oboists? a. Leon Goosens; b. Marc Lifschey; c. Andre Lardrot; d. Ray Still; e. Jimmy Caldwell.

9) Name and discuss as many interpretive techniques as you can.

10) What insights from studying Tabuteau's recorded lessons have been most helpful to you this semester and why?

These questions confirm that it was my intention to share with my students the same interpretive ideas that Marcel Tabuteau shared with me. Unfortunately, test results revealed that most of them had no idea what I was talking about! Despite conscientiously formulating lesson plans and syllabuses as other faculty members did—cataloging repertory; codifying reed-making and instrument maintenance techniques, etc.—I continued to focus on the **"how"** rather than the **"what"** of instrumental development. Five weeks of study with Marcel Tabuteau, during which I never played a single piece of music, convinced me that gobbling up piles of repertory is counterproductive if doing so only reinforces bad habits. In my own case, theory so preceded performance that, although years were required to incorporate Tabuteau's basic principles into my playing, his precepts proved ultimately to be more instructive than routine practice. My students have continued to complain through the years, however, that I never assigned them enough pieces of music to play.

The Clarion Wind Quintet

My successful first encounter with my new colleagues in the Clarion Wind Quintet—Philip Dunigan, flute; Robert Listokin, clarinet; Fred Bergstone, horn; and Mark Popkin, bassoon—was celebrated in their customary fashion with lunch at China City, where Popkin declared chopsticks to be mandatory. I could never again eat Chinese food with a fork in the company of these New York gastronomes! Popkin welcomed me as the quintet's first Tar Heel native son and described everyone else's dismay at still being stranded in the Piedmont Triad of "Grimsboro," "Die Point" and "Winstomb Salem!" (Greensboro, High Point, and Winston-Salem) The Clarion Wind Quintet had come from New York City in 1965 with no intention of staying very long in North Carolina. In fact, they were destined to be residents for the duration!

Mark Popkin was a Brooklyn College physics major turned bassoonist. His scientific bent expressed itself in the design and production of excellent bassoon reed-making tools. He was the pilot who guided and the engine that propelled the Clarion Wind Quintet. As the group's unofficial local manager, working with New York contacts and a Dutchman named Harry De Friese, he secured performance dates, booked international tours, and proposed recordings for the quintet on the Golden Crest label. His arrangements for woodwind quintet borrowed from all kinds of music composed for other instruments; but he also proposed and secured funding for the group's "American Music Project," a survey of unpublished American wind music that yielded thirteen programs for National Public Radio as well as an LP recording. Recording in the basement of his Arbor Road home on wintry mornings necessitated turning off the clanking furnace and draping blankets across our laps when the tape was rolling; but, despite our discomfort in the cold, listening to ourselves regularly on playbacks greatly refined our performance skills. Comparing my recordings to those of the best oboists in the world, I was able gradually to narrow the gap between my playing and theirs

Robert Listokin possessed dazzling technique and a distilled, supple tone that made his clarinet sound as if it played itself. He was a pleasant, good-natured fellow with a self-deprecating sense of humor and ready chuckle who could teach ANYONE to play the clarinet! It's a shame so few big-league talents came his way. Philip Dunigan could have been James Galway's younger brother—a bewhiskered Irishman with quick wit and twinkling eyes that trolled continually for pretty girls. (He married a few of them.) Phil attended Juilliard and toured with the Robert Shaw Chorale. He is the flutist playing the solo arias in Shaw's famous recording of J. S. Bach's *B Minor Mass*. Fred Bergstone, who also married a former student, was the most taciturn and steady member of the group. The Clarion Wind Quintet rehearsed regularly on Monday, Wednesday, and Friday mornings. Contributing to a music educators' journal concerning the group's repertory, I wrote, "Woodwind quintets are like children's cereals—cute and gimmicky and devoid of substance!" No wonder Mark Popkin adapted so much chamber music for us from other sources!

The first of two international tours I shared with the Clarion Wind Quintet happened in March 1975. It was a re-engagement for the others, who, along with my predecessor Roger McDonald, replaced a timid Netherlands ensemble in "singing the swan song of Dutch imperialism" in Suriname, Curacao, Aruba and Bonaire! My tour, a year after the Quintet's first one, coincided with independence and the creation of new regimes in these former colonies. At a party in Paramaribo, the exotic capital of Suriname, I met the newly-appointed Chief Justice of the country's Supreme Court. It reminded me of the governmental "role-playing" we had done as students at the Woodrow Wilson School.

Paramaribo's Dutch colonial buildings were incongruous set in the jungle alongside the indolent brown Suriname River, where houses presented ornate verandas and balconies like those in Charleston or Savannah, except that they were made entirely of wood. Cars rumbled along, as in Amsterdam, on the "wrong side" of the road. A beautiful School of the Arts violinist named Ann Bostian welcomed us to her parents' palatial home fronting the river. Her father was the CEO in charge of the extensive ALCOA bauxite mining operations that cut vast red gashes in the rain forest all across Suriname.

A pianist from nearby Curacao performed with us and helped arrange children's concerts for the rest of our tour. When some boys became too disruptive at one of them, Popkin whispered that they were preparing to cook us for dinner! I regained the boys' attention by challenging them to hold their breath while I played a famous long-winded second movement solo from Tchaikovsky's *Fourth Symphony*.

Looking out of my second floor Holiday Inn room window on the beach in Aruba, I saw a perfect postcard view of the blue Caribbean marred by supertankers all in a line on the horizon waiting to enter its deep-water port. Tanker trucks also patrolled our beach, watering grass and helping keep alive the pretty palm trees bent inland by incessant trade winds. Most of the island's topography was desert. When a brand-new Americana Hotel opened for business next door, I dropped five quarters in a slot machine that happily spat out $75. It was a little victory that would cost me many times that amount in years to come!

The Piedmont Chamber Orchestra

Despite its prosaic name, another important dimension of life at the North Carolina School of the Arts was the Piedmont Chamber Orchestra, a faculty performing ensemble augmented by professional "ringers" for concert tours Harsanyi conducted twice a year up and down the eastern seaboard. The first of these in the fall of 1974 ended at Lincoln Center in New York City.

Two notable violinists participating in that tour were Veda Reynolds and Marin Alsop. The Piedmont Chamber Orchestra was one of the finest *ad hoc* ensembles of its kind in America during the times it convened for concerts. (My taped recording of the Francaix *Flower Clock* with the Piedmont Chamber Orchestra in the spring of 1977 sounds almost as good as John DeLancie's.)

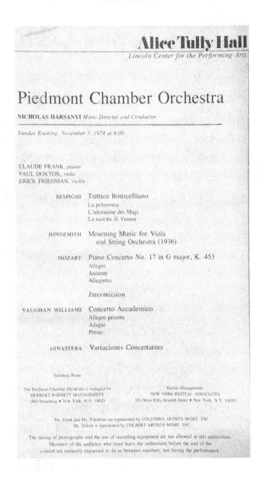

We always traveled together on a chartered bus, with Harsanyi sitting up front across from the driver. Even in the smallest towns, Mark Popkin could open a window and sniff out the local Chinese restaurant. One night in Kentucky, when the Big Muddy River crested so far above flood stage it threatened the tall bridge our bus was crossing, we outnumbered members of our audience. Next morning the river blocked the road out of a state park where we had spent the night. The best thing about that tour is that I mastered *Le Tombeau de Couperin* by fingering Ravel's most difficult passages with the reed-less oboe stuck in my ear, listening in the bus for hours to my keys clacking in proper sequence!

Homecoming in Winston-Salem

In June 1974 Mary Kay and I moved into a house at 3400 York Road, northwest of Winston-Salem on the corner of Peacehaven and Robinhood Roads, near a small shopping center and a barbecue restaurant. We bought the house from a black couple in a multiracial neighborhood. The four-bedroom split-level had an attached carport on a one-acre lot, the back part of which I fenced in hard labor for our new Cocker spaniel "Marcel." Four identical maple trees stood like soldiers at attention in a line on the front lawn, and a huge Asian pear tree that dropped prodigious amounts of rock-hard fruit each fall towered over the house on the west side. I hung a swing in it for Katie when she was old enough.

In Winston-Salem, the miraculous new dimension of our lives was parenthood, something admittedly more distracting and all-consuming for Mary Kay than for me. While "mommy" struggled 24/7 to mollify and satisfy our irascible, allergic little daughter, I came and went from home convinced that Katie Robinson was the most beautiful, the brightest, the most wonderful of all God's creations! I was crazy about her.

Living so near the "briar patch" where I was "born and bred," Mary Kay and I did not so much put down new roots in 1974 as revive old ones. Dad's insurance company changed its name from Security Life and Trust Company to "Integon," but Ed Collette was still its CEO. Wake Forest University snuggled more deeply into its now-verdant campus, shaded by towering pin oaks and magnolia trees, but its Georgian brick buildings still looked new. The familiar tangy sweet smell of R. J. Reynolds' tobacco still filled the air; and James Christian Pfohl's birthplace and Home Moravian Church were just down the hill from my office at the School of the Arts. It was an hour-and-a-half trip west to my parents' house in Lenoir and a half-hour trip east to my brother's in Greensboro. When Mary Kay participated in the fall tour of the Piedmont Chamber Orchestra, Katie stayed with my

Uncle Martin and Aunt Dorothy in Granite Falls.

Mother's career as a landscape painter developed as Dad's as a businessman (along with his ability to breathe) diminished. Her success was acknowledged in a book entitled *North Carolina Artists and Craftsmen*: "Nina J. Robinson . . . has attained considerable recognition with her oil paintings, particularly her landscapes of Western North Carolina. Her work has gone into private collections from New York to California, Texas, and most of the Southeastern states. In her own home area, where she has had several one-woman shows and won numerous awards, her paintings are extremely popular."

Brother Ed, meanwhile, whose daughter, Myra, was only a year older than Katie, had a good job with an industrial roofing company in Greensboro, working as its bookkeeper and bid-proposal writer. Mary Kay and I returned to WILDACRES in October to participate in the annual retreat of the Charlotte Oratorio Singers; and, at the invitation of Winston-Salem Symphony conductor, John Iuele, discovered Hot Springs and the Garth Newel Music Center on a spectacular autumn weekend in Virginia. We would return to that area with New York Philharmonic colleagues twenty-five years later for chamber music residencies at The Homestead.

At one time a trumpet player in the Atlanta Symphony, conductor John Iuele personified classical music in Winston-Salem. A portrait of him with his white mane flowing and a baton held exquisitely aloft filled a billboard next to Interstate 40, welcoming travelers to Winston-Salem. Iuele even propped a replica of it against the wall of his elegant home's living room, so that visiting fans and patrons could continue to admire it. He was a beautiful man with soulful eyes who reminded me of actor Victor Mature, except that Iuele was gentler and softer around the edges. I was a first-semester student at Davidson College when he first contacted me. He needed an English horn player to perform Cesar Franck's famous *D Minor Symphony* and wondered if I could do it. Iuele told me the Winston-Salem Symphony would provide an instrument. Senior fraternity brother Angus McBride generously loaned me his Studebaker for the gig.

Once settled in Winston-Salem, I began to resent the fact that Iuele's first chair oboist was a doctor who headed Radiology at Baptist Hospital. Like so many volunteer musicians in community orchestras everywhere, Dr. Leonard Nanzetta and his cellist/wife enjoyed "squatter's rights" by virtue of their long years of faithful service. But Dr. Nanzetta conceded nothing in terms of our relative training and instrumental competence. He called himself a bi-professional. My only choice was to join the Symphony's board of directors and assist Martha Brown and Tog Newman in oversight of the orchestra's educational activities.

A year later I pointed out to the board that, as a result of their employment at the School of the Arts, some of the country's best instrumentalists were already living in Winston-Salem. Their participation in the local orchestra could dramatically improve it for very little additional money. My recommendation was just to imitate the Rochester Philharmonic and Wichita Symphonies and entice conservatory faculty members with a premium rate of pay per service for each rehearsal and concert. John Iuele said he could easily find new foundation money to pay for that; and when I told Dr. Nanzetta he could have my salary if he moved over to the second oboe chair, he quickly agreed. That created the anomaly of a wealthy doctor's indulging his hobby for $60 a session while a professional oboist played for free! But it was worth it. I was thrilled to be able to perform the symphonies of Brahms, Beethoven and Tchaikovsky once again!

The Clarion Wind Quintet presented school concerts— eighteen in each cycle—to all sixth graders in Forsythe County's public school system each year. Watching from the stage as students filed in, I observed happily that busing had accomplished an almost consistent racial mix in every class. Our young listeners were generally well-behaved and attentive—especially during the "show-and-tell" part of the program when I did as I had in Aruba and challenged them to hold their breath during the long Tchaikovsky Fourth slow movement solo. A collective gasp of inhalation always anticipated my demonstration, followed by predictable little explosions of release (like popcorn popping) that accelerated the longer I played. One boy sitting in the front row held his breath so heroically, he turned blue and dropped onto the floor directly in front of me! I thought he was kidding until the school nurse and several teachers rushed to revive him.

"Do you think I killed him?" I whispered to Philip Dunigan sitting next to me.

"No way!" Dunigan said. "People **always** breathe again as soon as they pass out."

Nevertheless, fearing parental retribution, I never tried that trick again. The incident made me wonder if I might fall out of my own chair in a concert sometime!

Rev. David Burr and First Presbyterian were too conservative for Mary Kay and me, both in terms of church doctrine and social outlook. We shopped around for a couple of years before deciding on Home Moravian Church in Old Salem where we liked Wayne Burkett's preaching and the hymnody and liturgy of the denomination. John Mueller from the School of the Arts faculty was the church's excellent organist and Kay Phillips the choir's ebullient director. An oboe-playing assistant minister named Ken Robinson liked my reeds and called me "brother." After Mary Kay volunteered one time to roll up the little candles used in Moravian love feasts and other special occasions, I discovered that their mixture of beeswax and denatured beef tallow stayed tacky even in the coldest and driest conditions. The stuff was perfect on the thread I used for reed-making!

"Oboe Day in North Carolina"

John Mack and I first met at Salem College in 1959. Sixteen years later, in his tenth season as Principal Oboe of the Cleveland Orchestra, he returned to Winston-Salem. The reunion was an opportunity for me to honor and thank him.

Master classes by visiting artists were routine at the School of the Arts. Andre Segovia came the week before Mack to coach four classical guitar students; and, as valuable as that was, only the guitarists and their teacher knew it happened. In the spirit of James Christian Pfohl, I conceived of John Mack's visit in grandiose terms—hence, "Oboe Day in North Carolina!" Even if the self-designated proclamation was officially improper, it generated a tremendous amount of press. I sent a brochure describing the over-stuffed day's events to 1,500 band directors in a five-state area, as well as to all nearby college and university music departments. I ordered one hundred copies of an extensive article entitled "Effective Guidance for the Young Oboist," written by John Mack and published by the International Double Reed Society, and I arrayed dozens of LP recordings featuring Mack with the Cleveland Orchestra at a table for sale on campus. Seventy-five participants attended from as far away as Washington, D.C. and New Orleans, Louisiana. The $5.00 enrollment fees more than reimbursed me for printing, postage, and other expenses. The evening recital featured three of my oboe students from the School of the Arts; a former graduate who was a member of the Detroit Symphony; myself; and John Mack playing the Mozart Oboe Quartet with members of the faculty's Razoumovsky String Quartet. It was a big success.

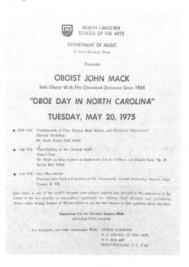

Dean Harsanyi and members of the Clarion Wind Quintet joined John Mack and me for lunch at the Salem Tavern on May 20, 1975.

Joseph Robinson with John Mack

Mack's visit was not all work and no play. We golfed on Wednesday at nearby Tanglewood Resort and. enjoyed a barbecue party at our house that went late into the night. Mack was still sipping mint juleps and working on Betty Camus's gouging machine ("Reed openings should look like something between a pancake and a diamond . . . ") at 3:00 in the morning. Sam Stone, Administrative Director of the School of the Arts and later head of its Foundation, wrote to me on May 28, " . . . it appears that the inaugural 'Oboe Day' was a very successful venture!"

On June 3, wrapping things up, I wrote Mack to thank him.

"It goes almost without saying that no one else would have undertaken so much for so many for so little! You jumped into 'Oboe Day' without complaint or reservation, knocking off one after another of the challenges of an impossible schedule . . . You belong to a handful of paragons in my experience—Fred Starr, Helmut Elliger, Seth McCoy, and Wyche Fowler . . . whose vitality and creativity are so hopeful and unreserved that the rest of us may dare to reach out a little farther, toss our hats a little higher, and laugh a little louder. It is difficult to say 'thank you' for something like that, except to acknowledge it. We are grateful not only for what you have done for us, but for **who you are**."

My first episode of atrial fibrillation occurred after too much turkey and a trip down the mountain from Blowing Rock on Thanksgiving Day 1975. Mary Kay and I were playing bridge and drinking coffee in Lenoir with my parents when my chest suddenly felt like a popcorn popper.

"I **can't** be having a heart attack!" I thought. "I'm too young for this!"

Dr. Troutman told me to calm down, take a warm bath, and go to bed. He said he would wire me up for an EKG the next morning; but I was already back in sinus rhythm by then. Three other episodes of A-fib occurred a few months apart—one in the spring that disrupted and postponed a Piedmont Chamber Orchestra/Haydn recording session. The doctor examining me then said, "Joe, don't worry about this. It's about as serious as dandruff!" Another asked me if I smoked (which I didn't); if I drank alcohol (which I almost didn't); or if caffeine bothered me. "Coffee drives me up the wall!" was my reply. **"Then don't drink it!"** was his adamant response. . . . and it worked! I didn't fibrillate again for twenty years.

In the summer of 1975, Mary Kay and I put Katie on our backs and traveled with Nicholas Harsanyi and the NCSA student orchestra to Italy. My job was to coach chamber music; lead a couple of wind sectionals; chaperon; and otherwise exult for four weeks in the cityscape, weather, and food of Rome, Assisi, and Florence. Marian Buswell's playing in the Mozart Oboe Quartet and the oboe soles of the Brahms and Barber Violin Concertos was so good it made me jealous. NCSA Board Chairman Dr. James Semans and his wife Mary, who sponsored the international program every year, accompanied us and were omnipresent, accessible, and congenial hosts. Mary Kay and I returned to Winston-Salem in love with Italy, appreciating the thousand-year-old allure of the sunny, salubrious Tiber River valley.

We also brought home with us deep tans, Deruta pottery, and an enduring addiction to *gelati misti*!

The John Mack Oboe Camp

During many weeks spent in musical retreats with the Charlotte Oratorio Singers at WILDACRES, I befriended owner Herman Blumenthal. Sometime in the winter of 1975, he revealed plans to renovate and rebuild his 1,600-acre mountain conference center and expand its activities. He asked me about enriching cultural programming at WILDACRES and whether the School of the Arts could become more involved in that.

"Tell him about 'Oboe Day in North Carolina!'" the ghost of James Christian Pfohl whispered! And so I did. I told Herman that John Mack's magnetism at School of the Arts the previous spring demonstrated that he could easily lure sixty to seventy oboists to the Blue Ridge Parkway for classes next summer. A "John Mack Oboe Camp" needed only John Mack's assent and a printed brochure to become reality!

Sitting alone at my kitchen table, I imagined what the curriculum and five-day schedule for sixty oboists at WILDACRES would look like. The second week of June seemed about right, following Cleveland Orchestra subscription concerts and the end of most academic spring semesters, and preceding summer festivals like Marlboro and Tanglewood. I knew Mack would prefer to begin with an introductory session on fundamentals, after which he would survey his favorite pedagogical material—the twelve articulation studies, forty progressive melodies and fifteen Grande Studies from the *Oboe Method* of A. M. R. Barret. Those exercises and etudes could be assigned to thirty oboists during morning sessions from 9:00 a.m. until noon, and solo pieces could be scheduled for thirty others in recitals at 5:00 each afternoon. Bruce Moss, a colleague from School of the Arts, could be the piano accompanist and Pat McFarland the resident repairman and a vendor of oboe paraphernalia. My most original idea was to explore orchestral excerpts in classes from 8:00 to 10:30 every evening, employing an audition format in which two oboists of similar age and ability played the same passages with John Mack acting as arbiter and coach. The days would end with "Tabuteau stories and refreshments in Laurel Cottage" until midnight, and we would postpone Mack's "tell-all" reed class until the final day, so that no one could even **think** of leaving early!

To establish early credibility and get the performance monkey off his back, Mack would want to "practice what he planned to preach" in a gala recital on the first evening, after which a champagne reception (for those old enough to drink) would welcome everyone in splendid fashion.

When the camp framework was complete, I drew a little oboe-playing bear sitting on a mountain overlook; wrote all the copy; arranged the layout on a bi-fold piece of letter stationery; and took everything to a neighborhood printer. All that I imagined was now **printed** and . . . voila! . . . the John Mack Oboe Camp was **real**!

JOHN MACK

OBOE CAMP

WILDACRES

"What do you mean **first annual?**" John Mack protested when he saw the brochure. "I didn't agree to do this more than once!"

In fact, Mack would preside at WILDACRES like a guru on a mountaintop for thirty ensuing years, until he died in 2006. Nothing confirmed and sustained his preeminence as a teacher more than the Camp. Passionate oboe players of all ages are still attracted to WILDACRES each summer, guided and inspired now by Danna Sundet and others of Mack's

most devoted and successful students. Except for replacing
my primitive oboe-playing bear with a clever logo designed
by a graphic artist at School of the Arts and updating relevant
dates and financial information, nothing has changed about
the brochure or the Camp's schedule since it began. Even the
format of the Camp directory remains the same.

Sixty-eight oboists attended the first John Mack Oboe
Camp in 1976—six days and five nights, with all meals and
twenty-five hours of instruction with John Mack included,
for the ridiculous price of $125! Blumenthal generosity made
this possible. WILDACRES charged only $90 per participant
for room and board for the week. I received no money to
create and administer the Camp in 1976; but, following the
second year, I presented $2,200 to the School of the Arts
Foundation for merit scholarships, making me the first
faculty member ever to do so. Many John Mack Oboe Camp
imitators emerged at WILDACRES—the Popkin/Glickman
Bassoon Camp; the William Bennett Flute Camp; the James
Houlik Saxophone Camp; and at other sites, the Thomas Stacy
Seminar and instrumental workshops in Hidden Valley,
California. Double Reed seminars are routine everywhere
now, but the John Mack Oboe Camp is the prototype that
started them all. It remains one of the most successful
specialty instrumental seminars of its type in the world.

The summer of 1976 gave Mary Kay and me another
reason to celebrate. Our second daughter, blue-eyed Jody
Diana (whom I called "Sweetness"), was born on July
13. Jody emerged from her mom as placid and content as
Katie had emerged irritable and impatient. Together the
two "Robinson girls" complemented each other perfectly—
something we rejoiced to see continue into adulthood. Jody
was christened in Home Moravian Church. Seventeen years
later she would return from New Jersey to Salem Academy
for her junior year in high school.

During our third year in Winston-Salem, life for Mary
Kay and me was a rich tapestry of family responsibilities
and social and musical opportunities; but its threads were
fraying, circumscribed by the parochial standards and

expectations that surrounded us. Although its variegated patterns still appealed to me, I was beginning to feel like a jack-of-all-trades and master of none. I missed playing in a major orchestra.

Midway through the fall semester, when the Clarion Wind Quintet was about to take a two-week tour of the Costa Blanca under sponsorship of a local Spanish bank, Mother called to say that Dad had suffered a second stroke and was hospitalized in Lenoir. He was too agitated and disoriented even to listen to the Wake Forest football game on the radio I brought to him. When Dr. Troutman refused to predict whether or when he would recover, despite Mother's protestations, I went ahead on tour.

As soon as our flight from Winston-Salem landed at Newark International Airport, a helicopter shuttled us across Manhattan to JFK. There my large, orange, leatherette suitcase came bouncing along on the baggage carousel with its torn handle sticking straight up in salute, so I had to rush around to find a replacement before boarding the trans-Atlantic flight to Spain. Once in Madrid, all five of us squeezed ourselves, our luggage, and our instruments into a Volkswagen station wagon and drove to Albecete, "The City of Cutlery." I bought a couple of kitchen knives for Mary Kay there. The weather was clear but cold in late November during the daytime and colder still when the sun went down. We slept in our coats in unheated hotel rooms that night.

The next day we descended from Spain's great mid-country plateau to its southern coastal plain, driving through movie-set badlands toward Alicante. Craggy fortifications encrusted half a dozen hilltops that gleamed at twilight, evoking images of medieval pillaging and plundering up and down the valley— crossbows, catapults, boiling oil and everything! Up and down the Costa Blanca, we performed in little towns called Altea, Benidorm, Denia, Orihuela, and Cartagena. Concerts took place in schools, churches, the large meeting room of a bank itself, and even at the Air Force Academy. I acted as host for the Quintet, welcoming audiences in a mixture of Central American Spanish and Umbrian Italian.

On December 3, 1976, a telegram arrived with news that Dad had died. Mother said he would be buried immediately—not to bother rushing home. (Of course, she was bewildered, hurt, and angry.) I took a predawn cab to Madrid, leaving my colleagues to play the last concert of the tour in Murcia without me, and arrived in Lenoir just in time for the funeral. I was thirty-six years old, fighting back tears the whole way home. My beloved adversary was gone.

Marian Buswell played second oboe in the Piedmont Chamber Orchestra until she graduated. After that, for our historic recording on VOX of the complete Nocturnes and Divertimentos by Josef Haydn in the spring of 1977, a student of John Mack's named Jon Dlouhy came from Cleveland to replace her. He was affable and eager, a young oboist possessing instrumental and reed-making skills equal to my own. Moreover, his instrument sounded stronger and deeper in the low register than mine did. Comparing oboes, we discovered that some of the cork pads on my bottom joint were leaking. Until then I supposed the only thing degraded by inadequate suction was **response**; but replacing those leaking pads proved that **sonority** was also adversely affected. By the time Jon visited a second time, my oboe sounded better than his.

maestoso

Audition in St. Louis

E xcept for the bad luck of working every day in the company of a talented but threatening flute player, Mary Kay and I might have remained in the Atlanta Symphony enjoying professional parity in one of our favorite Southern cities. And except for the growing antipathy I felt towards the North Carolina School of the Arts chancellor, we might have stayed comfortably at home in Winston-Salem. Beyond that, performing (even for free) in the Winston-Salem Symphony rekindled my love of orchestra enough to make me want to play full time again. That is why I heard "the sirens' call" when a notice appeared in the International Musician (the official publication of the American Federation of Musicians) announcing an opening for Principal Oboe in the St. Louis Symphony. Richard Woodhams (still owing me a new suit!) had auditioned for Eugene Ormandy and won the Philadelphia Orchestra job, replacing his teacher, John DeLancie. When he encouraged me to audition for his former position in St. Louis, I applied, confident that so much recording with the Clarion Wind Quintet distilled my tone enough to please a committee looking for Dick's kind of musical refinement and finesse.

I was invited to play in the audition finals, avoiding the preliminaries. Once again there was little time to prepare, but I was in good shape and felt optimistic. The beauty of Powell Hall and its splendid acoustics inspired me as soon as walked onto the stage. I sounded wonderful up there! Unfortunately, I once again chose Jacques Ibert's *Sinfonie Concertante* as an opener—determined to remedy the problems it caused in Boston, and once again playing it was a bad idea. The piece's athletic challenges, even if they had been flawlessly met (which they weren't), left my trump suit of coherent, expressive phrasing unrevealed; and the technical mistakes I made doomed me from the beginning. Auditions are tightrope walks—one misstep and you are dead!

Driving me to the airport afterwards, Woodhams was consoling, but he also told me that Peter Bowman from the Montreal Symphony had spent the previous summer performing at a festival with players from St. Louis who liked him a lot. He probably won the job before the official audition.

It was time to take stock. I was thirty-six years old. John Mack had supported me for nearly two decades in unprecedented ways, and Marcel Tabuteau himself had anointed me. Playing in the Mobile and Atlanta Symphonies inspired continual praise; but here I was, forgotten in North Carolina and on no major orchestra's radar screen. Meanwhile, my Marlboro buddy, Joe Turner, was ensconced in Baltimore; and Eric Barr, five years my junior, was thriving in Dallas. Dick Woodhams, ten years younger, was about to join the Philadelphia Orchestra; and twenty-four-year-old Elaine Douvas had already won Co-Principal Oboe in the Metropolitan Opera Orchestra. Young Peter Bowman was two-for-two in shoot-outs against me.

What went wrong? Early in my career I won four auditions in a row just by showing up and displaying my "Mack-reed tone" to conductors and committees. It never occurred to me to prepare diligently for auditions. Everything was too easy. Even when the standards and stakes rose in Boston (where I discovered the meaning of fear on the stage of Symphony Hall), at the National Symphony in Washington, D.C., in Montreal and Saint Louis, I still did not grasp the fact that I could no longer just walk onto a stage, play a few notes and win a job! When the audition to replace Harold Gomberg at the New York Philharmonic was announced that spring, I did not bother to apply. There seemed to be no point.

There was also little time for second-guessing or licking my wounds. Our VOX recordings of Haydn were imminent and engrossing, as was a rally by the faculty to fight administrative threats from Chancellor Suderburg to terminate the Piedmont Chamber Orchestra. Robert Hickok came from Brooklyn College to replace Nicky Harsanyi as dean of the School of Music and wasted no time rocking the School of the Arts faculty's boat. Thank goodness an orchestral consolation prize fell from the sky! John Mack invited me to replace retiring Robert Zupnik as Acting Assistant Oboe of The Cleveland Orchestra on a tour of Mexico and the Eastern United States in August. The repertory included most of the symphonies and concertos of Beethoven and Brahms, and Mack urged me to fly to Cleveland as soon as possible for coaching on all of this music. Unfortunately, when I arrived, I had a fever and bad sore throat. The concert in Severance Hall that night featured comic pianist/conductor Victor Borge, but it was more tedious than entertaining; and the obligatory after-concert dinner at Guarino's Italian restaurant dragged on forever. At last, miserable and shivering, I fell into bed in John Mack's guest room at midnight.

Next morning, Mack was his usual ebullient self. Cane and reeds were already soaking in his studio as he flew around fixing breakfast. His wife Andy sat safely out of the way in a corner of the kitchen, smoking and absorbed in the morning crossword. I woke up feeling better than expected, and after breakfast, could hardly wait to get to work. John Mack's enthusiasm for the oboe was irresistible. As we honked away on Beethoven's Seventh, he stopped, put down his instrument, picked up a cigar, and turned to face me.

"Listen, Joe," he said sternly. "No matter what is in your heart, you **must** congratulate the first oboe player following a concert!"

What? I could hardly believe my ears! Did I have to mainline praise right into his arm?

"Oh my gosh, I'm sorry," I mumbled. "I was so miserable last night I hardly heard a single oboe solo! Of course . . . what I **did** hear sounded great . . . rich . . . tone like mahogany . . . wonderful . . . amazing as always!"

Groveling in that way, I tried to fill his psychic maw. Too little; too late! His hunger reminded me of Harold Gomberg's when we met in Charlotte. Didn't Mack realize that, like Peter, James, and John at the Sea of Galilee when they heard the words, "Follow me," I obeyed?

Mack and I returned to the music and marked all of the places on the assistant parts where I should play. My job was to double the first oboe notes whenever their dynamic climbed to forte or above. Mack promised to fake illness at some point during the tour and give me a chance to be heard by his colleagues.

"Make twelve **very** flat reeds in anticipation of the 8,000-foot elevation of Mexico City," he said.

I told him that the reeds would fly with me from Italy, where Mary Kay and I and our girls would be once again with the North Carolina School of the Arts student orchestra.

Things were different about the International Summer Program in 1977. It had been easy to persuade Harsanyi to imitate Aspen and invite professionals (including me) to join the students and play principal parts in the orchestra, teaching by example, and Jim and Mary Semans' foundation paid the extra cost. The Pentagon Brass Quintet (Mark Gould and Ed Carrol, trumpets; Joseph Anderer, horn; Dave Langlitz, trombone; and Warren Deck, tuba—mostly from the Metropolitan Opera Orchestra) added great power to the back of the ensemble, and they also presented chamber music recitals of their own in Assisi, Florence and Spoleto. Clarinetist Steve Girko came from the Dallas Symphony with his bass-playing wife; bassoonist Benjamin Kamins came from the Minnesota Orchestra with his oboe-playing girlfriend. It was wonderful to perform the Mozart *Sinfonia Concertante* with Girko, Kamins and Anderer; but it was **not** wonderful to suppress the rebellion they instigated in Assisi, where they threatened to boycott a concert unless housing and working conditions improved immediately. It was also not so wonderful for Mary Kay to play violin and have to babysit at the same time. Worst of all was her return to New York with the girls, when tarmac delays in Rome extended their flight by so many hours the trip was almost unbearable for all of them.

By contrast, my flight to Mexico City was a breeze. In the luxurious hotel room assigned to me, I put my oboe together and soaked all twelve high-altitude reeds to see how they worked. Uh-oh! Nothing came out below second-line G— nothing at all! Had my instrument cracked in the airplane coming over? Retrieving a towel from the bathroom, I stripped all the keys from my oboe's top joint and laid them on top of it. Standing at the window in direct sunlight I stared at the naked grenadilla to see if cracks had opened between any of the tone holes. There weren't any. Low density air at high altitude was the entire problem. With so few molecules of air to activate, I was forced to scrape my reeds down to nothing to make them vibrate.

John Mack quickly swept me up into his exuberant Mexican train. I was the caboose that followed along wherever he went, charged with maintaining our daily store of scotch and peanuts. The first Cleveland Orchestra rehearsals on stage in Teatro de las Bellas Artes were thrilling and unforgettable. I could actually feel vibrations from the glorious sonority of the cello and bass sections tickling the soles of my feet. When I played (which was only in loud passages), I felt as if I was swimming inside a rushing torrent. Brahms and Beethoven never sounded so powerful!

I decided to grow a mustache. Dad had sported one as a young man, so it seemed a proper homage to try one on. Even though there weren't enough dark hairs in it to provide much definition or distinction, members of the Cleveland Orchestra who got to know me with that caterpillar on my lip asked years later what happened to it. I told them "Taco Joe Robinson stayed in Mexico!"

A couple of weeks of servile oboe underemployment gradually diminished the thrill of sitting in the center of one of the world's greatest orchestras. I began to doubt whether Mack would ever honor his commitment and give me something important to play. He was sick by then, exhibiting all of the symptoms of "Montezuma's revenge"— the nausea, diarrhea and raging fever—and Beethoven's *Pastorale* Symphony was next on the program. I practiced his part all afternoon in preparation for covering him. Half an hour before the concert, cooled down and stopped up, Mack wobbled onto the stage and said, "Move over!" His performance that night was not only dramatic proof of his love of music and his insatiable appetite for the oboe. It was also a warning.

Sitting next to me on a bus soon afterwards, Cleveland's assistant principal bassoonist, Matt Snell, introduced himself and whispered. "People have a good impression of you, Joe. There is talk that you might be interested in the permanent assistant job next year. Please let me give you some advice: **Don't even think about it**! This is the land of the living dead!"

During five weeks on tour that summer, I played first oboe on just one relatively unimportant piece—the Beethoven Triple Concerto. Two years later Matt Snell resigned his position in the Cleveland Orchestra.

Lorin Maazel (a.k.a. "Ma Szell") confirmed all of my negative impressions of him from my first year's observations at the Blossom Festival School. His performance on the podium was beyond confident; it was arrogant and self-aware. He continually flipped his left-hand pinky in a way that suggested conducting was child's play. In fact, many of the members of the Cleveland Orchestra believed that he **was** a child at play! (They knew, after all, that he conducted the New York Philharmonic in Lewisohn Stadium as a ten-year-old.) Most upsetting to Cleveland players trained by George Szell to perform with precision and classical restraint was Maazel's penchant for self-indulgent spontaneity. He could turn a Brahm's symphony upside down in a heartbeat!

Performers express more than musical notes when they play. They reveal who they are. Perhaps that is why the critical consensus regarding Lorin Maazel's legacy is that his music-making, despite unquestioned brilliance, was vapid and superficial—he was the most narcissistic person I ever met!

Fall semester of 1977 initiated a new affiliation for the Clarion Wind Quintet. Music Department Chairman Frank Tirro, in partnership with the Mary Duke Biddle Foundation, arranged for us to be in residence at Duke University every Monday throughout the academic year. The commute to Durham that took more than two hours in those days forced the five of us to cram ourselves and our instruments into a single car the way we had in Spain. Phil Dunigan usually sat in the middle of the back seat reading *Penthouse* magazine. Most of my eight oboists at Duke majored in pre-med and played either with Alan Bone in the Duke Symphony or with Paul Bryan in the university's celebrated Wind Ensemble.

The Mexican tour with John Mack and the Cleveland Orchestra had inspired and energized me enough to feel ready for the big leagues. Despite that, when an unofficial inquiry came from Maazel through personnel manager David Zauder inquiring whether I would be interested in the assistant principal oboe job in Cleveland next year, I said "No." Bench-warming, even for a player as great as John Mack, was not for me.

Instead, I wrote the New York Philharmonic asking to be permitted to audition there. On October 20, Jimmy Chambers, the orchestra's personnel manager who had been one of the greatest horn players of his era until his lip gave out, responded:

"Unfortunately, our limited amount of time is completely scheduled with highly qualified candidates . . . I am sorry that we are not able to hear you in this set of auditions."

I had applied **too late!** His letter nipped my emerging hopefulness in the bud.

Once again I contemplated the tapestry of life in Winston-Salem, where Mary Kay and I lived comfortably within the middle class. We owned a 3,600-square-foot home on a one-acre lot; drove two used cars; and spent part of each summer in Italy. We had two adorable little girls. My NCSA salary for 1977-78 was $16,000, and supplemented by income from all other sources—the Piedmont Chamber Orchestra, the Clarion Wind Quintet, the International Summer Program; and Mary Kay's and my private teaching, etc.—our total income was almost $22,000. It didn't matter to us that we ate out at the K & W Cafeteria and shopped Hanes and other outlet stores. We enjoyed the intangible benefit of proximity to our mothers and brothers. Things were good enough until I thought about the prospect of sending our daughters to private college. Furthermore, I was now convinced that I possessed the tonal power and dramatic range needed to follow Harold Gomberg in the New York Philharmonic.

Principal oboe auditions in New York began on October 25, when fifteen players were scheduled to compete. I called Eric Barr that morning to find out what was happening:

"Eric, have you played yet? How's it going up there?"

"Hey, man! Really great! I think I am going to win this thing! They've asked me to stay on and maybe play again."

If Eric's early success thrilled him, it also encouraged me.

"If they like him," I thought, *"they will love me! After all, I taught him half of what he knows!"*

Eric's winning would make me jealous to be sure, but I knew I would be proud of my dear friend and protégé. Eric hung around throughout the afternoon on October 25, without playing again; but, on his way out, Zubin Mehta told him he was the best oboist of day!

It was excruciating for me not to be able to compete, but I didn't just wait around to see what happened. I made formal application to the New York Philharmonic on October 29 and listed John Mack and Robert Shaw as references. I asked Jimmy Chambers to give me a chance to play if the auditions underway were inconclusive. I also went to work.

The Chart on the Wall

On a piece of Katie's poster paper, using a yardstick, I drew vertical lines from top to bottom. Between those lines at the top, I penciled in dates beginning with October 15. Down the left side of the paper, I described drills that would challenge every dimension of my basic oboe technique, and I separated those with horizontal lines drawn from left to right. Then I taped the chart to a wall in my studio at home.

First were octave long tone major scales, starting on low B at a metronome setting of quarter note = 60 beats per minute. These slow scales tested my potential to sculpt tones "up" or "down" with the greatest possible control of slope and dynamic range. Sometimes, every degree of the scale was expressed as a whole note "up;" sometimes as a whole note "down." Sometimes the notes alternated "up" and "down" in slow-motion diamond shapes. A few scales were traced like bannister rails continually "up" or continually "down." All of them exploited maximum use of breath and breath control; and after every 20-minute long-tone session, I checked the appropriate box on my chart.

Second were two octave scales tongued and slurred, starting once again on low B. In accordance with Tabuteau's instructions, I articulated low notes short and soft and higher ones longer and louder as they approached the top. The four quadrants of these scales were organized by volume as a "logically-inevitable phrase" would be—"1,2,3,2"—overrunning the center in the manner of a good golf swing! Slurred patterns were practiced as legato as possible, with the last pianissimo note at the bottom always lightly tongued.

Third were four sixteenth notes articulated on each degree of descending major scales, starting with high C. The first scale was played with lungs comfortably full; the next, after exhaling, with lungs nearly empty, and so on. This exercise, which helped with proper abdominal breathing, mainly strengthened my tonguing.

Fourth were all the major scales trilled, starting on low C. The tonic of each ascending scale was a trilled half note (with nachschlaeger) followed by quarter notes on each degree of the scale trilled twice.

Fifth was an arpeggio study from one of the Loyon etudes. An arpeggio ascended from third-space B to a turn at the top, then descended in B major down to B-flat, which repeated the pattern. The sequence of these arpeggios and descending scales was unbroken, with circular breathing practiced about halfway down in the key of E major.

Exercises two through five were practiced in sequence as an intact set at six separate metronome settings: 100, 104, 108, 112, 116, and 120. Completing the whole set took about 90 minutes.

Sixth were drills for two of the most difficult orchestral excerpts—*La Scala di Seta* and *Le Tombeau de Couperin*." For the allegro passage of *La Scala di Seta*, beginning with a metronomic setting of 112, except for slurring the ascending notes of the "scale" itself and the five notes preceding it, I articulated everything. I counted only the correct executions until I had played ten of them. Then I moved the metronome to 116 and repeated the process. By the time I succeeded ten times at 132, I had played the passage fifty times without error. *Le Tombeau de Couperin* was practiced in similar fashion. I played the notorious first movement passages correctly ten times each beginning at 76 and ending at 92. The point with both excerpts was to amass a huge body of correct executions at variable tempos.

Most of these training sessions started after Katie and Jody had gone to bed, at around 8:30 each evening, following a typical full day of teaching and performing. Before beginning, I whittled a reed that vibrated easily and crowed

"C"—one that would be entirely consumed by this particular practice session unless the cane was extraordinary, in which case I saved it for future use. Each training session lasted about two hours and fifteen minutes and I never missed a single one of them. The check marks filling up my chart helped sustain my momentum.

I received no direct report from New York when the next group of fifteen oboists auditioned on October 31. Eric still believed he was Mehta's favorite, but the "oboe grapevine" reported that audition committee members had voted for Joe Turner from Baltimore in order to create a deadlock. Some of them wanted older, more established players (like themselves) to audition. Personnel Manager Jimmy Chambers called to confirm that a few days later:

"We have decided when Zubin returns to New York in a couple of weeks to listen to a few other candidates. Do you still want to audition?"

"Yes, oh yes!" I said. *"Thank you very much."*

It was the opening I had been praying for.

Some family soul-searching ensued. With Mary Kay hoping to spare me additional audition heartbreak, she asked why I would spend money we did not have to take this chance in New York.

"The odds are no good," she said, and I knew she was right.

I responded, *"But if I don't try, I will regret it for the rest of my life."*

Chambers scheduled my audition with only two other oboists for November 14. The great Ray Still from the Chicago Symphony was one of them. I had already been in Olympic training for this moment for two weeks; and in another two weeks I would have drilled long tones, articulated and slurred two-octave scales, trills and arpeggios, etc. exhaustively for thirty-two straight days and played *La Scala di Seta* and *Le Tombeau de Couperin* correctly 1,500 times!

Three things stand out from this period of unprecedented self-discipline and focus.

First, I learned that investing in general rather than in

particular helped me apply my skills more successfully to the music itself—i.e., that excellence was attained quicker by indirect rather than by direct means.

Second, I learned that hard work dissipates anxiety. I slept soundly throughout my month of hard training and was not nervous at all when I walked onto the stage of Lincoln Center.

And third, I learned not to make the audition a pretext for mastering an especially difficult piece. No more Ibert! In New York I elected to open with the *Vivaldi D Minor*—a concerto recorded by Harold Gomberg with Leonard Bernstein twenty years earlier. It was a piece no other candidate would think to play, and I thought it might still resonate in the collective memory of my New York Philharmonic examiners.

Auditioning in New York

On November 14, 1977, I assembled my instrument in the men's woodwind dressing room on the first floor of Avery Fisher Hall, where no other oboist could be heard. My reeds worked well enough and sounded good. Choosing the weakest of them, I practiced my now-customary warm-up until the dressing room door cracked opened.

"Excuse me, Mr. Robinson. They are ready for you upstairs!"

Quickly exchanging reeds and putting the strongest one in my mouth, I grabbed my oboe and followed the young assistant out of the room.

We walked down the same hallway I used when entering—past the men's restroom and some other dressing rooms; turned left at a bank of mailboxes; and stepped into a switchback staircase leading up one floor to the Avery Fisher Hall stage. There I hesitated for a moment in the wings to test my new reed, then walked directly toward a music stand in the center of the stage and placed my Vivaldi part on it.

No carpet muted my footsteps, and no screen hid me from view. Zubin and most of the Philharmonic's woodwind players—including two legends of the orchestra world, flutist Julius Baker and clarinetist Stanley Drucker, sat scattered about in the seats in front of me. I nodded to the Philharmonic's brilliant accompanist, Harriet Wingreen, and we began to play.

At first no one seemed to notice; they were still whispering about the previous candidate. Bassoonist Manny Ziegler told me later that he walked down the aisle to Zubin to tell him to pay attention.

"This is the first real oboe tone we have heard in these auditions!" he said.

His comment initiated an interaction between Zubin and me that canvassed almost every important orchestral oboe solo in the repertory for the next thirty minutes. I could hardly hold my lips on the reed when Tchaikovsky's famous Fourth Symphony solo appeared on my stand. Seeing that, Zubin came up to the front edge of the stage and proposed a ten-minute break. Throughout the preceding audition marathon, Personnel Manager Jimmy Chambers sat beside me, turning pages and whispering encouragement. After the break, assistant principals and second chair players gathered on stage and formed a woodwind ensemble that accompanied me through the Brahms Violin Concerto solo three times; a Mozart Piano Concerto slow movement two times; and twice through sections of the first movement of Bruckner's Seventh Symphony. Testing my flexibility, Zubin shouted instructions and even conducted during this part of the audition, which lasted another thirty minutes. Two players in the accompanying group were already known to me—flutist Renée Siebert, a graduate of the North Carolina School of the Arts, and bass clarinetist Steve Freeman, with whom I performed at the Brevard Music Center. Everyone was cordial but noncommittal when I left the stage.

Jimmy Chambers whispered, *"Nice job, Joe. I will be in touch."*

In a cab on the way back to LaGuardia Airport, I gazed through the window at the urban wasteland of the South Bronx and thought with a shudder, *"Good grief! I might win this job!"* I had never heard of an audition half as long as mine! Back home in Winston-Salem I told Mary Kay the same thing.

The Clarion Wind Quintet left for a little tour of the Shenandoah Valley soon after I returned from New York. One of our concerts was at Washington and Lee University in Lexington, Virginia, and I was resting in my motel room when the front desk clerk asked me to come down to the lobby to take a call from my wife. My heart pounded as I pulled the privacy door shut and heard Mary Kay say:

"Jimmy Chambers just called from New York City. He told me Zubin Mehta wants to hear two players again . . . and, Hon, I'm sorry . . . but you are not one of them!"

(**Not** one of them; **not** one of them!? I couldn't believe my ears!)

"Eric Barr and Joe Turner are the two survivors. But Mr. Chambers gave me his home telephone number and made me promise you will call him. He wants to talk to you immediately!"

Stunned, I pondered the (212-***-****) number scribbled hastily on a piece of phone booth scrap paper. It was not the New York Philharmonic's exchange. Why would a personnel manager call to communicate the bad news of a failed audition, much less give out his private telephone number? But after getting change from the desk clerk, I dialed the number, deposited quarters into the pay phone, and waited.

"Mr. Chambers? This is Joe Robinson. My wife told me you wanted to talk to me."

For the next twenty minutes Jimmy Chambers praised my playing. He loved my tone and phrasing, thought my technique impeccable. And he said the audition committee agreed with him.

"Please take seriously this promise of a rave recommendation from me wherever you might audition again. I assure you, it will be worth something!" he insisted.

"Well, please tell me, Mr. Chambers . . . " (I pressed him.) *"Why am I not still in contention for this job?"*

At that moment if he had criticized my tongued triplets

in *La Mer* or the tempo of *La Scala di Seta,* I would have agreed with him and accepted my fate. But what he said was inconceivable.

"Mr. Mehta thinks your tone is too strong for the Philharmonic!"

(Too strong? Too strong for the most powerful orchestra in the world?)

"That's impossible. Harold Gomberg was the most dramatic oboe player in history!"

"You know it and I know it. Members of the audition committee know it. Zubin Mehta doesn't know it."

Jimmy Chambers was a kind man. His last words to me were:

"If anything—anything at all—is inconclusive in the next stage of these auditions, I will call you again. In the meantime, keep your chin up!"

At 3:00 in the morning on November 17, I gave up trying to sleep and got out of bed. I knew winning a once-in-a-lifetime position like Principal Oboe of the New York Philharmonic was like winning the lottery; but the numbers on my ticket almost matched and I was **so** close! My dismissal could not possibly have anything to do with tone! Discovering a piece of Holiday Inn stationary underneath the Gideon's' Bible, I penned the following letter to Jimmy Chambers (first draft):

Dear Mr. Chambers,

You are a busy man with a difficult job to do, and your dealing with me has been characterized by the utmost kindness and consideration. I am impressed in these principal oboe auditions by a style which goes beyond what is professionally necessary and I am grateful to you for that.

Please forgive me for presuming to have Mary Kay forward a tape of our last Piedmont Chamber Orchestra, Nov. 2 at Davidson College. The Francaix "Flower Clock" and Mozart Symphony #29 represent a different tonal conception than the one you heard, and speak directly to the grounds of my exclusion from the Philharmonic finals.

I know this is a long shot and a risky thing to do, but it could be helpful if the next round between Eric Barr and Joe Turner is disappointing or inconclusive.

Tonal diversity and flexibility have been among my greatest strengths as a player, and I feel honestly that creating a better woodwind blend would have been easy for me if I had not been trying deliberately in my audition to project a big musical personality. The tape shows playing more like deLancie's in the Francaix, and with a "lower profile" in the Mozart where only 14 strings are heard. (You could ask David Zander, on the other hand, about my ability to sound as big as John Mack when I have to.)

I will not "die hard" after this. I sat for 6 years on audition committees and know how difficult it is to have auditions actually preview the candidate in the job. You will not make a mistake by choosing Eric or Joe, but you might by excluding me if tone is the issue.

With best wishes and thanks again.

Sincerely, Joe

The most important sentence was, of course, the last:

"You will not make a mistake by choosing Eric or Joe, but you might by excluding me if tone is the issue."

A week later Jimmy Chambers telephoned me in Winston-Salem.

"Your letter arrived and it could not have been more fortuitous or persuasive. I called Zubin in Los Angeles and read it to him; and he said if you believe in yourself that much, he will hear you again!"

Being an English major had opened the door to Marcel Tabuteau's apartment for me in March 1963. Now it miraculously revived my candidacy for the New York Philharmonic principal oboe position in December 1977. Requisite hard work had indeed preceded this most important musical challenge of my professional career, and letters of recommendation from John Mack and Robert Shaw supported me. But it was Davidson College liberal arts that saved the day!

The showdown with Joe Turner and Eric Barr happened on December 8. This time I went to one of the soloists' dressing rooms on the third floor above stage level in Avery Fisher Hall to warm up. I heard Joe Turner around the corner doing the same thing. His reed sounded too bright; I thought, "No problem!" Then his room went quiet, and I realized he had been led below for his trial on stage. I never did hear Eric, but I knew all three of us performed the first movement of the Sonata for Oboe and Piano by Camille Saint-Saens with Harriet Wingreen, followed by a predictable list of orchestral excerpts and some passages once again with the assembled woodwinds. We were given thirty minutes each to play.

Offstage afterwards, standing with the others, I thought I detected encouraging signs from members of the audition committee as they walked past me on their way to Zubin's room upstairs—eyebrows flickering, sly grins, winks and nods—things like that.

Joe Turner was called first. He went upstairs, came down, and left the building. Eric Barr went up and came down next. He said he would wait to share an airport cab with me. By now, New York Philharmonic players were gathering around, patting me on the back and congratulating me openly.

Zubin beamed, shook my hand, and welcomed me to the New York Philharmonic. The audition committee's deliberations had lasted only ten minutes.

Administrative people quickly surrounded me and guided me into the hydraulic elevator accessing offices on the sixth floor. At the open door of Executive Director Carlos Moseley, the silver-haired patrician from Spartanburg saw me and ran from his desk to embrace me.

"Young may-en, young may-en!" he exulted in his honeyed Southern accent. *"Do you know what this muh-eens? Do you know what this muh-eens?*

(I was too stunned to know.)

Artistic Administrator Frank Milburn asked me which Baroque concerto I would like to play in my solo debut with the Philharmonic next December. Orchestra Manager Nick Webster pointed where to sign on the contract he shoved in front of me. (I noticed a line that read, "Salary, $48,000.")

Conversations about a mandatory executive physical exam, photographs for a press release, whether to begin playing in June or September, etc. were going on simultaneously. Everything was a blur! My head was spinning. All I understood clearly at that moment was that I won the audition.

"I won!"

In the plane flying home, I pondered Carlos Moseley's question and tried to imagine what it meant to be joining America's oldest and most prestigious orchestra. I knew that it meant inheriting a mantle of unremitting responsibility for the solo oboe parts of the greatest symphonic music ever written. Would it also mean that, like Brahms who heard the tramping feet of Beethoven behind him, I would always hear the heroic voice of Harold Gomberg echoing around me in Avery Fisher Hall?

Would 150 concerts a year; dozens of recordings; "Live from Lincoln Center" television broadcasts and international tours every year like the one with the Cleveland Orchestra overwhelm me? What about ten hours of commuting from New Jersey in and out of Manhattan every week and twenty hours a week of reed-making?

Teaching would come with the turf—one year eighteen students at Manhattan School of Music! Could my gut withstand the strain?

Then I remembered John Milton:

> *"Fame is the spur that the clear spirit doth raise*
> *(that last infirmity of noble mind)*
> *To scorn delights, and live laborious days."*

What an unbelievable honor and opportunity to perform

with the finest classical musicians in the world—colleagues, conductors, soloists; and to search for musical Truth at the highest level. Perhaps even, like Marcel Tabuteau, to play "a few good notes" for angels to enjoy!

Back in Winston-Salem, I feigned dejectedness as I walked into the den. Mary Kay took one look at me and turned back to her cooking.

Sitting down on the carpeted split-level stairs, I hugged Katie, who had jumped into my lap squealing **"Daddy! "You're home!"**

And in a very loud voice over her shoulder I asked, **"Darling, how would you like to move to New York City?"**

In the kitchen a pan lid crashed to the floor like a cymbal!

****

The end

Zubin Mehta

"I have conducted the world's greatest orchestras for almost sixty years and can say that oboist Joseph Robinson is one of the finest musicians I ever met. His natural musicality always inspired me, whether he was interpreting a Mozart Concerto, a Strauss tone poem, or one of the Brahms symphonies.

He was a great leader of the woodwind section of the New York Philharmonic, whose famous principal players such as flutist Julius Baker and clarinetist Stanley Drucker respected and loved him enormously. In addition, I know that he was a favorite of guest conductors Rafael Kubelik, Erich Leinsdorf, Leonard Bernstein, and many others.

No matter how physically demanding some of our tours to Europe, Asia, or South America were, Joe's standards of playing at evening concerts never lost their energy or tonal beauty.

I know that Joe, after leaving the Philharmonic in 2005, has continued contributing substantially to the world around him; and I embrace both him and his wonderful family with all my affection."

Zubin Mehta, July 5, 2017

Postlude

A call in April 1978 invited me to join the New York Philharmonic three months early—in June instead of September. Would I like to play first oboe on the orchestra's upcoming tour to Asia? Erich Leinsdorf was substituting for Leonard Bernstein, whose wife's death that spring forced his withdrawal; and the excellent New York free-lance oboist Ronald Roseman decided not to go.

"Of course, I will play!" I said, accepting immediately.

My first trip to Asia was an exciting re-discovery of the Cleveland Orchestra's kind of big league international concertizing. It introduced me to Snake Alley in Taipei; the Dog Market in Seoul; and the Imperial Palace in Tokyo. As I was packing up following our performance of *Eroica* in Tokyo's NHK Concert Hall, Johnny Shaeffer, Assistant Personnel Manager and Principal bass player of the Philharmonic, tapped me on the shoulder.

"Someone back here wants to meet the first oboe player," he said. "I guess now that's you!"

"Oh boy!" I thought. "Maybe I will meet my first 'fan' and sign an autograph!"

Dashing to the stage entrance, I confronted a young man with a large bouquet of roses. The fellow bowed stiffly and reached out to present his flowers, then intoned with great reverence and solemnity, "Beautiful 'praying,' Mr. GOMBERG!" (My famous predecessor's name was still in the program.) Of course my uproarious reaction embarrassed him; but Keisuke Wakao soon became my student and assistant teacher at Manhattan School of Music in New York City and eventually joined the Boston Symphony as Assistant Principal Oboe.

John Mack, always my guardian angel, wrote his pal Erich Leinsdorf before the tour to plead for the maestro's forbearance on my behalf. Thanks to him I survived my first concerts mostly unscathed.

Zubin Mehta, meanwhile, had not heard a note from his new principal oboist since my audition back in December. He HAD to be worried whether a mongrel like me could adequately replace the pedigreed Harold Gomberg! Zubin arrived in August to conduct two oddball run-outs to Buenos Aires and the Dominican Republic, and at his first rehearsal, said, "Good afternoon, ladies and gentlemen. Let's begin with Tchaikovsky 4—the second movement!"

Uh-oh! My worthiness was going to be tested immediately! Harold Gomberg had made a fetish of playing that 40-second opening solo without stopping to take a breath, and I had seen and heard him do it on television when I was a teenager in Lenoir. There was no question I would have to try to match his achievement. With great difficulty, turning all shades of red and purple, I succeeded, prompting the universal orchestra sign of approval from my New York Philharmonic colleagues, who shuffled their feet loudly on stage.

Piquantly over the din, Zubin sang out, "What are you trying to do, Mr. Robinson? Kill me? Maybe you don't have to breathe, but I do. This is **music**, not a circus!"

I withered in my chair, but realized at the same time that Zubin had taught me a fair lesson: **the content of one's musical expression is more important than the manner of its execution.** I never played that solo again without breathing until I recorded it with Leonard Bernstein for Deutsche Gramophone ten years later. By then I could circular breathe and play it all day long!

A week later, just before a twilight concert in the Dominican Republic, Zubin called me over.

"Run get your oboe part and bring it back here. I am going to mark all the places in your music where you must look at me."

He meant directly—eyeball-to-eyeball—and nothing less! (Could that have been a fetish of his own?) Performing a piece as tricky and unfamiliar to me as Ravel's *La Valse* while looking directly at Zubin completely unnerved me in the concert that evening. So much that I lost my place repeatedly and bombed just about every oboe solo in the piece. Afterwards, fearing the worst, I believe that Zubin may have remembered his own good advice: that the content of one's musical expression is more important than the manner of its execution! He never spoke to me about eye contact again.

Getting to know and trust each other on the New York Philharmonic high wire of relentless concert excellence was a learning experience for both of us. On my side, in many ways, ignorance was bliss—I had so few preconceptions about the great symphonic pieces that filled our schedule. And on Zubin's, it was gratifying to have a young principal player in front of him in the New York Philharmonic whom he could mold, inspire, and guide to one exhilarating musical mountaintop after another.

About the Author

In addition to fulfilling his instrumental duties with distinction for twenty-seven years as Principal Oboe of the New York Philharmonic, where he performed in more than 3,000 concerts and soloed frequently at Lincoln Center and abroad, Joseph Robinson received an honorary Doctor of Music degree at his alma mater, Davidson College, and a New York EMMY as Executive Producer of "Heroes of Conscience," a television concert/ documentary about Dietrich Bonhoeffer and other members of the German Resistance against Hitler. He has served on the governing or advisory boards of Davidson College, Union Theological Seminary, Oberlin Conservatory, the Curtis Institute of Music, the Brevard Music Center, the Grand Teton Music Festival, and many others. As President of the Grand Teton Orchestral Seminar he helped develop unique orchestral training that inspired imitation in the first Master of Orchestral Music degree in American higher education at Manhattan School of Music, where he was also Head of Oboe Studies. In 2006 he was named "Artist in Residence" in the Music Department of Duke University and in 2010 "Visiting Distinguished Professor of Oboe" at Lynn University in Boca Raton, Florida. He has been a keynote speaker and authored several published articles, the last in *Harmony Magazine* advocating competitive concerts as a way of increasing public interest in symphony orchestras.

Joseph Robinson is married to violinist Mary Kay McQuilkin, a Juilliard graduate and former member of the New Jersey Symphony. They are parents of three remarkable daughters and currently divide residency between Blaine, Washington, and Chapel Hill, North Carolina.